The Biblical Seminar
79

Religious Diversity
in the Graeco-Roman World

Religious Diversity in the Graeco-Roman World

A Survey of Recent Scholarship

Edited by
Dan Cohn-Sherbok
and John M. Court

Sheffield
Academic Press
www.SheffieldAcademicPress.com

For Lavinia and Kathleen

Copyright © 2001 Sheffield Academic Press

Published by
Sheffield Academic Press Ltd
Mansion House
19 Kingfield Road
Sheffield S11 9AS
England

www.SheffieldAcademicPress.com

Typeset by Sheffield Academic Press
and
Printed on acid-free paper in Great Britain
by The Cromwell Press
Trowbridge, Wiltshire

British Library Cataloguing-in-Publication Data

A catalogue record for this book is available
from the British Library

ISBN 1-84127-216-7

CONTENTS

ABBREVIATIONS

ABD	David Noel Freedman (ed.), *The Anchor Bible Dictionary* (New York: Doubleday, 1992)
ANRW	Hildegard Temporini and Wolfgang Haase (eds.), *Aufstieg und Niedergang der römischen Welt: Geschichte und Kultur Roms im Spiegel der neueren Forschung* (Berlin: W. de Gruyter, 1972–)
ANYAS	Annals of the New York Academy of Sciences
ASTI	*Annual of the Swedish Theological Institute*
BA	*Biblical Archaeologist*
BARev	*Biblical Archaeology Review*
BASOR	*Bulletin of the American Schools of Oriental Research*
BTB	*Biblical Theology Bulletin*
ConBNT	Coniectanea biblica, New Testament
CBQ	*Catholic Biblical Quarterly*
CRINT	Compendia rerum iudaicarum ad Novum Testamentum
CSR	Christian Scholar's Review
DSD	Dead Sea Discoveries
HeyJ	*Heythrop Journal*
HTR	*Harvard Theological Review*
HUCA	*Hebrew Union College Annual*
Int	*Interpretation*
JAC	*Jahrbuch für Antike und Christentum*
JBL	*Journal of Biblical Literature*
JES	*Journal of Ecumenical Studies*
JHS	*Journal of Hellenic Studies*
JJS	*Journal of Jewish Studies*
JRS	*Journal of Roman Studies*
JSJ	*Journal for the Study of Judaism in the Persian, Hellenistic and Roman Period*
JSNT	*Journal for the Study of the New Testament*
JSOT	*Journal for the Study of the Old Testament*
JSPSup	*Journal for the Study of the Pseudepigrapha*, Supplement Series
JTS	*Journal of Theological Studies*
LCL	Loeb Classical Library
NHC	Nag Hammadi Codex

NTOA	Novum Testamentum et orbis antiquus
NTS	*New Testament Studies*
RB	*Revue biblique*
Rel	*Religion*
RevQ	*Revue de Qumran*
RGG	*Religion in Geschichte und Gegenwart*
SBLSP	SBL Seminar Papers
SBT	Studies in Biblical Theology
SEÅ	*Svensk exegetisk årsbok*
SJLA	Studies in Judaism in Late Antiquity
SJT	*Scottish Journal of Theology*
SNTSMS	Society for New Testament Studies Monograph Series
SPB	Studia postbiblica
STDJ	Studies on the Texts of the Desert of Judah
TLS	*Times Literary Supplement*
TLZ	*Theologische Literaturzeitung*
TRE	*Theologische Realenzyklopädie*
TS	*Theological Studies*
TU	Texte und Untersuchungen
TWNT	Gerhard Kittel and Gerhard Friedrich (eds.), *Theologisches Wörterbuch zum Neuen Testament* (11 vols.; Stuttgart: Kohlhammer, 1932–79).
VC	*Vigiliae christianae*
WUNT	Wissenschaftliche Untersuchungen zum Neuen Testament
YCS	*Yale Classical Studies*
ZNW	*Zeitschrift für die neutestamentliche Wissenschaft*
ZTK	*Zeitschrift für Theologie und Kirche*

LIST OF CONTRIBUTORS

Graham Anderson is Professor of Classics at the University of Kent. He has a special interest in Apollonius of Tyana and is the author of *Sage, Saint and Sophist: Holy Men and their Associates in the Early Roman Empire*.

John M.G. Barclay is Professor of New Testament and Christian Origins at the University of Glasgow. His research on Diaspora Judaism culminated in the publication of *Jews in the Mediterranean Diaspora from Alexander to Trajan*. He is currently preparing a new translation and commentary on Josephus's *Against Apion*.

John M. Court has taught Theology and Religious Studies at the University of Kent for over 30 years, much of that as head of department. Sheffield Academic Press has also published his study guide on *Revelation* and *The Book of Revelation* and the *Johannine Apocalyptic Tradition*.

James D.G. Dunn is the Lightfoot Professor of Divinity at the University of Durham. He is the author of works on the Holy Spirit and Christology, several commentaries on Paul's letters and *The Theology of Paul the Apostle*.

Philip F. Esler is Professor of Biblical Criticism at the University of St Andrews. He has written extensively on social-scientific approaches to biblical interpretation. His works include: *Luke–Acts: The Social and Political Motivations of Lucan Theology*, *The First Christians in their Social Worlds: Social-Scientific Approaches to New Testament Studies* and *Galatians*.

Donald A. Hagner is George Eldon Ladd Professor of New Testament at Fuller Theological Seminary in Pasadena, California. He is the author of a two-volume commentary on the Gospel of Matthew in the Word Biblical Commentary series.

Charlotte Hempel held two post-doctoral research fellowships at the Universities of Birmingham and Cambridge and is currently a Fellow of the Meyerhoff Centre for Jewish Studies at the University of Maryland. She is the author of *The Laws of the Damascus Document* and *The Damascus Texts*.

Thomas O'Loughlin is a Senior Lecturer in Historical Theology at the University of Wales, Lampeter, specializing in the history of early Christian communities. His published work seeks to bridge the gaps that often exist between the history of societies, the history of ideas and the history of beliefs and doctrine.

Robert McL. Wilson is Emeritus Professor of Biblical Criticism in the University of St Andrews, and the author of several books dealing with the New Testament and Gnosticism. He has served as editor of *New Testament Studies*, and is a past President of the Society of New Testament Studies.

INTRODUCTION

John M. Court

Over the closing decades of the twentieth century there was an outpouring of books giving close attention to the variety of religious groupings that existed in the Graeco-Roman world, within the period of approximately one hundred years that pivots around the date of the birth of Jesus Christ. The phenomenon of religious diversity in itself has become a focus of attention, and a wide variety of scholars has attempted to untangle the complexities of religious interaction and conflict. Such scholarly investigation has frequently been stimulated by the quest to understand the earliest origins of Christianity, but it has also produced fresh understanding of the complex interrelationships between Jewish and Christian faiths, and the further dimension of their respective relations to pagan religions.

While there have been numerous specialized studies dealing with the specific religious issues of this period, the editors believe that there is a lack of an overall survey of this varied research. This book aims to fill that gap, and to provide an introduction to this vast field of scholarship, drawing together a kind of synopsis of this wide range of investigations, and charting possible new directions for the future. It is designed primarily for students on university courses, to serve as a textbook or a supplementary guide, for instance, in studies of the early period of Christian history. By drawing together these contributions from experts in their respective fields, we seek to provide an invaluable source of reference. Although our collection may be of particular interest to those engaged in biblical studies, it will also prove useful to those investigating the earliest stages of Jewish–Christian relations or seeking an understanding of pagan religions within the Graeco-Roman world.

At the start of our new millennium, it is in one important respect true that studies in this distant period, for example, of the origins of Christianity, must start with a freshly cleared field, or a blank sheet of paper.

That much is the moral, for instance, of the work of John Dominic Crossan (*The Birth of Christianity*, 1998). The point here is to resist habitual assumptions and traditional teachings, in reconstructing a perspective on how things began. But of course this is not to argue that generations of critical scholarship should be ignored, in the search for an innovative approach. Rather it is necessary to hold together, in a fresh conspectus, that material evidence about other religious traditions and cultures that has usually been pigeon-holed as known but unlikely to be relevant. One of the great gains of fresh thinking in recent years has been the recognition that theologians, historians and classicists should exchange views, because they have much to contribute from their own expertise when their areas of study overlap. It is hoped that the present volume, by its synoptic approach, will also contribute to that sharing of ideas.

This introduction will have served its purpose if it now supplies a ground plan of those areas of study in religious diversity in the Graeco-Roman world that are brought together by the contributors to this volume. Encouraged by a first sense of the importance of interrelating studies and making connections, the reader can proceed to study each area in greater detail.

It has long been recognized that Judaism in the first century CE was far from being a monolithic faith. Indeed, before the codification of the Mishnah around 200 CE, the pluralism of belief and practice defies the use of terms like 'orthodox' or 'normative'; in Matthew Black's grand phrase it was 'a widespread and dangerously proliferating and fissiparous heteropraxis'. It is therefore appropriate that the treatment of Judaism in the present volume embraces the first three chapters, on Palestinian Judaism, Diaspora Judaism and the Essenes.

At the outset, Philip Esler, in his overview of Palestinian Judaism, draws attention to the valuable contribution made to studies of religious diversity by the introduction of the powerful analytic methods of social-scientific research. The contribution made to biblical studies by the techniques of the social sciences received growing recognition towards the end of the twentieth century. This methodology is valuable in bringing into focus the vast difference in cultural terms between the first and twenty-first centuries and between the Middle East and the western world. In the first century religion, politics and economics are significantly interconnected, so that religion is 'an embedded phenomenon'.

An important distinction is made in this survey between political religion and domestic religion, corresponding to the social realms of the elite and the non-elite. For the elite the Temple and its cult are the unifying centre of 'common Judaism', but this is to ignore other areas of marked divisiveness, particularly in relation to domestic religion and the attitude of the non-elite towards the elite. The synagogue functioned to install the Great Tradition in the minds and hearts of the non-elite. In the first century especially diversity was reflected in unrest (for political and economic reasons); popular movements evoked the prospect of divine intervention in ways that recalled Israel's past. After the work of Johanan ben Zakkai at Jamnia, 'it is possible that the factionalism which had previously characterised Judaism was replaced by mutual tolerance' (at least for those who remained within the gathering at Jamnia, while those who did not were branded as heretics and accursed).

The chapters by Esler and Barclay both contain interesting (and divergent) views on nomenclature: 'Jew', 'Judaean', 'Israelite' and their historical and geographical complications. John Barclay starts by defending his use of the title 'Diaspora Judaism' against the older and misleading usage of 'Hellenistic Judaism'. 'Diaspora Jews had in common the fact that they lived as minority communities in a society governed by non-Jews' (p. 48)—a determining fact of Diaspora existence, even where social and political conditions varied widely. The term 'diaspora' may indicate too strong a dependence upon Jerusalem, but it also serves to indicate a mobility between Diaspora and Palestinian Judaism. The situation of a minority community necessarily raises further questions about the strategy that is adopted towards the majority or colonizing culture. Expressed again in the terminology of social science, the options include 'assimilation' (complete social engagement with others), 'acculturation' (adoption of the language—Greek instead of Hebrew—the literature and cultural values of others) or 'accommodation' (a more limited application of the others' cultural resources). 'A range of literary, historiographical, philosophical, theological and artistic "hybridizations" are evident in the Diaspora, whose object was not to ape Greek culture so much as to express Judaism within it, sometimes with a significant polemical edge against non-Jews (including "Greeks")' (p. 53).

New evidence for Diaspora Judaism has come from archaeology, including the spectacular synagogue discoveries at Dura Europos and

Sardis. Other available source material means that Philo, important though his work undoubtedly remains, is no longer regarded as the sole representative of Diaspora Jewish thought; his particular conflation of Scripture and Hellenistic philosophy is not to be taken as typical of Jews everywhere, even in his own era. Josephus can also be reassessed, regarded not as an abject renegade, but as a Jew honoured at the imperial court, while maintaining his social and emotional commitment to the Jewish people. Barclay quotes P. Trebilco's view of Asia Minor Judaism: 'A degree of integration did not mean the abandonment of an active attention to Jewish tradition or of Jewish distinctiveness. It was as *Jews* that they were involved in, and a part of, the life of the cities in which they lived' (p. 58).

Other questions remain about how others regarded the Jews, and whether Judaism sought positively to attract others. Literary sources offer a combination of positive and negative comments on the Jews. How do these sources relate to the opinions and actions of ordinary people? How do such comments on Jews compare with what might be said about, for instance, Egyptians or Syrians? Provided that 'mission' is not defined too rigorously, it is possible to argue that from time to time Jews attracted considerable numbers of Gentiles into conversion. Nor did the positive attraction of Judaism wither at the rise of Christianity; at least until the time of Constantine the synagogue continued in strong competition with the church. Jewish people seem to have exercised a multiple attraction, derived from (in our terms) both religious and non-religious factors.

Charlotte Hempel's account of scholarly study of the Essenes in the last century has a clear division into two phases, before and after the discovery of the Qumran library (the Dead Sea Scrolls) in the late 1940s. In the pre-Qumran phase of Essene study the main sources were the references to them in Josephus, Philo of Alexandria (describing also a group known as the Therapeutae of Egypt) and Pliny the Elder; the Damascus Document, discovered in Cairo in the late nineteenth century, was rarely associated with the Essenes, until comparisons were drawn more recently with the non-biblical texts found among the Dead Sea Scrolls. Since 1947 the key question has been whether the Essenes should be identified (or associated) with a community located at Qumran who might well have produced the scrolls. A majority of scholars (but by no means all) work with such links, and accordingly with a vastly enlarged database for Essene studies.

The flood of Qumran studies shows no sign of diminishing, indeed it has increased with the enlarged access to the texts. As the decades pass since the cave discoveries, there are many retrospective evaluations of the nature of the site, the contents and context of the scrolls and fragments, and the relationship to the Jerusalem Jews and the early Christians. It has long been conventional to refer to the Essenes as monks, but such a description of a pre-Christian Jewish phenomenon is an anachronism. The texts from Qumran clearly emanate from a fiercely conservative Jewish group, but this does not exclude the possibilities of foreign influences (e.g. from Iran or Hellenization). If the Essenes emanate from a Palestinian apocalyptic tradition, then according to the 'Groningen hypothesis', the Qumran community is a splinter group loyal to the Teacher of Righteousness. Alternatively, in H. Stegemann's latest view, the Teacher founded 'the main Jewish Union of Second Temple times', embracing all conservative Jews apart from the Temple establishment. As to the fate of the Essenes, there is more uniformity in ignorance as to what happened to them after the capture of Jerusalem in 70 CE. Theories that link them with early Christians, or Christian heretics, or even the Jewish Zealots at Masada, can only be arguments from silence at present.

The next three chapters form a triptych of studies on Christianity, examining in turn the Jesus of history, the apostle Paul, and the early church. Donald Hagner has written a lively and polemical piece in his analysis of recent studies of the 'historical Jesus'. His principal aim is to set the contemporary work of the Jesus Seminar in America within the framework of earlier quests of the historical Jesus. He examines the methodology with a critical eye, reviews examples of the work done, and proposes his own analytical observations in the light of the so-called 'seven pillars of scholarly wisdom' of the Jesus Seminar. Such an approach could be criticized as equally partisan, compared with the advocates of the Seminar. But, from the point of view of the student who can easily obtain access to much of this recent work, and indeed, will have seen it reflected in much popular writing and media presentation, it should be more helpful to be challenged by such a critical assessment to face the primary issues of such historical study.

I have recently encountered a comparison by Paul Trudinger of Winnipeg of work on Jesus and the Gospel by R.J. Campbell in the first decade of the twentieth century and by J.D. Crossan in the last decade. There are echoes in their respective presuppositions and methods that signal the key question as to what (if anything) has changed. A primary motive may be, as Hagner suggests, a quest for an 'alternate' view, given that the traditional view is felt to be old-fashioned and unconvincing. Albert Schweitzer's *Quest of the Historical Jesus* concluded that the nineteenth-century writers 'rather than having found the historical Jesus...had simply made Jesus over into their own image'. Schweitzer himself had no more room for the supernatural element when he argued 'that the historical Jesus was a radical apocalyptic preacher, more like an unkempt man standing on the corner'. Interest in the 'Jesus of History' should be open-minded, not presupposed for or against the supernatural. From the wider perspectives of our present book, one welcome change of method would be to move away from the 'criterion of dissimilarity', so popular with the 'New Quest', whereby authenticity is determined by the lack of parallels with first-century Judaism or early Christianity.

James Dunn makes the case for the apostle Paul as the patron saint of diversity, to whom this volume might well be dedicated! The outline of the case is in Paul's biography—'the diaspora Jew become Pharisee become apostle to the nations'. But Dunn also provides a fuller analysis of the rich diversity under three headings: Paul, troubler of Israel; Paul, second founder of Christianity; Paul, a consistent thinker?

'Paul is remembered as one who stretched the diversity which was Second Temple Judaism to breaking point' (p. 108). Here Dunn is usefully setting up for us a debate on the title 'Messiah' with Philip Esler, and on the fact of 'mission' in Judaism with John Barclay. But he pushes the issue further with the questions about Israel's identity and the binding nature of the Torah upon Gentile converts. Paul's sense of his own prophetic commission maintains his claim of a place within the diversity of Judaism. The stretching effect applies equally to infant Christianity, between the Christian Jews who kept within the pale, and the acute-Hellenizers and Gnostics who broke the bounds. It is Paul's voice within the New Testament that gives a harder edge to thinking about Jesus, and stimulates such diverse reactions. But 'if Christianity commends itself as a coherent system of thought, it is primarily Paul we have to credit for that' (p. 117). Dunn argues this third part of his case with regard to diversities and tensions in Paul's Christology, his ideas of salvation, his concept of the church and his principles of praxis.

In a book of this kind, a chapter on the early church in the perspective of a century of scholarship might readily take one of two forms: either a narrative account of the early church as it is now seen in the light of progress in patristic scholarship; or a survey of major contributions in the form of an annotated bibliography with a focus on the major reference works and series (e.g. Lampe's Patristic Lexicon and the *Corpus Christianorum*). In either way the perception of the century might be one of a gradual liberation of church history from preoccupation with the study of heresies. But Thomas O'Loughlin offers something different from either, by concentrating on the earliest church and demonstrating the interface between New Testament and early church history, between the realms of the biblical theologian and the Classical historian.

O'Loughlin's chapter concentrates on two processes. The first is the discovery of new evidence, from newly discovered documents, such as *The Didache*, the Nag Hammadi library of texts, particularly the *Gospel of Thomas* and the Dead Sea Scrolls. The inclusion of the last two categories in this list must alert the reader of this book on diversity to the interrelationships that also exist, here with the chapters on the Essenes and Gnosticism. In addition to texts, new evidence also comes from archaeological research into the social context of Christianity in such centres as Corinth. And the second process is to approach 'the past [as a foreign country] from a different angle and attitude to the sources of information'. O'Loughlin illustrates the ways in which the emerging picture will be totally different, by comparison with Joseph Bingham's *The Antiquities of the Christian Church*, published in 1870 and remaining as a standard undergraduate text well into the twentieth century. Maps in the back of Bibles tend to retain the older focus for the early church, first on Palestine, then on Asia Minor and Greece, Rome and the western perspective; where are the maps of the spread eastwards to Syria, or south down the Nile? The moral of the changing perspective is that 'we cannot make ourselves into the centre of the universe' and recreate the Christian past in our own western image. There are echoes here of the critique of quests of the historical Jesus.

The final group of three contributions to this volume are concerned with religious diversity within the pagan and syncretistic phenomena of the Roman world, treating political, philosophical and practical aspects in the legacy of Greek religion, in Gnosticism, and in Mithraism as an example of the Mystery Religions. In the first of these, Graham Anderson summarizes his approach by the title of his chapter: 'Greek

Religion in the Roman Empire: Diversities, Convergences, Uncertainties'. Evidence is drawn from a variety of sources, not only from papyri and inscriptions but also from literary texts and ancient fiction. Examples characterize a 'multi-ethnic religious pluralism' and seek to analyse not just the fact but its internal tensions, seriousness and vibrancy. One cannot simply assume that with the rise of Christianity paganism is exposed as an empty sham, apart from the later counter-activities of the Emperor Julian. There is an interesting comparison here between the studies by E.R. Dodds, Robin Lane Fox and Ramsay MacMullen on what makes conservatism and radical renewal vital one moment and sterile the next.

Ancient writers are ready to accept the integration or equivalence of Greek and foreign deities, and indeed to alternate between the singular and plural forms of the word for god. Syncretizing situations may well have contributed to the later imperial tendencies to monotheism. Anderson compares samples of urban populations (Ephesus and Athens— including cross-references to the New Testament) with pictures of rural religious belief and practice. Speedy success for a cult is evidence of the rapid adaptability of pluralist religion. Anderson's other comparison is between the popular world of dreams, magic and oracles and the intellectual attitudes of the upper classes. There are indications of 'religious tourism' that one would otherwise have regarded as the prerogative of Christian pilgrims or as a modern phenomenon. The Imperial cult is discussed here, as a special case for the interpretation of intellectual reaction, with reference to the work of Simon Price. It is a traditional view of Christian prejudice to regard this cult as a purely political device, but the sense of communal security and power, associated with the deification of even a living emperor, is unlikely to have been just political 'spin'.

Robin Wilson offers, from his own decades of research, a sharply focused picture of Gnosticism as it relates to the particular concerns of this volume. The subject is one that is almost indefinitely extendable, beyond Mandaism, Manichaeism and the Hermetica, to Merkabah mysticism and the Kabbala, and on to the modern relevance of Gnosticism as a *Nachwirkung* in the work of Blake and Jung and in New Age religion. On the other hand, it is rarely given its proper critical attention within historical studies of the first century. Christian church historians often try to trace an 'orthodox' pathway and thus wait for manageable 'heresies' such as that associated with Arius. Wilson discusses the development of scholarly attitudes to Gnosticism, from the view of a 'bizarre and outlandish Christian heresy' (Christian faith untrammelled by Judaism) to the idea of a pre-Christian Gnosticism and its subsequent relations with the New Testament. Two further phases transformed the picture: one was the phenomenological studies of Hans Jonas, recognizing in Gnosticism a new way of thinking; the other was the discovery in 1945 (paralleling the Qumran discoveries) of the Nag Hammadi texts, written in Coptic. Not all these primary texts are gnostic, and some that are gnostic are non-Christian; some are Hermetic texts and some are classified as Wisdom literature. Wilson discusses the relation of this library to the literary genres of the New Testament, and highlights the special interest in the *Gospel of Thomas*.

The main characteristics of gnostic teaching are summarized under five headings. These are then illustrated by a summary of the Valentinian system, as described by the Christian adversary Irenaeus, and documented in the *Gospel of Truth* and the *Gospel of Philip*. It can be seen that Gnosticism was 'not a counsel of despair, but a religion of hope and deliverance, at least for those who were fortunate enough to possess the divine spark, to hear and respond to the call of the gnostic redeemer' (p. 179). In a final section Wilson discusses the arguments for alternative origins of Gnosticism, in today's debate between the Jewish element and the Platonic tradition, especially Middle Platonism. It is clear that it 'soon came into contact with the developing Christian movement, and the two interacted in various ways. We have still a long way to go before we can finally claim to have traced out all the lines of development on either side' (p. 181).

Much of the debate about the Mystery Religions has also centred on the relationship with the New Testament. In the study of Gnosticism the *religionsgeschichtliche Schüle* made a very positive contribution by exploring the possibilities of contributions to the thought of the Mediterranean world from other religions of the ancient Near East. By contrast their over-enthusiastic comparison between Christianity and the Mysteries provoked a strong counter-reaction, from which the subject has scarcely recovered. But as new evidence became available, particularly in later iconography and archaeological explorations of sites, so the Mysteries regained an independent interest. The interpretative work of Franz Cumont and M.J. Vermaseren were particularly significant for the understanding of Mithraism. The use of literary evidence for the study of the Mysteries can be compared with what Graham Anderson writes about Greek religion.

A major difficulty for research is inherent in the nature of the Mysteries, that they are intended to be secret. The modern comparison with revelations about secret cults from brain-washed or hostile witnesses may illustrate, but overstate, the problem. After observations about the methodology of modern study and the diversity of religions encompassed by the designation of Mysteries, this chapter focuses on one particular example, that of Mithraism. There could be several justifications for this selection, not least the importance of the cult for the military in the Roman Empire, and the fact of rivalry between it and Christianity. As is the case with Gnosticism, questions of origin and development are fiercely contested with regard to the Mysteries. There is some evidence here, and reasonable speculation, for a process of transformation from a local and 'primitive' religion to a more intellectualized ideology spreading out from Rome as the centre. But David Ulansey's recent decoding of Mithraism in terms of astronomy will require more evaluation before it can be established as a revolution in Mithraic studies. Ancient science may yet be seen to have such a constructive relationship with an ancient religion, but, as with Gnosticism, the modern enthusiasm may outrun the historical evidence.

PALESTINIAN JUDAISM IN THE FIRST CENTURY

Philip F. Esler

1. *The Meaning and Context of 'Palestinian Judaism'*

a. *Introduction*

To seek to describe 'Palestinian Judaism' within the context of religious diversity in the Graeco-Roman world—both looking at how the subject has developed in the last hundred years and charting its likely future course—necessitates at the very outset that we recognize the current methodological ferment in the study of the biblical world.[1] New ways of examining the evidence relating to ancient Israel and, indeed, Greece and Rome, especially those deriving from social-scientific research that bring into focus the vast cultural distance between the subjects of our investigation and us, constitute such a watershed in the study of the field that many of the older authorities now need to be used with considerable caution. Accordingly, rather than offering a catalogue of scholarly monuments and concluding with a brief survey of future prospects, in this essay I will situate the field within the new perspectives that are emerging and refer to earlier scholarship in relation to them.

Both terms in the phrase 'Palestinian Judaism' require explanation. 'Palestine' derives from 'Philistia', the name for the coastal plain lying between Joppa and Gaza once inhabited by the Philistines. In time 'Palestine' came to refer to a larger area, roughly comprising the regions known as Judaea, Samaria and Galilee, while it could also even cover Idumea in the south and parts of the area east of the Jordan as well.[2]

---

1.   For further details, see Esler (1998a: 1-28).
2.   So Ptolemy in the mid second century CE; cf. Stern (1980: 166-71). Feldman argues that 'Judaea' could be used for the whole of this area in the first century (1990). After the defeat of Bar Kochba in 135 CE official Roman policy was to replace 'Judaea' with Palestine.

But the term 'Judaism' and the related words 'Jew' and 'Jewish' raise more serious problems, to be considered below.

b. *Historical Overview*

The critical period for the study of 'Palestinian Judaism' within the Graeco-Roman world begins in 332 BCE when Alexander the Great captured Palestine, which resulted in the intensive Hellenization of the region, and ends in 135 CE with Hadrian's legions suppressing the revolt led by Bar Kochba and establishing a pagan city in Jerusalem closed to Israelites. A number of pivotal events can be identified in this period. In 167 BCE the Seleucid king Antiochus IV Epiphanes launched an onslaught on the people, precipitating a successful revolt by the Maccabaean family and the institution of the Maccabaean/Hasmonaean rule, which persisted for nearly 100 years before it collapsed into internecine strife that was brought to an end with the capture of the Temple by Pompey in 63 BCE, thus marking the beginning of Roman control of Palestine. Herod the Great reigned, with Rome's blessing, over much of Palestine from 37–4 BCE, while his son Herod Antipas enjoyed rule over Galilee and Perea from 4 to 39 CE. For most of the period from 6 to 66 CE Judaea was actually a Roman province and suffered the exigencies of rule by prefects of various quality, including one Pontius Pilate (26–36 CE). Then came the disastrous war with Rome from 66 to 70 CE, which resulted in Jerusalem and the Temple being sacked and much of the population killed or sold into slavery. Finally, there was the unsuccessful revolt led by Bar Kochba in 132–35. Many works cover the tumultuous historical framework of Palestine in the Graeco-Roman world, ranging from the very detailed (Schürer 1973, 1979; Smallwood 1976; Grabbe 1994) to the more schematic (Grabbe 1996: 1-28). All of these events reveal a striking connection between religious, political and economic phenomena in a way that demands consideration, initially in relation to the broad social system of ancient Palestine. To bring this essay within manageable proportions, its focus will be on the first century CE.

c. *Elite and Non-Elite in the Advanced Agrarian Society of Palestine*

It is necessary to begin our investigation of the social system in Palestine at a suitably high level of generality, with its broad nature, so as to bring out its basic arrangements and interconnections. Lenski and Lenski (1982) employ a macrosociological approach to analyse the development of social systems from a preindustrial stage, beginning with hunting and gathering societies, proceeding to horticultural societies, and then agrarian (simple and advanced) before moving on to industrial and industrializing societies. Palestinian society, throughout the ancient period, fell into the advanced agrarian type, characterized at a technological level by the use of the plough, which allowed permanent cultivation of a much larger area of land than among horticulturists and which thus led to the production of agricultural surpluses.

A distinctive social and political structure developed in response to these surpluses. In short, a tiny ruling elite (2–5 per cent of the population), based in cities, took control over the rest of the population, who were mainly peasants, and extracted a hefty proportion of their surplus to support their often luxurious life in the city and the religious cult or cults that it contained. The ruling elites provided little in return, except military protection aimed at preventing anyone else seizing the surplus; roads running from villages to towns were to facilitate the movement of produce from the former to the latter (Kautsky 1982: 156). This type of land use, especially in relation to numerous large estates, persisted in Palestine from earlier times under each succeeding dynasty during the Graeco-Roman period, whether Seleucid, Hasmonaean, Herodian or Roman, as Fiensy has argued from literary and archaeological evidence (1991: 21-73). Illuminating details of how the system worked to the detriment of the peasantry can be seen in Neh. 5.1-13.

At an early stage elites in the ancient Near East, including Palestine, discovered that a religious ideology proclaiming that a particular god required some of the agricultural produce was a powerful inducement for the peasants to turn over part of their surplus. In addition to the means of economic production, the elite controlled virtually all political power and status and had a virtual monopoly on literacy, through their control over trained scribes. Everywhere the elite presented themselves as aristocratic and treated the rest of the population with contempt (Kautsky 1982: 177-87). Although there were a large number of priests in first-century Palestine, we should probably distinguish between ordinary priests, generally living in towns in the countryside and receiving the tithe direct from local peasants and perhaps being on reasonably good terms with them, and the high priests dwelling in Jerusalem at an altogether higher level of wealth and luxury, and profiting (probably in various questionable ways) from the Temple cult and the commercial activities associated with it. There is evidence they had indeed turned the Temple into a 'robbers' den' (Bauckham 1988; C.A. Evans 1989b).

Over time, especially with the introduction of iron ploughs, which increased production even more, the number of 'retainers' catering directly to the needs of the elite, such as household servants, stewards and scribes, together with other groups serving them indirectly, such as artisans and merchants, grew considerably. Expanding wealth and a growing urban population provided conditions for the growth of trade. Large empires in particular, such as those in Mesopotamia, the Helle- nistic east and Rome, which all affected Palestine, constituted large trading areas where exchange and transportation could be facilitated. The result was widespread commercialization (Kautsky 1982: 28-47). There is strong evidence, increasingly archaeological in nature, for first- century Palestine, including Galilee, having been characterized by vig- orous trade and commercialization (Overman 1993). With this came an increasing monetarization of economic relations, a phenomenon that usually worsens the condition of rural peasants (Freyne 1995: 37-44).

The elite comprised high Roman officials, the priesthood, especially the high priests, and the various Herodian rulers (client kings, eth- narchs and tetrarchs) and rich, aristocratic landowners. It was in the interests of both of these groups to maintain the existing system (Horsley 1993: 9-12), which essentially meant keeping the tithes and taxes flowing in without interruption or disturbance. The elite were assisted by retainers of various sorts, beneath whom were the peasantry and a limited urban population of merchants, artisans and labourers, while unclean, degraded and expendable persons constituted the lowest level.

d. *Distinctive Mediterranean Culture*
In addition to the material conditions of life in first-century Palestine, and the advanced agrarian system that constituted their foundation, there was an ensemble of features of non-material culture that must briefly be noted. The delineation, at an appropriate level of generality, of a distinctive Mediterranean culture that characterized the ancient Graeco-Roman world, including Palestine, and that is very different from modern North Atlantic or North American cultures (which we tend unconsciously to deploy when reading texts from the first century CE) constitutes one of the most important developments in the field in the last 20 years. Following its inauguration in Bruce Malina's 1981

work, *The New Testament World* (revised edition 1993), which produced a model of Mediterranean culture using modern anthropological
research into the region, the interpretation of texts and other data from
ancient Palestine as productions of a culture alien to our own has
become a flourishing field of research with major and unavoidable
implications for the study of religious phenomena (see Elliott 1995;
Esler 1994: 18-36; 1995a). Chief among the cultural features highlighted are the prominent group orientation of Mediterranean people
(in sharp contrast to individualism), as seen particularly in the strength
of kinship ties, honour as the primary social value, the belief that all
goods are limited, the importance of patron/client ties and the significance of purity boundaries.

e. *Religion as an Embedded Phenomenon in First-Century Palestine*
One aspect of the introduction of anthropological research into the field
is the realization that our contemporary view that phenomena like
'religion' or economics have an existence separate from politics or the
family is quite anachronistic when applied to the ancient Mediterranean
world. Right across the region at that time, the features we refer to as
'religious' institutions and ideas were primarily embedded either in
structures of political dominance, such as the Temple in Jerusalem, put
in place by local aristocratic elites, as discussed above, or in the household. There was political religion and domestic religion, but not really
'religion' per se. Political religion used the roles, values and goals of
politics in the articulation and expression of religion and was characterized by functionaries who mixed cultic and political roles and who
attended to powerful deities providing well-being and prosperity, or
their opposite if provoked. It was legitimated in 'the Great Tradition'
(Redfield 1956: 68-84), the high and learned culture of the elite.
Domestic religion used the roles, values and goals of the household in
the articulation and expression of religion. To the extent that it featured
religious functionaries, they were family members, and the focus was
on the deities as the source of familial solidarity and commitment, and
well-being for the kin group (Malina 1986; 1994; 1996). Domestic
religion was legitimated in 'the Little Tradition', the low or folk culture
of the non-elite. The synagogue (discussed below) is perhaps best seen
as representing a form that mixed political and domestic religion.[3]

3.   To the extent that in the first century the synagogue was a locus for the

Nevertheless, in preindustrial societies like this one run by an aristocratic elite, even though the lives of the peasants and those who lived off their agricultural surplus were quite segregated, it was common to find a measure of formal identity between the two types of religion (so Kautsky 1982: 161), no doubt because the rulers socialized the ruled to accept forms of religiosity that preserved the *status quo*. This was certainly true of ancient Israel, which exhibited an uncommonly close connection between the two traditions, as reflected in institutions like the synagogue, pilgrimages to Jerusalem, sacrifices offered for the people as a whole or for individuals, and the fact that the ordinary priests spent most of the year living in rural communities. In spite of these features, the distinction remains an important one, as seen in the frequent assertion by the non-elite of traditions demanding justice from the rulers (ultimately stemming from Amos, Isaiah, Micah and Hosea; Chaney 1989; Esler 1998b) and the use of prophetic and messianic elements of the great tradition at times of popular unrest, as discussed below. Phenomena like these indicate the very different interests at stake and the extent to which the Palestinian non-elite managed to voice their predicament, which is very unusual among peasants (Scott 1985: 36-37 *et passim*). Thus, while the 'Great Tradition' worked its way down and became part of the Little Tradition, the process was slow and always incomplete (Fiensy 1991: 2).

Accordingly, to speak of 'Judaism' as a functioning religion (so Sanders 1992: ix) entails anachronistically separating religious phenomena from the social and economic issues with which they are inextricably connected and also misses the distinction between political 'religion' and domestic 'religion', the respective realms of the elite and the non-elite. If 'Judaism' is to be retained in this connection, it should have reference to a more inclusive reality.

f. *'Judaism' and Ethnicity*
One explicit perspective capable of usefully bringing together the diverse data relevant to the notion of 'Judaism' is that of ethnicity. As a result of the work of Fredrik Barth (1969), older views of ethnicity as a primordial phenomenon in which cultural features established the distinctive identity of an *ethnos* have largely given way to the idea that

dissemination of Great Tradition throughout Palestine, especially in the form of the Mosaic law, it was perpetuating political religion, while its role as a gathering point for local families must also have given it a domestic dimension.

the primary issue is a people's sense of itself as distinctive, with various cultural features, sometimes changing over time, being employed to designate and realize this separation. The boundary (more like a process than a physical obstacle) between the *ethnos* and other groups provides for some areas of interaction and others where this is prohibited. On this approach, religious practices and beliefs (political or domestic), incorporating the Temple cult and the taxation system run by the elite at one extreme, to the practice of circumcision, dietary habits, practices of daily prayer and a unique set of ethical norms at the other, constitute some of the panoply of cultural features making 'Judaism' a distinctive form of ethnicity.[4]

None of this is to downplay the undoubted diversity that characterized 'Judaism' in first-century Palestine, which we will consider below. As long ago as 1914 C.G. Montefiore (1914: 3-5) suggested that several 'Judaisms' existed in the first century, and he mentioned 'apocalyptic', 'Hellenistic', 'Palestinian' and 'Rabbinic' Judaisms. This notion has become popular (Nickelsburg 1986: 2). On the other hand, some of those who speak of 'Judaisms' (including Montefiore) fall into the error already mentioned of working with an implicit model of 'religion' that largely—and unacceptably—separates it as a phenomenon from its necessary political, economic or domestic contexts.[5]

g. *Nomenclature*
There remains the question of whether the words 'Jew', 'Jewish' and Judaism are appropriate in relation to the ethnic group under discussion. These are translations of the very common *Ioudaios* and and the rather uncommon *Ioudaismos*. The first problem with 'Jew' and 'Jewish' is that they fail to convey the territorial flavour of the word *Ioudaios*. In the first century CE this word referred to a member of the ethnic group who lived in, or originated from, Judaea and which worshipped its god in the temple in Jerusalem.[6] This usage is very clear in

4. I have recently argued this position with respect to Israel (1998a: 78-86), while Hall (1997) has adopted a similar approach in relation to ancient Greece. Stern (1994) and Cohen have recently argued against Barth's approach in relation to Judaism, but it is not possible to enter this debate here.

5. Nickelsburg (1986), on the other hand, takes a broad view of 'Judaism' as encompassing social, political and economic, as well as religious issues.

6. Thus, Josephus refers to the people from Galilee, from Idumea and so on who travel as pilgrims to Jerusalem as *Ioudaioi*, 'Judaeans' (*War* 2.41-43). Their

Josephus, who only drops *Hebraios* and *Israelitês* and begins to use the word *Ioudaios* regularly (indeed almost invariably) of the people after the beginning of Book 11 of the *Jewish Antiquities*, when Cyrus gives them permission to return to *Ioudaia* and to rebuild the Temple in Jerusalem.[7]

But one also observes the same usage in ancient Gentile authors, such as Hecataeus of Abdera (writing c. 300 BCE; Stern 1974: 20-24), Clearchus of Soli (c. 300 BCE)[8] and Manetho (an Egyptian writer from the third century BCE).[9]

On this basis, the most appropriate translations of the words in question are 'Judaean' and 'Judaeanism'. The second problem with using 'Jew', 'Jewish' and 'Judaism' is the extent to which they now carry meanings indelibly shaped by events after the first century, such as the development of a different identity for the people around the Mishnah, their experience in mediaeval Europe and the watershed of the Holocaust, so that they are anachronistic in connection with the ancient period. For those who are not willing to go as far as 'Judaean' and 'Judaeanism', 'Israelite' and 'Israel' probably represent a reasonable compromise. Some might object that using 'Judaean' as the translation for *Ioudaios* means losing a way of referring to an inhabitant of the geographic region of Judaea. But Josephus himself faced this issue and it did not deter him from using *Ioudaios* more generally.[10]

---

primary ethnic designation is 'Judaean' because of their close links with Judaea and the Temple there, but they happen to live in Galilee and elsewhere.

7.   Harvey (1996), in his interesting coverage of the names for members of the people in Josephus, largely misses this important aspect.

8.   Clearchus has Aristotle state that the *Ioudaioi* are descended from Indian philosophers who in India are called Calani but in Syria 'by the territorial name of Judeans' (*Ioudaioi, tounoma labontes apo tou topou*: literally, 'Judeans, taking the name from the land'), for the district which they inhabit is called Judaea' (Stern 1974: 50). Stern (1974: 50) unhelpfully translates *Ioudaioi* as 'Jews' in spite of the statement in the text directly linking *Ioudaioi* and Judaea.

9.   According to Josephus in *Contra Apionem* 1.228, Manetho (an Egyptian writer from the third century BCE) at one point describes how 'our ancestors' were driven out of Egypt, 'occupied what is now called Judaea, founded Jerusalem, and built the temple' (Stern 1974: 81). This is again consistent with a strongly perceived connection between the name of the people and the name of the land in which was located their capital city and sacred temple.

10.   When he was describing crowds of *Ioudaioi* gathering in Jerusalem both from outside and inside Judaea in 4 BCE after the people had been provoked by the

h. *Sources*

Lastly, we should mention the sources for the study of the Judaean *ethnos* in first-century Palestine. The principal literary sources are the *Jewish War* (written between 75 and 79 CE) and the *Antiquities of the Jews* (written between 93 and 94 CE) of Josephus. They are available in the Loeb series in Greek and English (by Thackeray *et al.*), and an older translation by Whiston (1737; 1987) has frequently been reprinted. Other important literary sources are the works of Philo (in the Loeb version, translated by Colson and Whitaker [1929–43], and a nine-teenth-century translation by Yonge, recently reprinted 1993). There is also a rich collection of Jewish intertestamental literature in Charles-worth (1983, 1985), which includes Judaean historians other than Josephus (1985: 775-919), of which Holladay has provided an edition (1983). The last century has proven a fertile field for the study of Israelite literature of the Second Temple period, with texts emerging from monasteries in places as far apart as Ethiopia and Armenia, the Cairo Geniza and, most dramatically, the caves around Qumran. Convenient translations of the non-biblical manuscripts found at Qumran include those by Vermes (1995) and Martinez (1994), with the latter containing clearer line numeration. Helpful secondary treatments of the Judaean writings composed during the period in question include Nickelsburg (1981), Stone (1984) and Kraft and Nickelsburg (1986: 221-436). M. Stern has edited an important collection of Graeco-Roman authors on 'Jews' and 'Judaism' (1974, 1980, 1984). Lastly, there has been an explosion of information about first-century Palestine from archaeological and other non-literary research. There are introductions

conduct of Sabinus, the Roman procurator of Syria, he stated (as translated in the Loeb edition): 'So on the arrival of Pentecost...it was not the customary ritual so much as indignation which drew the people [*dêmos*] in crowds to the capital. A countless multitude flocked in from Galilee, from Idumaea, from Jericho, and from Peraea beyond the Jordan, but it was the native population of Judaea itself [*ho gnêsios ex autês Ioudaias laos*] which, both in numbers and in ardour, was pre-eminent (*War* 2.43; Loeb: II, 339).'

The word *gnêsios* means 'belonging to the race (*genos*)', hence 'genuine' or 'legitimate'. Accordingly, the Loeb translation does not convey quite the right meaning. Josephus does not have in mind simply those who happened to live within Judaea, 'natives' in that sense. He is referring to such of the people belonging to the particular ethnic group in question who lived in Judaea itself (as opposed to those who did not). Perhaps a more accurate translation would be 'but it was the membership of the people from Judaea itself'.

to this field by Meyers and Strange (1981) and Meyers and Kraabel (1986), and a more recent review in relation to Galilee by Overman (1993). Since some of this work fails to take sufficient account of the distinctive socio-economic features of Palestine as an advanced agrarian society where the elite extracted the agricultural surplus of the non-elite (see next section), the writings of Sean Freyne (1980, 1995, 2000), who is very sensitive to the nature of the system, and the recent jointly authored work by K.C. Hanson and Douglas E. Oakman (1998), repay consideration.

2. Political Religion, Temple and Elite

a. The Functions of the Temple

The Temple in Jerusalem was the institutional heart of Judaean identity. Originally constructed when the Israelites returned from their captivity in Babylon late in the sixth century BCE (Ezra 3), it was massively rebuilt and magnificently adorned with white marble, gold and cedar by Herod the Great, in a project that was begun in 20 BCE and largely completed within 18 months, that work continued for nearly 70 years. As already noted, Josephus regarded the decision of Cyrus to permit the people to return to Judaea and rebuild the Temple as inaugurating a new epoch for the *ethnos*, marked by his adoption of the name *Ioudaioi* for the people from then on, which had persisted into his time.

The Temple had a political function in as much as it was the institution that legitimated the control the priestly elite exercised over Palestine, in conjunction with Roman and Herodian authorities. The high priestly elite controlled religious operations and religious symbols, and the vast economic resources they required, in a way that benefited them directly. For this reason it is appropriate to refer to Judaism (or 'Judeanism') as a political religion.

In spite of its central role, we should be alert to the extent to which the Temple represented very distinct interests and could be a focus for division rather than harmony. In suggesting that the Temple and its sacrificial cult formed a unifying centre of a 'common Judaism', E.P. Sanders (1992: 47-76) is correct in underlining the cultic importance of the Temple, but errs in focusing too closely on cultic practices—where there was a measure of Judaean solidarity—while ignoring other areas characterized by a marked divisiveness. I have already proposed that it is helpful to distinguish between political and domestic 'religion' in first-century Palestine, and that religious issues were closely integrated with administration and economics, as well as politics. The recent work by Hanson and Oakman (1998: 135-54) very clearly sets out the patterns of relationship involved. Nevertheless, it is in the interests of conceptual clarity to deal these with elements separately.

1. *Cult*. The underlying idea of the Herodian Temple, like others in the ancient Near East, was that here, in some mysterious sense, God dwelt on earth and human beings could get close to him (Esler 1987: 152-54). Sacrifice was the particular mechanism chosen for achieving this end. Malina (1996) has recently offered a useful interpretation of the meaning of sacrifice within the political religion represented by the Temple as a ritual in which an offering is rendered humanly irretrieveable and ingestible and then directed as an inducement to God in the guise of king or lord by someone lower in social status to have some beneficial life-effect.

There were two broad types of sacrifice in the Temple. First, every day there was a morning and evening sacrifice of a lamb on behalf of the whole people (the *tamid* offering). Secondly, numerous other sacrifices were made on behalf of individuals, either (a) burnt offerings to thank or honour God; (b) sin or guilt offerings, to atone for various forms of transgressions or to purify the transgressor; (c) shared sacrifices, for various purposes, including thanks and praise, where the animal was apportioned on the altar for consumption by the priest, the offeror and his family and friends, or in expiation for sin (atonement sacrifices) (Sanders 1992: 103-18).

The personnel required for these cult included priests, Levites, singers and gatekeepers.

2. *Administration*. The Temple was the locus of the Sanhedrin, a court convened by the high priest and comprising representative of priestly families and people with legal and scribal expertise. It also required a considerable staff to maintain the order and purity of its precincts, including a police force of Levites.

3. *Economic Dimension*. The existence of the Temple and an elite who profited from it had a decisive impact on the production and distribution of goods in Palestine. According to Josephus (*Ant.* 12.140), the Temple needed large supplies of animals (calves, rams, lambs and doves), incense, flour, wine, oil, salt and water, which originated in

Judaea or Galilee, or farther east (in Nabatea or Mesopotamia). Also needed were wood, linen, wool and precious metals (Hanson and Oakman 1998: 151). The high priests obtained these from their own estates, from tithe and tax (like the Temple tax) and through trade. The burden of taxation on the peasants, although underestimated by some commentators like E.P. Sanders (1992: 146-69), was no doubt severe, and peasant indebtedness grew during the Roman period. The *prosbul* measure attributed to Hillel abolished the protection afforded by Deut. 15.1-2 and thereby greatly improved the position of the creditor in relation to the debtor (Neusner 1973: 16-17).

One particularly profitable line of business was the monopolistic sale of sacrificial animals and the exchange of Greek and Roman coinage into the Syrian half-shekel used for payment of the Temple tax. This business must have required considerable personnel. There is a strong chance that it was run at excessive profit levels (Bauckham 1988). The money spent by the large numbers of pilgrims who visited Jerusalem each year made a signficant contribution to the Judaean economy (Broshi 1987).

It is difficult to assess the reaction of the peasantry to the tithes and taxes they were required to pay. Although the Temple was the place where they could discharge various forms of indebtedness, it might also be the occasion of their children going hungry. There is good evidence (Evans 1989b) that the high priestly families were regarded as being corrupt and taking more than they were entitled, a phenomenon having a long history in Israel (1 Sam. 2.12-17). Little wonder, then, that Jesus should complain that the Temple had been turned into a robbers' den (Mk 11.17).

b. *Members of the Elite*
1. *High Priests.* The Temple was run by the high priests. During the Roman period high priests were appointed by Rome or its agents from certain aristocratic families, of which a number were particularly prominent, as can be seen from lists in Josephus and the Mishnah. The high priests profited hugely from the Temple and it was in their interests to cooperate with Rome quite closely to ensure that nothing happened to disturb the *status quo*. Archaeological excavations in Jerusalem have revealed extremely luxurious houses from the first century that must have belonged to the elite, quite possibly the high priests (Avigad 1983).

2. *Sadducees.* There are few sources concerning the Sadducees (see the discussion in LeMoyne 1972). Even the meaning of their name (Greek: *Saddoukaios*; Hebrew: *Saddûqîm* and variants) is uncertain (LeMoyne 1972: 155-63). On one view, they traced their descent to Zadok, a high priest in the time of David, although the forms of their name do not necessarily support this view. Another possibility is that the name characterizes them as 'just' or 'righteous'.

Sadducees enter the historical stage in Josephus's account of the reign of John Hyrcanus, in the context of a struggle for power with the Pharisees in which they were successful, to the extent that their practices and policies replaced those of the Pharisees (*Ant.* 13.293-298).[11] They clearly numbered some members of the elite among their members, either lay (such as Jonathan the Sadducee, who was a friend of John Hyrcanus) or priestly (such as the high priest Ananus who had James the Just put to death in the interim period between the procuratorships of Festus and Albinus in the sixties of the first century [*Ant.* 20.199-203]). This does not mean that all Sadducees belonged to the governing class (although that is a reasonable possibility, as Sanders has proposed [1992: 318]), or that all members of the governing class were Sadducees (Saldarini 1988: 106). Yet the fact that they were less popular with the people than the Pharisees may indicate that they were more closely aligned to the ruling elite, rather than serving the elite as retainers. On the three occasions they are mentioned in Acts they are associated with the Jerusalem elite (4.1; 5.17; 23.6-8).

Very little is known of their beliefs, which are usefully discussed by Sanders (1992: 332-36). The main sources are those places where Josephus discusses them in relation to the Pharisees (*War* 2.164-66; *Ant.* 13.171-73) and a few New Testament passages (Mk 12.18 and parallels; Acts 23.6-8). While they rejected additions to the written law, it is unlikely that they did not follow any beliefs and practices not found in Israelite scripture, since this would have left them without a particular calendar. Perhaps the better view is that they rejected non-biblical traditions (such as the Pharisaic 'traditions of the fathers') of which they did not approve (Sanders 1992: 334). The execution of James the Just by Ananus tends to confirm their reputation for being

---

11. For the references to the Sadducees and Pharisees in Josephus, see Schalit (1968).

very strict enforcers of the law. They certainly denied the survival of the soul after death and the resurrection of the body.

While it is difficult to find an adequate description for the Sadducees, Saldarini usefully refers to them (and the Pharisees) as a 'political interest group who wished to influence the way Jewish life was lived religiously, socially and politically' (1988: 106).

3. *Herodians*. At various times in the first century BCE and the first century CE members of the Herodian family held power in Palestine as vassal rulers under Roman control. The main periods were the reign of Herod the Great from 37–4 BCE, followed by the reigns of his three sons after his death: (a) Archelaus in Judaea, Samaria and Idumea from 4 BCE to 6 CE; (b) of Herod Antipas in Galilee/Perea from 4 BCE to 39 CE, and (c) Philip over the non-Israelite area northeast of Galilee from 4 BCE to 33/34 CE. Herod Agrippa I also reigned over most of Palestine for the brief period 41–44 CE.

Their place in the Palestinian social and political system must be seen in terms of their role as clients of Rome, continuously working to maintain their elite status in cooperation with Roman interests (see Hanson and Oakman 1998: 82-86). The word *Herodianoi*, 'Herodians', which appears in Mark (3.6; 12.13) and Matthew (22.26), although never in Josephus, covers both the Herods themselves and also their extensive circle of clients and retainers, who are actually referred to in Mk 6.14-29 in attendance at the birthday party of Herod Antipas as power elites (*megistanoi*), senior military leaders (*chiliarchoi*) and the leaders (*prôtoi*), probably village elders, of Galilee. The Herodian kings were situated at the centre of networks consisting of members of the elite and retainers that stood over against the peasants who supplied the agricultural surplus needed to underpin their power and lifestyle, even if they also benefited from taxes imposed on goods and travellers passing through their territories.

c. *Retainers of the Elite*
1. *Scribes*. Scribes (Hebrew: *sofer*; Greek: *grammateus*) were significant figures in Palestinian Judaism at all periods, as they had been throughout the ancient Near East from the times when ruling elites first came to accumulate peasants' agricultural surpluses in cities. Essentially retainers of the elite, they served such functions as drawing up legal documents, copying sacred texts, serving as administrators and

accountants, recording taxes and even offering legal advice. They also aided the illiterate non-elite by writing letters for them. Josephus employs the word *grammateus* for officials at all levels from village to the royal court. Scribes were not a cohesive group, but persons located at various parts of the social system wherever skills of literacy, numeracy and management were needed. Saldarini plausibly suggests that most scribes were middle-level officials, agents of the elite and serving in various bureaucratic posts. Their positions gave them power and influence, but they were dependent on the priests and leading families in Jerusalem and the Herodian leaders, like Herod Antipas in Galilee during the time of Jesus. The very highest level of scribe, on the other hand, may have come from the elite itself and would probably have been well educated in the law and in the cultural and religious traditions of the people (Saldarini 1988: 274-75).

2. *Pharisees.* The last century has witnessed a lively discussion on the identity and characteristics of the Pharisees.[12] The issues are troubled by difficulties surrounding the sources and the very different methodologies adopted by various commentators, many of whom rely on unexamined (and usually anachronistic) assumptions about how Palestinian society functioned, as Saldarini has shown (1988).

Our three main sources are Josephus, the New Testament and rabbinic literature. Among a number of passages referring to the Pharisees, Josephus offers detailed (and parallel) descriptions of them, in the context of discussing various groups in Palestine (including the Sadducees and the Essenes), in the *Jewish War* (2.162-66) and in the *Antiquities of the Jews* (18.12-17). In each case he singles out features relating to their way of life, thought and influence. Elsewhere he notes that they adhered to customs handed down by their ancestors and this led to conflict with the Sadducees, who recognized only the written law (*Ant.* 13.297-98). Josephus presents them as one of number of groups in Palestine who sought to increase their influence during opportune periods, such as the reign of John Hyrcanus (*Ant.* 13.288-89), when Queen Alexandra sought to maintain control after the death of her husband Alexander Jannaeus in 76 BCE (*Ant.* 13.398-407), and at the transition to Roman rule in Judaea after the death of Herod in 4 BCE

---

12. Useful recent treatments include Neusner (1971, 1973), Bowker (1973), Saldarini (1988), Goodblatt (1989), Sanders (1990a, 1990b), and Stemberger (1995).

(*Ant.* 18.4). He refers to them using a number of words of which the most prominent is *hairesis*. It is difficult to find an appropriate translation. 'Sect' is no help, since in social-scientific terminology a sect means a group that has split from a parent religion so that joint membership is no longer possible. This was not the case with the Pharisees, who remained a part of Israel. To translate *hairesis* as 'school of thought' over-emphasizes their thoughts and beliefs to the detriment of other aspects of their identity.

Pharisees appear frequently in the New Testament (see Saldarini 1988: 144-98). It is interesting that the earliest extant use of *Pharisaios* comes at Phil. 3.5, in Paul's claim to have been one before his conversion. He says he is a Pharisee in relation to the law, and this aspect of his previous life might be connected with his assertion at Gal. 1.15 that he had been excessively zealous for his 'ancestral traditions'. In the Gospels and in the Acts of the Apostles the Pharisees come into contact, even controversy, with Jesus. They often seem to act as retainers for the elite, for example, by encouraging the payment of tithes to the priests. In the Gospel of John they play a heightened role as opponents of Jesus, especially since John deletes the scribes and elders from this role, which they had in the Synoptics. This seems to represent an unhistorial simplification by John of a more complicated picture.

It is frequently stated that the rabbis were the direct descendants of the Pharisees. Yet if there was a strong connection like this we would expect the rabbis to refer to their predecessors as *perushim* (a Hebrew equivalent of *Pharisaioi*, meaning separatists), but they hardly ever do, preferring the word *Hakamim* (the Wise) for this role (Bowker 1973: 4-5). On the other hand, if the Pharisees had survived the war of 66–73 CE as the major group, they would thenceforth be mainstream rather than merely one among a number of elements. Certainly there are strong grounds for believing that the *Hakamim* are related to the *Pharisaioi* of Josephus, given the general similarities between his accounts and what is said of the *Hakamim* in the rabbinic sources and the fact that particular incidents are told of both (Bowker 1973: 5; Sanders 1992: 413).

An important recent discussion of the nature of the Pharisees was inaugurated by Jacob Neusner, who proposed that the Pharisees had begun as a politically active group, but left the political arena in the time of Herod the Great and turned to more religious issues (1971, 1973). He argued that when one subjected rabbinic traditions to form-critical analysis (an approach he pioneered) it was apparent that the main themes in the strata of material relating to the first half of the first century CE were ritual purity, tithes, food laws and sabbath and festival observance. The Pharisees seem to have advocated a holiness in domestic settings similar to that of the priests in the Temple. This latter aspect has been challenged by E.P. Sanders, who argues that although the Pharisees aspired to a level of purity above the ordinary, they did not go as far as the Jerusalem priesthood (1992: 438-40).

Perhaps a useful term for the Pharisees is that of 'reform movement', referring to a group who stays within a parent religion but advocates the reform or intensification of its ideas and institutions (Esler 1987: 47-53). At the same time, Saldarini is right in seeking to set the Pharisees within the larger social system of Palestine as retainers to the elite, sometimes seeking and occasionally achieving wider political influence.

3. *The Non-Elite and Domestic Religion*

The vast mass of the Israelite *ethnos* living in Palestine belonged to the non-elite. While many, if not most, of them looked to the Temple as the cultic centre of their religious beliefs, as shown by the large numbers that went on pilgrimage to Jerusalem at the time of the three great feasts each year, this was a sign of the extent to which they had been socialized to accept the Great Tradition of the elite to an unusual degree. Yet we have already considered evidence for a resentment toward the avarice of the high priests in some quarters at least. Accordingly, E.P. Sanders's bland description of 'normal' or 'common' Judaism as that which 'the priests and the people agreed on' (1992: 47), while being accurate to a degree, rather obscures the politics of the situation. One needs to take into account the social context in which religious beliefs and practices were pervasively embedded and to consider the other manifestations of religiosity, in the synagogue and the home, to get a fuller picture.

a. *Village, Subsistence and Taxation*
The non-elite of Palestine, the peasants especially, but also fishermen, petty traders and artisans, produced the products that the elite taxed and tithed to maintain their position. Understanding how the system worked necessitates examining in detail the various aspects of production, distribution and mechanisms of control (Hanson and Oakman 1998: 101-25), a task beyond the scope of this essay other than in very general terms.

Agriculture was the basis of the economy, but it was not very productive. Palestinian peasants could expect a yield at best 10–15 times the grain seed sown, whereas modern farmers can obtain 40 times or better (Oakman 1986: 63). In first-century Palestine there was tension between the need of the peasantry to produce subsistence crops and the desire of the elites to have crops for sale (Hanson and Oakman 1998: 106); just the same tendency by the elite had been castigated by the prophets of the eighth century BCE (Esler 1998b: 151-62). Much of the land in Palestine was under the control of the various sections of the elite—Romans, high priests and Herodians (Fiensy 1991), which a large number of peasants worked as tenants or even day labourers. Yet we should not make the mistake of imagining a free labour market, since much of this labour was supplied to discharge indebtedness (Hanson and Oakman 1998: 113). Although money was not central to the system and much distribution among the peasantry was done by barter, there are signs of increasing monetarization in the early first century (Freyne 1995). There is no reason to think that the level of taxation on the peasants was anything other than onerous and oppressive (Hanson and Oakman 1998: 113-16). Arguments to the contrary by Sanders (1992: 146-69) and Udoh (1996) unfortunately proceed without reference to comparative perspectives.[13] Josephus contains a graphic description of the onerous taxation policy of Herod the Great (*Ant.* 17.306-308), as well acknowledging the extractive practices of Roman governors (*Ant.* 18.176).

b. *Synagogues*
An inscription found in Jerusalem and almost certainly to be dated to the period before 70 CE runs as follows:

> Theodotus, son of Vettanos, priest and *archisynagôgos*, son of an *archisynagôgos*, grandson of an *archisynagôgos*, built the synagogue for Torah-reading and for the teaching of the commandments. Furthermore, the hostel and the chambers, and the water installation for lodging needy strangers. Its foundation stone was laid by his ancestors, the elders and Simonides.[14]

13. Thus Sanders can contemplate (1992: 167) a taxation level of 28 per cent without any suggestion from comparable peasant experience of what this would actually mean to the lives of the peasants concerned.

14. This translation is given by Hanson and Oakman (1998: 79); for the Greek text and discussion, see Riesner (1995: 192-200).

Here we have evidence for the existence of the synagogue as an Israelite institution in Palestine centring on the teaching of the Mosaic law during the first century CE and probably earlier. This is matched by a reasonable amount of literary evidence for the existence of synagogues, such as Mk 6.1-6 (Nazareth), Acts 6.9 (Jerusalem) and Josephus, *War* 2.285-91 (Caesarea). One gains the impression that the synagogue was an important gathering place for first-century Palestinian Israelites.

There is at present under way a lively reassessment of the origins of the synagogue. The view that it originated in the time of the Babylonian exile and during the return to Palestine in the sixth century BCE, which has been very popular from the sixteenth century until quite recently, has been subjected to heavy attack as resting on a virtually nonexistent evidentiary basis (Urman and Flesher 1995: xx-xxiii). There is even evidence for believing that synagogues only appeared in Palestine at all after the Maccabaean revolt (Grabbe 1995: 19-23). Our earliest evidence for synagogues hitherto comes from Egyptian papyri dated to the third and second centuries BCE (Griffiths 1995), on the assumption that the expression *proseuchê*, originally meaning 'prayer' but used in this material with reference to a building, is actually an abbreviation for *oikos tês proseuchês*, 'house of prayer'. This is a reasonable view to take of the evidence.

One of the Egyptian papyri referring to the *proseuchê*, from the second half of the first century BCE, distinguishes it from the assembly of Israelites itself, the *synagôgê* (Kasher 1995: 209). Hengel has made a good case for the proposal that *synagôgê* was actually used of the building itself in Palestine up to the first century CE (as in the Theodotus inscription) and thereafter largely supplanted *proseuchê*, which had been employed in the Greek-speaking Diaspora (Hengel 1971: 171-80). This meant that the word, which had originally referred to an Israelite group, came to be applied to the building in which it met.

There is still very little archaeological evidence for synagogues in Palestine for the first century CE, let alone earlier. Uncertainty remains as to whether the structures identified as synagogues at Masada and Herodium actually fulfilled that function (Flesher 1995: 34-38). The only archaeologically solid evidence for first-century Palestinian synagogues is that referred to in the Theodotus inscription from Jerusalem and the remains from Gamala (Flesher 1995: 38-39) and Migdal (Groh 1995: 58-59), both in Galilee. Nevertheless, the growing archaeological activity in the Galilee is proving an important source of understanding of ancient Palestinian synagogues (Groh 1995).

The synagogue was clearly a vital institution for the installation of the Great Tradition in the minds and hearts of the non-elite, which we have already noted was an essential feature of the Palestinian Judaism. At the same time, it probably functioned in a conservative way to confirm local roles and statuses. Jesus soon felt the pressure to conform when he spoke in the synagogue at Nazareth otherwise than in keeping with his accustomed role as a craftsman (*tektôn*), the son of Mary and the brother of other villagers (Mk 6.3).

4. *Diversity, Unrest and Messianic Expectations*

a. *Unrest in First-Century Palestine*
No picture of Palestinian Judaism would be complete without mention of the diversity and unrest that characterized it, especially in the first century, and again for a brief period in 132–35 CE. Fuelling the instability were many factors, but no doubt two critical ones were non-elite dissatisfaction with the prevailing social and economic arrangements, especially in the form of Herodian and Roman taxation, and widespread dislike of rule by Rome and not by God.

The difficult conditions of the peasants led to much indebtedness to the elite and their retainers. Security for such debts could be taken in to the form of crop liens or mortgages over land, with default leading to dispossession. This was probably the main cause for the rise of banditry in the first century. Bandits in this sense are not the mere plunderers portrayed by Josephus but most commonly peasants who have been repressed, especially through high taxation, and forced from their land and village (Hobsbawm 1981). They respond by organizing themselves into gangs that prey upon the interests of the elite. The phenomenon in Palestine is well described by Hanson and Oakman (1998: 86-90), with fuller details in Horsley (1993: 37-39). Josephus has 14 separate references to bandits (named or unnamed) in his writings for the period from 47 BCE to 67–70 CE.[15] Bandit activity increased in the forties, fifties and sixties of the first century and bandits played a vital role in the revolt against Rome.

In particular, many peasants who had turned to banditry because of

---

15. For full details, see the chart in Hanson and Oakman (1998: 91).

the advance of the Romans in Galilee in 67–68 CE fled to Jerusalem where they formed a coalition called the 'Zealots', where they tried to set up an alternative rule to that of the high priests. They advocated a purified Temple and freedom from Roman rule, regarding themselves as being 'zealous' for all that was good. They perhaps drew inspiration from Phinehas in Num. 25.6-15, who is called a 'zealot' in the Septuagint.[16] An alternative view of the 'Zealots', associated especially with the writings of Martin Hengel (1961), which saw them as an organized movement of resistance going back as far as 6 CE, has been strongly criticized by Horsley (1993: x-xi, 77-80).

Yet there was also an urban context for unrest. Interesting examples of the populace of Jerusalem, swollen by pilgrims, taking direct action to rectify perceived injustices, can be seen in (a) the disturbances in the Holy City in 4 BCE relating to their protest to Archelaus following the funeral of Herod the Great;[17] (b) the consternation caused by Pilate's introduction of imperial standards into Jerusalem;[18] and (c) their unhappiness at the provocative act by a Roman soldier during the governship of Cumanus (48–52 CE).[19] Secondly, Jerusalem in the fifties witnessed the rise of the 'Sicarii' ('Dagger-men'; *Ant.* 20.186). The Sicarii engaged in assassination of members of the Jerusalem elite, beginning with Jonathan the high priest (*War* 2.254-56), and kidnapping for ransom. Their actions clearly reflect extreme dissatisfaction in one part of the Palestinian non-elite with the way the country was governed by the high priests and Rome (Horsley 1993: 39-43).

b. *Millennial Dreams, Prophets and Messiahs*
Much of this unrest crystallized around visions of a future soon to be transformed that drew upon themes from Israel's Great Tradition. The experience of colonized peoples in modern times reveals how often indigenous cultures that have suffered dislocation at the hands of foreign rulers generate millennial dreams of a new future, generally formulated by a charismatic leader of the Weberian type, in which the intruders will be removed and the old ways restored. Examples range

---

16. For the Zealots, see Goodman (1987: 219-220) and Horsley (1993: 56-58, 77-78).

17. Josephus, *Ant.* 17.204-207; *War* 2.4-7.

18. Josephus, *War* 2.169-74.

19. Josephus, *Ant.* 20.108.

from the Cargo cults of Melanesia to the Ghost Dance of North America (Esler 1994: 98-104). Millennial movements from other contexts, such as seventeenth-century England (Rowland 1988), are instructive, but lack the relevant colonial dimension to these phenomena. While there is no inevitable connection between relative or absolute deprivation produced by colonization and visions of this kind, such a social context often accompanies and helps to explain them. Similarly, in first-century Palestine there were a number of popular movements led by particular individuals who evoked for their followers the prospect of God's decisive intervention into history on behalf of his people in ways reminiscent of great moments in Israel's past.[20]

Barnett (1980–81) usefully coined the phrase 'sign prophets' to describe one type of first-century phenomenon, to which Rebecca Gray has devoted a useful monograph (1993).[21] There are three examples described by Josephus. During Pilate's reign a Samaritan led his armed followers to Mount Gerizim to see sacred vessels allegedly buried there by Moses, but they were crushed by the Romans (*Ant.* 18.85-86). In the mid-forties a self-styled prophet named Theudas led his followers from the common people (*ochlos*), with their possessions, to the river Jordan, telling them that it would divide, apparently as the Red Sea had done for Moses. The scene is like a latter-day exodus from the bondage of Egypt. The Romans also destroyed this group (*Ant.* 20.97-98; Acts 5.36). Thirdly, in 56 CE another self-styled prophet, allegedly from Egypt, told his followers that at his command the walls of Jerusalem would fall down, as as had happened with Joshua outside Jericho. Again, they were defeated by the Romans, although the Egyptian escaped (*Ant.* 20.169-70; *War* 2.261-62; Acts 21.38).

Much interest has focused on a particular kind of millennial expectation referred to in the field as 'messianism', the view that a future figure acting as God's anointed agent (*masiah*, 'anointed one' in Aramaic,

20. Many commentators use the word 'eschatological' to refer to the future-orientated and transformative content of first-century phenomena analogous to modern millennialism, and 'apocalyptic' to refer to literature dealing with the direct revelation of the divine will that often characterized the genre of 'eschatological' texts. Both of these terms are now so overloaded with various theological and literary agendas, however, that they should only be used with care.

21. In *Ant.* 20.168 Josephus speaks of 'imposters and deceivers' who called upon others to follow them out into the desert where they would display signs and wonders done according to God's plan.

messiah in Hebrew and *christos* in Greek) would soon arrive bringing with him a radical change in the current dispensation, in the inter-related areas of religion, politics and social and economic arrange-ments. Such a role suggests that the ruling elite would have been antipathetic toward messiahs and messianic movements as posing a threat to the *status quo* on which they depended. The word *messiah/ christos* does not occur in relation to the three movements just de-scribed in Josephus. Indeed, we are rather handicapped in our under-standing of actual messianic movements, however, by virtue of the fact that our major source, Josephus (himself originating in the Palestinian elite), was not interested in providing details about them.

Yet there is a reasonable variety of messianic texts, although not all of them actually use the word messiah. It is preferable to work with messianism in the functional sense just outlined than to concentrate too closely on the word itself. While many of these texts envisage a Davidic messiah: *Psalms of Solomon* 17 (see Davenport 1980), Sibyl-line Oracle 5 (see Collins 1984: 187-91) and Philo (see Borgen 1992), a non-Davidic messiah can be found in the Parables of Enoch (*1 Enoch* 37–71, on which see VanderKam 1992: 169-91). A variety of messi-anic figures are represented at Qumran, such as the Messiah of Israel, the Messiah of Aaron, the Prophet and the angelic figure of Michael/ Melchizedek (see Talmon 1987; Schiffman 1992). Most of these texts were written before 70 CE, but some, such as 4 Ezra came after. We are faced with a great variety of ideas expressed in texts treasured by diverse interests within Israel, so that we should not imagine that there was any monovalent understanding of messiahship in Palestine in the period in question. Nor should we try to cobble together a composite picture ourselves from the sources, representing as they do different periods and different groups.

Perhaps the most interesting of all the messianic texts is *Psalms of Solomon* 17, written in the middle of the first century BCE, since in vv. 21-45 it presents a very full picture of a messiah (described as such in v. 32). God will raise up this Davidic king, giving him strength to destroy unrighteous rulers and purify Jerusalem of Gentiles. He will gather a holy people and end injustice. He will distribute the people 'on the land according to their tribes'. He will judge in righteousness, enslave the Gentiles and honour God in a purified Jerusalem. He will not 'concentrate hopes in a multitude for a day of war', but will 'strike the earth with the word of his mouth forever'; free from sin, he will

condemn rulers and drive out sinners by the strength of his word. He
will be powerful in the Holy Spirit and the blessing of God. It is clear
how unpalatable such sentiments would have been to the high priests
and Romans ruling Palestine from Jerusalem, even though the extent to
which the text may have been used by representatives of the non-elite
against the elite between the date of its composition and 70 CE is completely unknown.

5. *The Significance of the War with Rome (66–70 CE)*

a. *Reasons for the Revolt*
There were three moments of revolt against local and/or Roman rule in
Palestine: in 4 BCE (on the death of Herod the Great), in 66–70 CE
(although Masada did not fall until 73 CE) and in 132–35 CE. In each
case the question of the reason for the revolt is well worth asking, although most attention has focused on the war with Rome in 66–70 CE.
Richard Horsley interprets the events of this time as the culmination of
non-elite antipathy to the repression that they experienced (1993: 49-
58), triggered by the violence and ineptitude of the last Roman prefects
before the revolt (especially Florus in the period 64–66). There is much
to be said for this type of interpretation, as it rests upon a socially real-
istic understanding of the extremely difficult situation of the Palestinian peasantry to which many other commentators fail to pay sufficient
attention. A very different view is that of Goodman (1987), who down-
plays the factors of economic distress and religious ideology and
argues that the most significant cause lay in faction-fighting within the
ruling Judaean elite.

b. *The Consequences of the Revolt*
Whatever the causes of the revolt, its course (for which see Smallwood
1976) and consequences, especially the destruction of Jerusalem and
the Temple, described in graphic detail by Josephus in Book 7 of *The
Jewish War*, proved catastrophic for Judaeanism in Palestine. Apart
from the large numbers of people killed in the fighting, many thousands
more were sold into slavery. With the institutional heart of Israel
destroyed, and the sacrificial cult no longer possible, Israelites were
deprived of their major form of redemptive media. In this context,
accordingly, it is not surprising that there seems to have been an
upsurge in the use of other modes of access to the divine will, such as

through the creation of apocalyptic texts that told of the revelations by God or his angels to seers. Three such texts, *4 Ezra*, *2 Baruch* and the *Apocalypse of Abraham* have recently been interpreted as responses to the destruction of Jerusalem in 70, although they were written a few decades thereafter (Stone 1981; Esler 1995b). Furthermore, unlike many other indigenous peoples who have been crushed by a colonizing power, the Israelites had a theological tradition that stressed that they were God's chosen people among all the nations of the earth. Given their total defeat by Rome, this doctrine of election produced a powerful dissonance, an agonizing disjunction between what their religious beliefs suggested should happen and their actual experience (Esler 1994: 128). *4 Ezra* in particular, a magnificent religious text on any basis, arguably had the social and religious function of reducing this dissonance (Esler 1994: 128-30).

c. *Jamnia*
Yet one of the primary ways in which *4 Ezra* sought to manage this sense of dissonance was by re-endorsing the Mosaic law as the source of life for Israel. It encouraged Israel to rediscover its identity by gathering round the law in the quiet fulfilment of its obligations (Esler 1994: 129). That process was to culminate in the compilation of the Mishnah around 200 CE, which supplemented the law with the collection of a huge body of oral tradition.

I will end this essay with a brief review of the beginnings of that long process. A rabbinic legend, which probably has some foundation in fact, recounts how Rabbi Johanan ben Zakkai, having escaped from Jerusalem when the city was under Roman siege during the revolt of 66–70 CE, sought and obtained permission from Vespasian to found a school at Jamnia (Saldarini 1975), a city (known in Hebrew as Yavneh) located on the coastal plain of Judaea between Joppa and Azotus (Schürer 1979: 109-10). A group of scholars gathered around him, many of them no doubt from among those whom Josephus and the New Testament calls Pharisees, although the precise connection between the rabbis and the Pharisees of earlier times is hard to specify (Cohen 1984), as noted above.

Unfortunately, no contemporary documents survive that relate what transpired at Jamnia, and we must depend on a variety of (often much) later rabbinic sources. Nevertheless, the evidence suggests that Ben Zakkai ran his school for about ten years, until Gamaliel II took over.

The school moved to Usha in about 135 CE, after the disastrous Bar Kochba revolt.

The sources that are extant suggest that Ben Zakkai's primary interest was to stabilize and to an extent redefine Israelite legal traditions, which was an urgent task now that the Temple lay in ruins. The previous leading role of the priests was taken over by the rabbis, and cultic practice replaced by a culture of intense study of the law and group decisions as to its content and ambit in a wide variety of situations.

It is possible that the factionalism that had previously characterized Judaism was replaced by mutual tolerance within Judaism, at least for those who were happy to remain among the gathering at Jamnia, with those who did not being branded as *minim* (heretics) and accursed (Cohen 1984).

Although the view argued by Ryle (1892) that the third part of the Israelite canon of scripture, 'the writings', was closed at Jamnia in about 90 CE has been widely influential, it lacks convincing demonstration (Lewis 1992: 634; McDonald 1995: 28-30).

DIASPORA JUDAISM

John M.G. Barclay

1. *What's in a Name: 'Hellenistic' or 'Diaspora' Judaism?*

What term shall we use to describe the Judaism that is not 'Palestinian Judaism'? For a long period scholars have contrasted 'Palestinian' with 'Hellenistic' Judaism, thus conveying the impression that Palestinian Judaism was not 'Hellenized', whereas Judaism outside Palestine was, to a more or less uniform degree. But most scholars now recognize that this is seriously misleading: Palestinian Judaism was, in varying respects and to varying degrees, significantly 'Hellenized', while Jews outside Palestine were enormously varied in their 'Hellenization' (see below, section 3). With the work of E. Bickerman (1939), V. Tcherikover (1961), S. Lieberman (1962) and M. Hengel (1969) in the middle of this century, the realization began to dawn that to contrast 'Palestinian' with 'Hellenistic' Judaism was to over-simplify a highly complex cultural map and, more fundamentally, to confuse *geographical* with *cultural* boundaries. 'Hellenization' was a process too subtle and multiform to be so neatly demarcated.

But if all Second Temple Judaism was 'Hellenistic', though in a highly variegated manner, can we find a less misleading term for its non-Palestinian forms? The most obvious contrast to 'Palestinian' would be another geographical term, and here we most naturally turn to the traditional label for existence outside the homeland: 'the Diaspora'. A critic would immediately and rightly point out that the boundary between 'homeland' and 'Diaspora' was not constant or always self-evident in antiquity, as the sphere of Jewish territorial control fluctuated over time. But even if one grants some local ambiguities around the edges of the Jewish state, for the vast bulk of Diaspora Jews it was clear enough that they were *not* in the 'homeland'. A critic would also assert, again rightly, that terms like 'homeland' and 'Diaspora' seem to connote a particular understanding of Jewish 'belonging' that not all

Jews in antiquity (or today) would share. 'Diaspora' means, in Greek, 'scattering' (English-speakers used to employ the term 'the Dispersion'), and it has been shown that in ancient Jewish usage it generally had connotations of 'exile', brought about by divine judgment (van Unnik 1993). But we know that some, perhaps many, Jews in the ancient 'Diaspora' did not think of their location in that way, nor did all necessarily regard Palestine as their 'homeland' in any meaningful sense. Again we may grant this, but continue to use the term 'Diaspora' in as neutral a sense as possible; there seems to be no better alternative.

The most awkward critic would object that the single term 'Diaspora' suggests that all Jews outside Palestine lived in the same conditions or shared the same views. Would it be better to refuse any single term, and to place alongside Palestinian Judaism simply 'Egyptian Judaism', 'Babylonian Judaism', 'Roman Judaism', etc.? This question of the unity and diversity of Diaspora Judaism will concern us below (section 4), but we may here justify the use of the general category on the grounds that, for all their differences, Diaspora Jews had in common the fact that they lived as minority communities in a society governed by non-Jews. That basic fact could give rise to varied social and political conditions, but it determined Diaspora existence nonetheless.

Of course, to place 'Diaspora Judaism' alongside 'Palestinian Judaism' is not to suggest that they were watertight compartments. Many Jews moved between Palestine and 'the Diaspora' (e.g. Paul and Josephus), and there is no necessary ideological difference between Jewish outlooks inside and outside Palestine. Nonetheless, the history of Jews in the Diaspora is to a large extent distinguishable from that of Jews in Palestine and worthy of separate treatment. Curiously, many books on Judaism in antiquity concentrate only or almost exclusively on Jews in Palestine (e.g. Grabbe 1994; Schäfer 1995); their more numerous and highly creative relatives in the Diaspora certainly deserve full and separate analysis (see e.g. Collins 1986; Barclay 1996).

2. *Value Judgments on Diaspora ('Hellenized') Judaism*

The old contrast between 'Palestinian' and 'Hellenistic' Judaism often conveyed an implicit value judgment, which affected scholars' attitudes to the 'Hellenized' Diaspora. The values conveyed by these terms varied in accordance with scholars' perspectives on another and more basic purported contrast, between 'Judaism' and 'Hellenism'. This conceptual contrast has its roots in the Maccabean literature (e.g. 1, 2 and 4 Maccabees), where it was used it for rhetorical and political purposes to defend a particular version of Judaism against 'Hellenistic' pollution. But it was taken up again in nineteenth-century scholarship to serve new ideological ends, and to this day the false impression abounds that 'Judaism' and 'Hellenism' encountered one another only as enemies.

The values attached to the two abstractions, Judaism and Hellenism, sometimes depend on scholars' faith commitments and the particular variant of Judaism or Christianity to which they subscribe. In its post-Enlightenment Christian use, 'Judaism' came to stand for what is narrow, national and particularistic, a religion of the 'flesh' not the 'spirit' (so e.g. Baur 1878). However, 'Hellenistic' Judaism, as found in the Diaspora, could be accorded some merit, as it represented an 'open', 'liberal', 'spiritualized', 'cosmopolitan' or 'universalistic' expression of Judaism (Simon 1948). Its engagement with the surrounding Hellenistic culture could be applauded, and its apologetic and missionary success emphasized (Georgi 1964). From a Christian viewpoint, this might even seem a kind of 'preparation for the Gospel', a development of a universal Judaism that Christianity could utilize and surpass. This acculturated Judaism was also attractive to European Jews engaged in the struggle for 'emancipation', indicating that Jews did not have to withdraw into seclusion to maintain their identity, but could confidently partake in all manner of Gentile cultural pursuits *as Jews*. Viktor Tcherikover, one of the most brilliant Jewish scholars of the twentieth century, carefully assessed the Jews' reaction to Hellenistic civilization in both Palestine and the Diaspora (1961); he also edited the Jewish papyri from Egypt that demonstrated the engagement of Egyptian Jews in their Hellenized environment (with A. Fuks, 1957–64). His positive appreciation of their achievements in this arena was clearly influenced by his commitment to Jewish cultural and political 'emancipation'.

On the other side, such 'Hellenization' of Judaism could be portrayed as a dangerously 'heterodox' phenomenon. Assuming that 'Judaism' and 'Hellenism' were fundamentally incompatible, an influential train of thought, both Jewish and Christian, considered the Palestinian—and specifically the Pharisaic/rabbinic—form of Judaism to be 'normative' (e.g. Moore 1927–30; Wolfson 1948). Here was the expression of 'pure', 'native', 'orthodox' or 'mainstream' Judaism against which all other forms of Judaism were to be measured. If Diaspora Jews used Greek in preference to Hebrew, if they read and appreciated Greek philosophy, if they mixed freely with Greeks in political and social affairs, that only shows how 'assimilated' they had become, and how dangerous it was to contaminate Judaism with any kind of 'syncretism' (a negatively loaded term).

The evidence of Jewish life in the Diaspora could in fact be interpreted in various ways. In the early decades of this century many scholars thought that Diaspora Jews were typically citizens in Greek cities and that there was considerable evidence of Jewish 'syncretism' (e.g. mixing the worship of the Jewish God with the worship of Sabazius). The discovery (in 1932) of the lavishly painted synagogue in Dura Europos, dating from the mid-third century CE, made many wonder whether the rabbinic strictures against representative art had any influence in the Diaspora. Erwin Goodenough employed this evidence, combined with his studies of the Jewish philosopher Philo (from Alexandria, c. 20 BCE–50 CE), as part of his exhaustive garnering of Jewish iconography on tombs, sarcophagi, amulets, etc., to argue that there was a common 'mystical' and 'sacramental' Judaism in the Diaspora, which daringly incorporated pagan symbols and concepts from the mystery cults (1953–68; selected portions, 1988). Not many people were convinced by his specific proposals, but his insistence that the artefacts be taken seriously and his refusal to accept the rabbinic material as 'normative' helped create a sea change in opinion. On the other side of the argument, scholars maintained that there was little or no evidence for 'syncretistic worship', that Jews in the Diaspora continued to look to Jerusalem for leadership and that Diaspora Jews neither were nor wished to be citizens of their host cities. Thus, for instance, Wolfson (1948) interpreted Philo's philosophy as closely related to, even dependent on, that found in rabbinic Judaism, while recently Kasher has urged that no true Jews in the Diaspora could possibly have wanted to gain local citizenship (1985).

It seems that the best way forward is to deconstruct the traditional, value-laden *antithesis* between 'Judaism' and 'Hellenism', and to assess the varied cultural developments of the Diaspora with as little pre-judgment about 'syncretism' and 'orthodoxy' as possible. One useful method is to adopt analytical tools developed *outside* the traditional discourse of Judaism and Christianity, thus minimizing their specific value judgments. For many decades now, sociologists and anthropologists have been studying minority communities and their varied interaction with dominant or host cultures, and scholars of ancient Judaism are just beginning to explore how such disciplines could clarify and illuminate the phenomena they seek to understand.

3. *'Hellenization' and Forms of Acculturation*

One of the greatest weaknesses in analysis of the Diaspora has been the assumption that 'Hellenization' is all of a piece: that 'Hellenization' in one respect implies 'Hellenization' in another and that all are of equal weight in altering the character of Judaism. In fact the discussion has been bedevilled by a lack of consensus on what is meant by 'Helleniza-tion' and 'Hellenism', as well as a general failure even to recognize and address this lack of consensus. Some find the Jewish use of Greek, especially in the Septuagint translation, a striking example of 'Helleni-zation', while others focus on Jewish knowledge of Greek literature and philosophy, on Jewish use of Gentile names, artistic symbols and legal formulae, on Jewish participation in Gentile athletics and politics, on Jewish accommodation to Gentile religious customs or Jewish involvement in the concoction of 'magical' formulae. Generally these are all lumped together and treated as of equal significance; occa-sionally they are put in some hierarchy of importance, but without defensible reasons. Four things may be said on this matter:

1. In the first place, it is questionable whether in reality all these phenomena should be included under the heading 'Hellenization'. The 'Hellen-' component in that term suggests something originally Greek, or at least something resulting from the cultural shifts inaugurated by the conquests of Alexander the Great (d. 323 BCE). Thus, strictly speaking, such a term would be irrelevant to the conditions of Jews in the Romanized (western) portions of the Mediterranean, while, even in the east, Alexander's conquests, and the later expansion of Roman power, produced such a complex intermingling of cultures that it is often impossible to unpick what was distinctively 'Greek' from what was, for instance, 'Egyptian', 'Syrian' or 'Anatolian'. The Maccabaean rhetoric and its later echoes have caused us to be fixated on 'Jews' and 'Greeks', and to over-simplify the multiple frontiers on which Jewish acculturation took place.

2. Even if we focus on phenomena that can be vaguely defined as 'Hellenistic', we still need to discriminate between different forms of

'Hellenization' and different degrees of depth. We sense that it is somehow unproductive to label as parallel forms of 'Hellenization' the mere ability to speak Greek, regular participation in worship of, say, Dionysus, knowledge of Greek literature and intermarriage with a Gentile family. As noted above, the best means of sorting different forms of 'Hellenization' may be derived from the social sciences, where minority and colonized societies have been observed in the different strategies they adopt towards the majority or colonizing culture. In this direction, I have mapped out (1996) some basic distinctions between 'assimilation' (social engagement with others), 'acculturation' (adoption of others' language, literature and cultural values) and 'accommodation' (the use to which the others' cultural resources are put). Although these terms are not used consistently by social scientists, the realities they describe are generally distinguishable, indicating, for instance, how and why it was more dangerous for the continuance of Jewish culture when Jews married Gentiles than when they learnt their language and literature. Such an analysis serves to highlight certain ancestral customs as significant 'boundary markers' between Jews and non-Jews, such as refusal to participate in 'alien' or iconic worship, the observance of dietary laws, sabbath customs and the practice of male circumcision. Slackening of practice in these matters seems to have been particularly damaging to the preservation of the Jewish tradition, and was recognized as such by both Jews and non-Jews.

3. This form of analysis might help us to avoid imposing judgmental criteria derived from modern forms of Judaism, or from species of ancient Judaism that were irrelevant to the Diaspora. There is nothing to be said for applying rabbinic forms of assessment if what counted was the standard applied by local and contemporary Jews. 'Apostasy' and 'unorthodoxy', if we may use such terms at all, are to be defined not by our judgment, but by local contemporary standards: an 'apostate' Jew was one so labelled by his/her contemporaries, who may also have disagreed in their judgment (as they did, for instance, about Paul). Unfortunately, scholarship is replete with hidden value judgments, imported from the scholar's own assumptions about 'legitimate' expressions of Judaism. If we pay close attention to what was acceptable to local Jewish communities in their own environment and at their own time, we may be able to dislodge some of our anachronistic preconceptions (Barclay 1995).

4. Dissolving the assumption of a necessary contrast between 'Judaism' and 'Hellenism' could enable us better to appreciate the richly embroidered identity woven by many Jews in the Diaspora, who could be as intensely 'Greek' as they were intensely 'Jewish'. A range of literary, historiographical, philosophical, theological and artistic 'hybridizations' are evident in the Diaspora, whose object was not to ape Greek culture so much as to re-express Judaism within it, sometimes with a significant polemical edge against non-Jews (including 'Greeks'). With fine gradations of cultural antagonism and cultural convergence, Diaspora Jews advanced their Jewish cause in diverse forms, with considerable innovation precisely in the close entwinement of multiple cultural traditions (Barclay 1996). To unpick such tapestries into their constituent threads would be to destroy what made them creative and important. Rather we should accent the multi-layered complexity of Jewish identity in the Diaspora, and the constant shifts in Jewish self-definition that history and circumstance required.

4. *Unity and Diversity in the Diaspora*

If we break down generalizations about 'normative' Judaism, will our studies result in purely localized portraits of variant 'Judaisms'? In the last few decades, study of Diaspora Judaism has shifted from generalization about 'Diaspora Jews' into greater and greater particularity, with increasing consciousness of differentiation among the phenomena studied. This has been caused partly by an increase in knowledge about the Diaspora, accompanied by more detailed local studies, and partly by an intellectual affirmation of pluralism and a corresponding distrust of attempts at unifying theories.

The last 100 years have seen a remarkable growth in our knowledge about Jews in the Diaspora. A large number of archaeological discoveries—inscriptions, papyri, tombs and synagogue buildings—have enriched our appreciation of Diaspora Jews, even if no single find has been quite as spectacular as the discovery of the Dead Sea Scrolls which revealed so much about Palestinian Judaism. We have already noted the discovery of the Dura Europos synagogue (in 1932), whose paintings were far more lavish than anyone could have anticipated; they also suggested a carefully constructed artistic symbolism, although there remains wide disagreement about what meaning(s) the paintings convey (Kraeling 1956; Goodenough 1953–68: IX–XI). Since that date, the unearthing of numerous synagogue mosaics in Galilee, some with Zodiac signs centred on the sun-god Helios, has confirmed our sense that the second decalogue commandment was by no means as restrictive as we might have thought. Fresh discoveries of catacombs in Rome and Venosa at the beginning of this century opened up new light on the character of the Jewish communities in those cities (Leon 1960), while Jewish tombs have also been found in quantity in Cyrenaica (modern Libya, Lüderitz 1983) and the province of Asia (western Turkey, Trebilco 1991). At Sardis, archaeologists discovered the largest known synagogue, whose dedicatory inscriptions and central position in the city indicated that the Jewish community there in the third and fourth centuries CE was both wealthy and socially respected (Kraabel 1983). Further confirmation that Jews in this period were socially influential was discovered at Aphrodisias, where a long list of donors, both Jewish and Gentile, signified close social ties (Reynolds and Tannenbaum 1987; see further below, section 7). At an earlier point, the great bundles of papyri discovered in Egypt at the turn of the century included enough about Jews to indicate their participation in many levels of Graeco-Egyptian society, and individual papyri threw important light on their political fortunes (Tcherikover and Fuks, 1957–64). As new Jewish inscriptions are continually being discovered (e.g. in the Bosphorus, Levinskaya 1996), there is every reason to hope that excavations will continue to uncover evidence about the Diaspora, in the form of papyri, inscriptions, synagogue buildings and other artefacts.

It is not always easy to determine which of our evidence *is* Jewish. Jews did not always bear distinctively Jewish names, and some that appear Jewish might not be so. Moreover, Jewish symbols are not always present on stones or tombs, or, where present, not always clear or unambiguous, especially after Gentile Christians began to copy them. (Even in relation to texts, disputes still continue as to which texts are to be attributed to Jews: in some cases, there is room for suspicion that works attributed to Greeks are really by Jews, in others that Jewish texts have been subtly adapted by Christians.) Thus, increase in evidence always brings increase in complication: just when we hope issues might be resolved, they are often rendered more puzzling! But the more we know, the more detailed local knowledge we can amass, which helps us to see that the condition of Diaspora Jews did not remain constant over time, and varied considerably from province to province or even from town to town. Thus we become increasingly conscious of the hazards of anachronism and the dangers of generalization. With every additional piece of information, we become more cautious, in the realization of how much else we would like to know but do not! And we are constantly facing the awkward question of the *value* of our sources, both literary and archaeological: do these represent wider phenomena or are they to some extent skewed or idiosyncratic? How much other Jewish evidence do we not recognize as such because it was in fact indistinguishable from the contemporary norm? We accept as Jewish only what is labelled as such; but that might lead us to a one-sided notion of Jewish distinctiveness.

Recent years have seen the publication of highly valuable collections of source material. Following the publication of the Egyptian papyri by V. Tcherikover and A. Fuks (1957–64), the Egyptian inscriptions have been excellently re-edited in W. Horbury and D. Noy (1992) and the inscriptions from Western Europe in subsequent volumes by Noy (1993; 1995). There have also been several fine studies of local Diaspora communities, such as the monographs by S. Applebaum on Jews in Cyrenaica (1979), P. Trebilco on Jews in Asia Minor (1991), L. Rutgers on Roman Jews (1995) and J.M. Modrzejewski on Egypt (1995). Each of these invites closer attention to specific historical and local conditions, and the most recent local studies show a welcome tendency to treat Jews alongside other contemporary groups and not as an isolated or unique phenomenon. But each also illustrates local diversity in Jewish experience and expression, and indicates how perilous it may be to generalize over time or across disparate locations.

But the reluctance to generalize is also fostered by the (postmodern) distrust of 'totalizing explanations' that gloss over the particularities of time, place and person. The pluralistic condition of modern Judaism, and resistance to orthodox attempts to legislate for other Jews, have led some Jewish scholars to emphasize the diversity in ancient Judaism, and many scholars (both Jewish and Christian) now insist one should talk not of 'Judaism' in antiquity but of 'Judaism*s*'. Unfortunately, it is not always clear what is implied by the use of the plural, whether, for instance, it is being asserted that there were distinct and incompatible Jewish *groups*, or whether we are viewing only varied interpretations of common Jewish symbols (texts, customs and artefacts) that need not imply social divisions. The problem lies partly in the different nuances given to the term 'Judaism', which can be viewed primarily as a web of

beliefs, with multiple variants, or, perhaps more realistically, as an ethnic community whose shared symbols were powerful and enduring
precisely because they were open to diverse interpretation. In the latter
case, it is hard to justify using a plural noun.

In relation to the Diaspora, scholars no longer use Philo as *the*
representative of Diaspora Judaism; it is widely recognized that his
particular conflation of Jewish Scripture and Hellenistic philosophy,
although not wholly unique, cannot be taken as typical of Diaspora
Jews everywhere, even in his own era. Within his Alexandrian community at the beginning of the first century CE we can trace a variety of
Jewish perspectives on cultural and political matters, including internal
dissensions on the way to respond to Roman power. Yet we also find
the whole Jewish community apparently caught up in the Alexandrian
'pogrom' of 38–39 CE, and Philo indicates a large measure of una-
nimity on such matters as circumcision and sabbath rest. What is more,
Jews throughout the Diaspora seem to have been able to recognize one
another as Jews when they travelled from city to city or went on
pilgrimage to Jerusalem together, and we find a regular list of Jewish
practices commented on by non-Jews in a variety of locations and
times. Thus, while we should remain ever alive to diversity in the Diaspora, and while we should resist notions of Palestinian control unless
there is good evidence to support it, we might be justified in proposing
certain generalizations about how Jews in the ancient Diaspora constructed and maintained their Jewish identity (Barclay 1996). As Cohen
has noted (1990), a number of factors, including temperament, induce
some scholars to be 'unifiers' and others 'separators'; realism and
scholarly competition suggest that these will never be fully reconciled,
although we can hope for the ability to recognize a measure of truth in
others' opinions.

Thus far we have discussed a number of interrelated issues which have
shaped the foundations of scholarship on the Diaspora. We may now
turn to a number of specific topics which have been the focus of
scholarly debate regarding the interface between Jews and Gentiles in
the Diaspora.

5. *Jewish Isolation or Integration*

As Kraabel has noted (1982), a common conception in older
scholarship on the Diaspora was that Jewish communities were largely

isolated from their host societies, or, if individual Jews were socially integrated, that was only on terms that decreased their Jewish commitments. The underlying assumption was that of Jewish social and cultural weakness, expressed either in a self-protective, 'ghettoized' lifestyle, or in capitulation to superior cultural forces.

It is easy to see how evidence *could* be cited to support this rather doleful view of Diaspora existence. The mass of Jewish catacombs in Rome could be taken to represent a self-enclosed community with its own burial facilities, just as occasional evidence for predominantly Jewish streets or even 'quarters' (e.g. in Alexandria) could be used to suggest general social isolation. In stressing the ubiquity of 'pagan' practice and iconography in city life (in public buildings and festivals, at artistic and sporting performances, in political activities of many kinds), it could be noted how difficult this made participation by Jews who were faithful to their ancestral strictures against 'idolatry'. It could also be noted that non-Jews, such as Tacitus and Juvenal, sometimes commented on Jewish 'separatism' and complained about the difficulty of eating with a Jew. Thus whatever evidence was found for Jews taking political office or undergoing citizenship training was either explained away (they were not really Jews, or not really doing what the evidence suggested) or interpreted as signs of 'apostasy'.

In recent years, however, the mass of evidence for Jews breaking the bounds of what we impose as 'norms' has contributed to a growing appreciation of Diaspora Jews as integrated, active participants in their environment, and participants from a position of strength, not weakness. For instance, it is now widely (but not universally) recognized that Philo and some other socially elite Jews in Alexandria were also citizens of the city, but negotiated their engagement in civic life on terms that enabled them to maintain their Jewish monotheism and the confidence of their Jewish community. Similarly, Josephus in Rome is now less often regarded as an abject renegade, but as a Jew honoured by the imperial court who *also* maintained his social and emotional commitment to the Jewish people (Rajak 1983). Even the catacombs in Rome show by their artistic features and by the nomenclature of the deceased that Jews in that city interacted at many levels with their cultural environment (Rutgers 1995). Moreover, alongside Tacitus's and Juvenal's hostile remarks, one has to account for the mass of evidence, both Jewish and non-Jewish, that Jews in Rome attracted admirers and imitators, who could hardly have adopted Jewish customs without enjoying friendly relations with Jews.

However, the most significant evidence in this connection has come from Asia Minor, where archaeological material concerning Jews indicates their distinct seating in a theatre (Miletus), their acquisition of patronage from highly placed Gentile officials (e.g. Julia Severa, at Acmonia) and even influence on the coinage of their host cities (Apamea, with the figure of Noah). The single most spectacular example of Jewish confidence and integration has been the discovery of the synagogue at Sardis, whose central location in the city, massive scale and use of local cultural symbolism indicate a large, respected and integrated Jewish community. Moreover, inscriptions here and elsewhere in the province indicate the participation of Jews in civic administration (as councillors etc.), and their announcement of such roles *within the synagogue* suggests the acceptability of that role among the rest of the Jewish community. We do not know how such Jews negotiated their way through the 'idolatrous' aspects of their civic roles, but the evidence suggests that they did not abandon their Jewish identity in the process. As Trebilco concludes, in sentences that summarize the new consensus:

> A degree of integration did not mean the abandonment of an active attention to Jewish tradition or of Jewish distinctiveness. It was as *Jews* that they were involved in, and a part of, the life of the cities in which they lived (his italics, 1991: 187).

Besides the social integration of individual Jews, there is also some evidence concerning the legal status of Jewish communities in the Diaspora. Following the work of J. Juster (1914), it became common to talk of a general constitutional basis for Jews through the Roman empire (a kind of Magna Carta), formulated by Julius Caesar and continued by his successors. But this and the associated notion of Judaism as a 'permitted religion' (*religio licita*) have been shown to be unsupported by the evidence, which indicates only certain common trends in Roman protection of Jewish ancestral customs, a protection that had to be reasserted in individual cases by emperors and provincial governors (Rajak 1984). As regards the status of Jewish communities at a local level, it has been common to assert that they generally constituted *politeumata*, which were taken to be semi-autonomous organizations of ethnic minorities recognized by the local civic administration (e.g. Kasher 1985). In recent years, however, this thesis has been exploded: it was based on scattered fragments of evidence, connected only by a term with multiple and variant senses (Lüderitz 1994). It appears that if the Jewish community (or communities) in a particular city had any official status, that varied from place to place and time to time, depending on the size of the community and the history of its relationship with the host city.

6. 'Philo-Judaism' and 'Anti-Semitism'

Traditionally, both Jews and Christians have tended to portray a 'lacrymose conception' of Jewish history in the Diaspora, sometimes perhaps with the underlying assumption that Jews should never have been there in the first place. Since we are better informed about crises than about the normal patterns of life, it is comparatively easy to pick out moments when Diaspora Jews came under intense political pressure, suffering expulsion from Rome (19 CE), violent persecution in Alexandria (38–39 CE) and virtual obliteration across the whole of Cyrenaica, Egypt and Cyprus (115–17 CE). Also, given the history of anti-Semitism in the nineteenth and twentieth centuries, it is not surprising that there has been intense study of its parallel phenomena in the ancient world, together with their causes and consequences. It has been difficult, however, to get a balanced perspective on such a topic.

Earlier collections of Graeco-Roman comments on Jews have now been superseded by the magnificent work of M. Stern (1974–84, arranged by author; a briefer collection, presented by topic, is provided by M. Whittaker 1984). This provides as good a conspectus as we could wish of what non-Jews said about Jews. What it does not (and cannot) provide are the answers to three related questions: (1) How are we to assess the combination of positive and negative comments on Jews in these sources? (2) How do these literary sources relate to the opinions and everyday actions of ordinary people? (3) How do such comments on Jews compare to what might be collected of comments about, for instance, Egyptians or Syrians? In other words, were Jews a special case or did they fare much the same as other oriental non-Greeks? We may take each of these questions in turn.

1. *The combination of positive and negative references to Jews.* There have been various analyses of the positive and negative comments about Jews, with attempts to find historical shifts or a general predominance in one direction or another. Thus, for instance, Gager

(1983) and others have stressed that the early Greek response to Jews was largely complimentary, and that it was only under Roman rule that hostile attitudes to Jews began to emerge. Whether the evidence of all the authors can be interpreted this way is a matter of debate (in some cases negative passages have to be treated as late additions), but it is noticeable that many scholars now place greater emphasis on 'philo-Judaism' than on 'anti-Semitism', except in very specific historical contexts. Thus L.H. Feldman (1993), while he divides up the sources into 'Prejudice against Jews' and 'The Attractions of the Jews', finds even within the hostile comments about Jews some elements of admiration or respect. However, it is somewhat artificial to divide up the material so neatly into two categories (pro- and anti-Jews). In the ancient world people rarely lined up squarely 'for' or 'against' Jews or Judaism, but expressed their combinations of admiration, puzzlement, interest and disdain in highly variegated forms. Stern was wise to avoid categorizing his authors.

2. *Literary sources and the opinions of ordinary people*. It is important to remember that our literary sources may be entirely *unrepresentative* of the mass of the population, and fail to reflect ordinary social relations. If some Greek philosophers treated the Jews as an intriguing philosophical race, that does not say anything about the character of contacts between Jews and Greeks in everyday life. Conversely, the hostile comments of Roman *literati* like Juvenal and Tacitus may mask the fact that the Jews in Rome were actually quite popular and influential at the time in which they wrote; in fact, a careful look at their invective suggests precisely that. Thus a proper analysis of Jew–Gentile relations has to take all the evidence together, giving due allowance to variations in local conditions and possibly variant opinions at differing social levels. As we shall see below (section 7) some Jewish communities in the Diaspora drew a penumbra of admirers and imitators whose attitude to Jews and Jewish customs often had nothing to do with the political and intellectual stances adopted by our extant authors.

3. *Were Jews a special case*? When we make collections of comments about Jews in antiquity, we perpetrate the impression that they were singled out for special attention. However, wider reading of the contexts from which Stern or others cite texts about Jews often reveals that they were placed alongside other ethnic groups and were given special attention only when social or political factors gave them

unusual prominence (e.g. tensions in Alexandria or the Jewish War in Palestine). As Josephus complained, Greek historians actually made extremely little reference to Jews, but his own collection of comments on Jews, and his attempts to refute some ludicrous accusations against them (in his *Against Apion*), established an approach to the topic that remains influential to this day. The fact is that Jews were often noticed only in passing by our authors, and then often in association with other 'eastern' nations whose strange habits were commented upon with a mixture of interest and snobbish distaste. If we were to collect all the references to Egyptians in antiquity, we would find a similar range from interested respect to haughty abuse, and the number of anti-Egyptian jokes would probably outnumber those we count 'anti-Jewish'. It is perhaps only the tragic history of European Jews that has given such prominence to 'anti-Semitism' in antiquity. Indeed hostile comments about Jews in ancient sources are misleadingly termed 'anti-Semitic', since Jews were not the only 'Semites', nor was hostility based on notions of their *racial* inferiority. If, rather, we term such remarks 'anti-Jewish', we must remember that the targets may be very diverse. As a living people (not just a 'religion'), Jews won enemies (and friends) for all sorts of reasons.

7. *Jewish Mission (?) and the Attraction of Gentiles*

A vigorous debate has broken out in recent years over the 'missionary' interests of ancient Judaism, especially in the Diaspora. On one side it has been stressed (e.g. by Feldman 1993) that Judaism was extremely attractive to Gentiles and that mission to 'pagans' was a natural activity for Jews. Evidence has been found in references to converts in Roman authors, in Jewish literature said to have an 'apologetic' purpose, in stories and tombstones referring to proselytes, in the apparent reference to Pharisaic mission in Mt. 23.15, and (most controversially) in estimates of the rise in the Jewish population in the Roman Empire, which is attributed to successful mission among Gentiles. On the other side, M. Goodman (1994; cf. S. McKnight 1991) stresses the lack of Jewish motivation for mission (e.g. tolerance of Gentile idolatry, at least before 100 CE), and has dismissed or reinterpreted each piece of evidence advanced by the other viewpoint, including the so-called 'apologetic' literature.

Various extraneous factors may be influencing this debate, such as a desire in some quarters to present Judaism as the precursor to Christian mission (or alternatively, as innocent of the Christian aggression in this matter), as well as scholars' convictions concerning whether present-day Judaism *should be* engaged in mission or not. To a considerable extent, the debate is also clouded by different understandings of 'mission'. Goodman adopts an extremely stringent definition: 'a universal mission to bring people perceived as outsiders into a particular community and to convert them to the views held by that community' (1994: 14). He finds the historical evidence for proselytism and the ideology of ancient Judaism failing to satisfy such a condition. Others would define 'mission' less rigorously, without, for instance, a universal dimension and without a positive quest for converts beyond assisting into Judaism those who approach of their own volition. Any argument from the supposed growth in Jewish numbers is worthless: all guesses about population figures, ancient and modern, are unreliable, and even if we could document growth, proselytism need not be its cause. But it is not so easy to dismiss evidence from the city of Rome for the significance of proselytes and proselytism. In general, if we avoid generalizations about 'missionary religions' and allow a loose definition of 'mission', it is possible to argue that, in certain locations and at certain times, Jews attracted considerable numbers of Gentiles into conversion (Carleton-Paget 1996). What role, if any, their literature played in this process is not so clear: only a small percentage of our extant literature seems to be aimed *directly* at Gentiles, but a good deal else may be framed with a view to oral interaction between Jews and Gentiles and thus, while intended for Jewish readers, may serve an *indirect* apologetic purpose.

Whatever one may conclude about the extent and significance of proselytism, it is clear enough from both Jewish and non-Jewish sources that many Gentiles were inclined to respect Jews, some to the point of offering their support or patronage to Jewish communities, some to the point of imitating Jewish customs, and some attending Jewish synagogues and festivals. It is common to lump all such people together in one category with a single label, either 'God-fearer' or 'sympathizer'. The label 'God-fearer' has occasioned much dispute since it seems to be used by Luke in his *Acts of the Apostles* in a more clearly defined sense than was found in other literary and archaeological sources. There the notion of 'fearing God' (meaning 'being religious') could be expressed in a variety of ways and used of a variety of people (Jews and non-Jews); only occasionally, in disputed cases, did it seem to designate a 'class' of Gentile 'friends' or sympathizers. Recently, the discovery of a long inscription from Aphrodisias (Reynolds and Tannenbaum 1987), dating from the third century CE, has indicated that this term could be used in this semi-technical sense: it heads a list of Gentiles who contributed to a Jewish institution, but are clearly distinguished from proselytes. This has put paid to the theory that Luke *invented* this category of people (Kraabel 1981), though he may still have over-schematized a fluid phenomenon (see Cohen 1989; Levinskaya 1996).

The fact is that, whatever label they may or may not have been known by, a variety of Gentiles contributed to the support and success of Jewish communities in a variety of ways without becoming Jews (proselytes). This is, in fact, an entirely understandable phenomenon. Jewish communities sometimes attained size, wealth and local influence, so it is not surprising that a variety of social, political and economic motives might encourage sponsors, patrons and hangers-on. They also practised customs of great antiquity, supported by an ancient Scripture, and did so sufficiently publicly to be regularly noticed; not surprisingly, some people imitated attractive features of these customs (e.g. stopping work or lighting lamps on the sabbath) or at least adopted similar practices. Jews also had special religious customs based on a strenuously 'philosophical' notion of the 'one God', and it was natural that some Gentiles should find this concept, and the accompanying Jewish worship, attractive.

Thus a whole variety of positive responses to the Jewish people and their culture can be imagined and documented, and it has rightly been emphasized that the positive attraction of Judaism did not wither at the rise of Christianity (Simon 1948). Rather, the synagogue continued at least until Constantine in strong competition with the church, and ordinary Christians themselves were frequently to be found enjoying closer links with Jewish custom and community than their leaders would approve (Meeks and Wilken 1978). In all this, we must remember that 'the Jews' designates both an ethnic and a religious community. Recently, some have argued that the relevant Greek and Latin terms should really be translated 'Judaeans', highlighting the ethnic, and even geographic, connotations of the term. The term may well have carried such nuances in many circumstances, though the geographic connotation may have weakened in the Diaspora over time, and the fact that non-Judaeans could become 'Judaeans' (by proselytism) indicates that 'ethnicity' should not be construed in a narrowly racial sense. In any case, it is important to remember that the power of attraction exercised by the Jewish people was multiple, derived from both (what we would call) 'religious' and (what we would call) 'non-religious' factors.

8. *Prospects for Future Research*

Much remains to be discovered about Jewish life in the ancient Diaspora and, given average luck, more will be unearthed by future archaeology. Further knowledge may increase the concentration on specific, localized manifestations of Jewish community, making generalizations about 'the Diaspora' harder or more complex. Current trends in leading scholarship suggest greater and greater caution concerning the use of all our sources, as critical questions are posed about their value as evidence.

At the same time, there is great potential in further thematic and cross-cultural studies that compare the Jewish Diaspora with other ancient Diasporas (see the title of Cohen and Frerichs 1993). Granted that there were certain things distinctive of Jews, there was also much else in their communal life, their use of iconography, their boundary maintenance and their exposure to social disdain that they had in common with other ethnic groups, whose existence has never been studied with the same intensity as Jews and Christians have employed in studying ancient Judaism. In this matter, much will depend on whether the study of ancient Judaism (and Christianity) remains semi-detached from the wider historical study of the period, or whether the current trend towards its increasing integration continues. There is certainly much to be gained from the careful insertion of Diaspora studies into the broader social and cultural analysis of the Hellenistic and Roman worlds. There is also much to be learned in this sphere from sociological and anthropological analyses of ethnicity, identity and acculturation. Thus, on several fronts, there is a large agenda yet to be explored.

THE ESSENES

Charlotte Hempel

The scholarly study of the ancient Jewish group of the Essenes during the last hundred years falls into two distinct phases. A major turning point occurred around the middle of the twentieth century with the discovery of what a majority of scholars still believe to be an Essene library and community settlement at Khirbet Qumran by the shores of the Dead Sea. The Qumran library comprises the remains of approximately eight hundred scrolls, some very fragmentary, which were discovered in 11 caves between 1947 and 1956. The first half of the period this volume is concerned with may, therefore, be described as the pre-Qumran phase of research on the Essenes whereas the second half of the twentieth century can be summed up as the post-Qumran phase of research on the Essenes. In what follows I shall attempt to deal with the most salient aspects of the scholarly debate on the Essenes that has characterized the last hundred years.

Sources

Our main sources on the Essenes are found in the writings of three classical authors: the Jewish historian Flavius Josephus (38 to after 93 CE), the philosopher Philo of Alexandria (30 BCE–45 CE), and Pliny the Elder (23/4–79 CE). Neither the New Testament nor the corpus of rabbinic literature include a reference to the Essenes, although scholars have sometimes attempted to identify the Essenes with one or other group mentioned in the latter two corpora. Moreover, it has been one of the concerns of scholarship over the last hundred years to identify the Essenes' own literature among the apocrypha and pseudepigrapha and, since around the middle of the twentieth century, the Qumran scrolls in particular. The evidence on the Essenes as contained in the classical sources is most conveniently accessible in the volume edited by

G. Vermes and M.D. Goodman, which collects all the statements on the Essenes in the classical sources in their original languages accompanied by Goodman's English translation.[1]

Name

The name Essenes occurs only in Greek and Latin in the writings of the classical authors. What is more, the writings of Josephus, Philo and Pliny attest two different forms of the name. Thus, Philo refers to the Essaeans (Greek: Ἐσσαίοι) whereas Josephus knows both the form Essaeans as well as Essenes (Greek: Ἐσσηνοί). The use of two different forms in the writings of Josephus has been taken by some to indicate Josephus's use of different sources describing this group.[2] Finally, Pliny employs the term Essenes (Latin: *Esseni*). As far as the etymology of the term is concerned most scholars are in agreement that it is almost certainly of Semitic origin. Much less agreement reigns, however, when it comes to identifying the particular Semitic root from which the name was derived, and a number of suggestions have been made. The most popular of these suggestions are a derivation from the Aramaic אָסִין, 'healers', or the Aramaic חָסִין, 'pious ones', and finally the Hebrew עוֹשִׂים, 'doers', abbreviating a longer expression עוֹשֵׂי התורה, 'the doers of the Torah'. The evidence of the Qumran scrolls has not been able to bring this ongoing debate to a satisfactory conclusion, although some have argued that the Semitic form of the name Essenes can be found in the scrolls.[3]

---

1. G. Vermes and M.D. Goodman, *The Essenes according to the Classical Sources* (Oxford Centre Textbooks, 1; Sheffield: JSOT Press, 1989).

2. Cf. W. Bauer, 'Essener', in *Pauly-Wissowa, Real-Encyclopädie der classischen Altertumswissenschaft*, supp. vol. IV (ed. W. Kroll; Stuttgart: Metzler, 1924), cols. 386-430, esp. col. 419, and R. Bergmeier, *Die Essener-Berichte des Flavius Josephus: Quellenstudien zu den Essenertexten im Werk des jüdischen Historiographen* (Kampen: Kok Pharos, 1993).

3. For an excellent and up-to-date survey of this debate, see most recently J.C. VanderKam, 'Identity and History of the Community', in P. Flint and J.C. VanderKam (eds.), *The Dead Sea Scrolls after Fifty Years: A Comprehensive Assessment*, II (Leiden: E.J. Brill, 1999), pp. 487-533, esp. pp. 490-99. For an earlier survey see G. Vermes, 'The Etymology of "Essenes" ', *RevQ* 2 (1960), pp. 427-43.

Essenes and Therapeutae

Another area of scholarly debate that continued throughout the twentieth century, although it began much earlier, is the relationship between
the Essenes of Palestine and the Therapeutae of Egypt as described by
Philo in his work *De vita contemplativa*.[4] In this treatise Philo includes
a most favourable description of a group of Jewish ascetics who lived
in many places, but he singles out a colony in the vicinity of Alexandria in particular. Philo's account of the Therapeutae displays both
similarities as well as some differences to what we know about the
Essenes. A number of scholarly positions have been put forward to
explain the evidence. First, there are those who argue that both groups
are entirely unrelated. Thus, J.W. Lightley maintained that, 'it is quite
improbable that the two communities were in any way connected with
each other'.[5] Moreover, W. Bauer cautiously comments that Philo produced stylized accounts of both groups in order to emphasize their
similarities, which should not be taken to suggest an actual closeness of
both.[6] Finally, W. Bousset and H. Gressmann conclude that both movements represent fundamentally different phenomena, the Essenes being
a monastic order whereas the Therapeutae appear to be a guild of her-
mits.[7] A second position is represented by M.-J. Lagrange. Lagrange
begins by describing the Therapeutae as a counterpart of the Palestinian Essenes but subsequently expresses the suspicion that Philo's
description of the Therapeutae may be his own creation of an idealized

4.   The relevant sections of Philo's treatise are included as an appendix in
Vermes and Goodman, *The Essenes*, pp. 75-99. For an outline of the earlier scholarly debate on the Therapeutae, see S. Wagner, *Die Essener in der wissenschaftlichen Diskussion: Vom Ausgang des 18. bis zum Beginn des 20. Jahrhunderts*
(Berlin: Alfred Töpelmann, 1960), pp. 194-202. One prominent feature of the
nineteenth-century debate was the question of the authenticity of *De vita contemplativa* as a genuinely Philonic work. For a more recent contribution on this debate, see
E. Schürer *et al.*, *The History of the Jewish People in the Age of Jesus Christ*, II
(Edinburgh: T. & T. Clark, 1979), pp. 593-97.
5.   J.W. Lightley, *Jewish Sects and Parties in the Time of Jesus* (London:
Epworth Press, 1925), p. 277.
6.   Bauer, 'Essener', IV, col. 416.
7.   W. Bousset and H. Gressmann, *Die Religion des Judentums im späthellenistischen Zeitalter* (Tübingen: J.C.B. Mohr [Paul Siebeck], 1926), pp. 467-68.

contemplative Jewish group.[8] Thirdly, and finally, a sizeable group of scholars hold that the Therapeutae and the Essenes are very closely related to each other. Thus, G. Vermes concludes that the Therapeutae are best seen as 'an off-shoot of the Palestinian ascetic movement of the Essenes'.[9] Vermes's position has recently received support from P. Bilde.[10]

Essene 'Monks'?

It is interesting to note that monastic language is prevalent in the secondary literature on the Essenes both before and after the discovery of the Dead Sea Scrolls. This puts a criticism levelled against the pioneers in the study of the scrolls, some of whom were Catholic priests, into perspective. Members of the first generation of Qumran studies have been criticized for portraying the community associated with the Qumran settlement and some of the scrolls in monastic terms.[11] Their perspective on the discoveries, it is further sometimes maintained, was coloured by their own clerical background.[12] Although there might be some truth in this argument, it is noteworthy that the use of monastic terminology with reference to the Essenes has a much longer history.

8.   M.-J. Lagrange, *Le judaïsme avant Jésus-Christ* (Paris: J. Gabalda, 1931), pp. 581-86.

9.   Vermes and Goodman, *The Essenes*, p. 17. For an earlier representative of a view along such lines, see M. Friedländer, *Die religiösen Bewegungen innerhalb des Judentums im Zeitalter Jesu* (Berlin: Georg Reimer, 1905), pp. 121, 151. Further J.T. Milik, *Ten Years of Discovery in the Wilderness of Judaea* (ET J. Strugnell; London: SCM Press, 1959), p. 92, and M. Hengel, *Judaism and Hellenism: Studies in their Encounter in Palestine during the Early Hellenistic Period* (London: SCM Press, one-vol. edn, 1974), p. 247.

10.   Cf. P. Bilde, 'The Essenes in Philo and Josephus', in F.H. Cryer and T.L. Thompson (eds.), *Qumran between the Old and New Testaments* (JSOTSup, 290; Copenhagen International Seminar, 6; Sheffield: Sheffield Academic Press, 1998), pp. 32-68, esp. pp. 65-66.

11.   Cf. Milik, *Ten Years of Discovery*, pp. 84, 90, 103. See further E. Sutcliffe S.J., *The Monks of Qumran: The People of the Dead Sea Scrolls* (London: Burns & Oats, 1960).

12.   See, for instance, P.R. Davies, 'How Not to Do Archaeology: The Story of Qumran', *BA* 51 (1988), pp. 203-207 (reprinted in *idem, Sects and Scrolls: Essays on Qumran and Related Topics* [South Florida Studies in the History of Judaism, 134; Atlanta, GA: Scholars Press, 1996], pp. 79-87).

The first generation of Qumran scholars continued a well-established tradition that conceived of the Essenes, with whom the people behind the scrolls were identified, in terms of a monastic order.[13] It seems fair to say, for instance, that the majority of writers on the Essenes in the first half of the twentieth century employed monastic terminology to describe them.[14] An early critique against employing monastic terminology to describe the Essenes is voiced by Bauer.[15] This tendency to describe a pre-Christian Jewish phenomenon in monastic terms is indeed anachronistic and is only now beginning to change, although it still persists today in the work of some writers.

Foreign Influence

A great deal of the scholarly debate on the Essenes in the nineteenth and early twentieth centuries was concerned with attempts at identifying foreign influences, predominant among them Greek and Persian, on the Essenes.[16] Friedländer goes as far as to state that the Essenes were more Hellenistic than Jewish in nature.[17] Bauer, on the other hand, promotes the view that the Essenes were doubtlessly a Jewish group but one that was very much shaped by the syncretistic atmosphere of the time.[18]

Since the discovery of the scrolls, which most experts hold to be an Essene library, we now have an extensive corpus of ancient Essene literature composed almost exclusively in Hebrew and Aramaic rather than being forced to rely on secondary accounts of the Essenes written in Greek and Latin and aimed at introducing this Jewish group to a Gentile audience. The study of the primary evidence of the scrolls

13. The view that the Essenes, who were frequently identified with the Therapeutae, were the first monks was popular already in the eighteenth and early nineteenth centuries, cf. Wagner, *Essener in der wissenschaftlichen Diskussion*, pp. 3-4.

14. Cf., for example, Bousset and Gressmann, *Religion des Judentums*, p. 456; Friedländer, *Die religiösen Bewegungen*, pp. 145, 147, 159; Lightley, *Jewish Sects and Parties*, pp. 283-85, 292; E. Schürer, *Geschichte des jüdischen Volkes im Zeitalter Jesu Christi*, II (Leipzig: J.C. Hinrichs, 3rd edn, 1898), p. 559.

15. Cf. Bauer, 'Essener', col. 424.

16. See Bousset and Gressmann, *Religion des Judentums*, pp. 458-65; Lagrange, *Judaïsme avant Jésus-Christ*, pp. 325-28; Lightley, *Jewish Sects and Parties*, pp. 307-18; Schürer, *Geschichte des jüdischen Volkes*, pp. 574-84.

17. Friedländer, *Die religiösen Bewegungen*, p. 114.

18. Bauer, 'Essener', cols. 427-28.

allows us, therefore, to examine any possible foreign influences on these writings without being led astray by the Hellenistic garb their portrayal may have been given by the classical authors. Thus, Bergmeier has argued, for instance, that both Philo and Josephus made use of a Hellenistic-Jewish source and that the bulk of Josephus's description of the Essenes further relied on a Pythagorizing source.[19] Whether or not Bergmeier's conclusions are accepted in their entirety, his results do alert us to the complexity that is involved when trying to establish a case for foreign influences on the Essenes rather than on the classical authors to whom we owed our knowledge of the Essenes in the first half of the twentieth century. The texts from Qumran clearly emanate from a conservative Jewish group. The authors of a number of Qumran texts not merely stress the importance of keeping separate from non-Jews but stress the impurity and wickedness of fellow Jews who are not members of the same group. Moreover, the archaeologist J. Magness has shown that the pottery excavated on the Qumran site shows a distinct lack of imported vessels.[20] Nevertheless, a number of areas of foreign influence have also been the subject of study in the post-Qumran era. Thus, M. Weinfeld has argued at some length for the presence of organizational parallels between the Qumran community and Graeco-Roman associations.[21] Whereas most scholars would acknowledge a Babylonian background for a number of astrological and calendrical compositions attested at Qumran,[22] J. Murphy-O'Connor has attempted to make a case for the inception of the Essenes in the Babylonian exile on the basis of his analysis of the Damascus Document.[23]

19. Bergmeier, *Essener-Berichte*, pp. 66-107.

20. J. Magness, 'The Community at Qumran in Light of its Pottery', in M.O. Wise *et al.* (eds.), *Methods of Investigation of the Dead Sea Scrolls and the Khirbet Qumran Site: Present Realities and Future Prospects* (ANYAS, 722; New York: New York Academy of Sciences, 1994), pp. 39-50.

21. M. Weinfeld, *The Organizational Pattern and the Penal Code of the Qumran Sect: A Comparison with Guilds and Religious Associations of the Hellenistic-Roman Period* (NTOA, 2; Göttingen: Vandenhoeck & Ruprecht; Fribourg: Editions Universitaires, 1986). For an earlier suggestion along the same lines see H. Bardtke, 'Die Rechtsstellung der Qumrangemeinde', *TLZ* 86 (1961), pp. 93-104.

22. Cf. for example, M. Albani, 'Horoscopes in the Qumran Scrolls', in P. Flint and J.C. VanderKam (eds.), *The Dead Sea Scrolls after Fifty Years: A Comprehensive Assessment*, II (Leiden: E.J. Brill, 1999), pp. 279-330.

23. J. Murphy-O'Connor, 'The Essenes and their History', *RB* 81 (1974),

Moreover, Iranian influence is frequently discussed with reference particularly to the teaching on the two spirits in the *Community Rule* (1QS 3.13–4.26).[24] Finally, M. Hengel has attempted to show that, even though the Qumran library emanated from a group that was fiercely conservative, it nevertheless shows traces of having been influenced by a number of trends that may be defined as a product of Hellenization.[25] It needs to be borne in mind that many such alien influences pertained more widely in contemporary Palestine rather than characterizing the Qumran texts and groupings in particular.

Identification of Essene Writings

Prior to the discovery of the scrolls scholars offered a number of varied hypotheses on the question of identifying Essene writings among the known corpus of Jewish literature. On the one hand, Bauer maintained that no Essene writings survived and dismisses anything that has been stated to the contrary as mere conjecture.[26] P. Riessler, by contrast,

pp. 215-44. For a critique see M.A. Knibb, 'Exile in the Damascus Document', *JSOT* 25 (1983), pp. 99-117. Babylonian origins for the Essenes had already been argued for prior to the discoveries at Qumran by W.F. Albright, *From the Stone Age to Christianity* (New York: Doubleday, 1957 [reprint of 2nd edn, 1947]), pp. 374-78.

24. Cf. S. Shaked, 'Qumran and Iran: Further Considerations', *Israel Oriental Studies* 2 (1972), pp. 433-46. For a more reticent position that prefers to find the background of Qumran dualism in the Jewish wisdom tradition see J. Frey, 'Different Patterns of Dualistic Thought in the Qumran Library. Reflections on their Background and History', in M. Bernstein, F. García Martínez and J. Kampen (eds.), *Legal Texts and Legal Issues: Proceedings of the Second Meeting of the International Organization for Qumran Studies Published in Honour of Joseph M. Baumgarten* (STDJ, 23; Leiden: E.J. Brill, 1997), pp. 275-335, esp. p. 300.

25. Cf. M. Hengel, 'Qumran und der Hellenismus', in M. Delcor (ed.), *Qumrân: Sa piété, sa théologie et son milieu* (Paris: Duculot; Leuven: Leuven University Press, 1978), pp. 333-72. On the issue of Hellenization see further the discussion and literature referred to in L.L. Grabbe, *Judaism from Cyrus to Hadrian* (London: SCM Press, one-vol. edn, 1994), pp. 147-70. For further literature on foreign influence on the Essenes see also Schürer *et al.*, *History of the Jewish People*, II, p. 589.

26. Bauer, 'Essener', col. 389. See also G.F. Moore, *Judaism in the First Centuries of the Christian Era in the Age of the Tannaim*, II (3 vols.; Cambridge, MA: Harvard University Press, 1932), p. 280: 'The opinion entertained by some scholars that the apocalyptic literature originated with the Essenes lacks evidence.'

argued in favour of considering the bulk of the Old Testament apocrypha and pseudepigrapha as going back to the Essenes.[27] Most other scholars held a midway position and argued in favour of an Essene provenance for a limited number of the writings from among the apocrypha and pseudepigrapha.[28]

Very soon after the discovery of the first Dead Sea Scrolls in 1947, the Israeli scholar E.L. Sukenik suggested that the non-biblical texts from Qumran cave 1 go back to the Essenes as known from the classical sources.[29] The case for an Essene background to this newly discovered library was spelt out at greater length in a monograph by the French scholar A. Dupont-Sommer.[30] An identification of the movement behind the Qumran library with the Essenes is based on an impressive catalogue of correspondences between the description of the Essenes in the classical sources and the practices and beliefs that can be culled from the Dead Sea Scrolls, especially the *Rule of the Community* (1QS).[31]

27. P. Riessler, *Altjüdisches Schrifttum ausserhalb der Bibel* (Heidelberg: Kerle Verlag, 1966 [reprint of 1928 edn]), pp. 1266-339.

28. Cf. G.H. Box, *The Apocalypse of Abraham* (London: SPCK, 1918), p. xxi (*Apocalypse of Abraham*); R.H. Charles, *The Apocrypha and Pseudepigrapha of the Old Testament in English with Introductions and Critical and Explanatory Notes to the Several Books*, II (Oxford: Oxford University Press, 1973 [reprint of 1913 edn]), p. 280 (*1 Enoch* 108); Lagrange, *Judaïsme avant Jésus-Christ*, pp. 329-30 (parts of *1 Enoch* and the *Assumption of Moses*); W.O.E. Oesterley and G.H. Box, *The Religion and Worship of the Synagogue: An Introduction to the Study of Judaism from the New Testament Period* (London: Pitman & Sons, 1907), p. 263 n. 1 (*The Life of Adam and Eve*). See further Lightley, *Jewish Sects and Parties*, pp. 275-76, and Wagner, *Essener in der wissenschaftlichen Diskussion*, pp. 216-18.

29. E.L. Sukenik, *Megillot genuzot I* (Hidden Scrolls) (Jerusalem: Bialik Institute, 1948), p. 16.

30. A. Dupont-Sommer, *Les écrits esséniens découverts près de la mer Morte* (Paris: Payot, 1959), which subsequently appeared in English under the title *The Essene Writings from Qumran* (ET G. Vermes; Oxford: Basil Blackwell, 1961).

31. For a thorough analysis of the correspondences between Josephus and the scrolls, see T.S. Beall, *Josephus' Description of the Essenes Illustrated by the Dead Sea Scrolls* (SNTSMS, 58; Cambridge: Cambridge University Press, 1988). For a briefer summary see Schürer *et al.*, *History of the Jewish People*, II, pp. 583-85. See also H. Stegemann, 'The Qumran-Essenes—Local Members of the Main Jewish Union in Late Second Temple Times', in J. Trebolle Barrera and L. Vegas Montaner (eds.), *The Madrid Qumran Congress: Proceedings of the International*

Something of a special case among the Dead Sea Scrolls is the *Damascus Document*.[32] Two mediaeval manuscripts of this work were recovered at the end of the nineteenth century from the storeroom of a synagogue in Old Cairo (the Cairo *genizah*) and brought to Cambridge by the Talmud scholar Solomon Schechter, where they are housed to this day in the University library.[33] Ever since the discovery of the first Dead Sea Scrolls scholars were struck by the close resemblances these displayed to the Cairo *Damascus Document*. Since ten fragmentary ancient copies of the same composition were subsequently discovered in Qumran caves 4, 5 and 6 the *Damascus Document* is now studied as part of the Qumran library. We cannot know with certainty how the text of the *Damascus Document* reached mediaeval scribes and Cairo but the most likely explanation draws on reports of earlier manuscript discoveries in the Judaean desert.[34] With the notable exception of P. Riessler, who favoured something of a pan-Essene approach to the provenance of the pseudepigrapha, the Cairo *Damascus Document* was rarely associated with the Essenes prior to the discoveries at Qumran.[35]

The Essene hypothesis to explain the provenance of the scrolls, though still the most widely held among Qumran scholars today, has not gone unchallenged, and a number of alternatives have been suggested. Thus, on the basis of the legal positions advocated in a recently published text from Qumran cave 4 known as *Miqsat Ma'aseh ha-Torah* (4QMMT; the customary Hebrew title of this text is usually

Congress on the Dead Sea Scrolls, Madrid 18–21 March 1991, I (STDJ, 11; Leiden: E.J. Brill, 1992), pp. 83-166.

32. For an introduction to this text, see C. Hempel, *The Damascus Texts* (Companion to the Qumran Scrolls, 1; Sheffield: Sheffield Academic Press, 2000).

33. On the Cairo *genizah*, see S. Reif, 'Cairo Genizah', in *Encyclopedia of the Dead Sea Scrolls*, I (ed. L.H. Schiffman and J.C. VanderKam; New York: Oxford University Press, 2000), pp. 105-108. I am grateful to Professor Reif for kindly making his entry available to me prior to its publication. On the Cambridge University holdings from the Cairo *genizah*, see further the website http://www.lib.cam.ac.uk/Taylor-Schechter. S. Schechter's edition of the Cairo manuscripts appeared in 1910 under the title *Documents of Jewish Sectaries*. I. *Fragments of a Zadokite Work* (Cambridge: Cambridge University Press, 1910).

34. Cf. J.C. VanderKam, *The Dead Sea Scrolls Today* (Grand Rapids, MI: Eerdmans; London: SPCK, 1994), pp. 1-2.

35. Cf. Riessler, *Altjüdisches Schrifttum*, pp. 1323-24. See also Wagner, *Essener in der wissenschaftlichen Diskussion*, pp. 218-20.

rendered into English as 'Some of the Precepts of the Torah'), L.H. Schiffman has advocated a Sadducean background to the scrolls.[36] Schiffman's proposal in the 1990s received as little support as an earlier suggestion of a Sadducean background for the scrolls in the 1950s.[37] Finally, it is instructive to observe that J.M. Baumgarten, another expert on Jewish law, who was moreover among the first to point out halakhic correspondences between 4QMMT and the position attributed to the Sadducees in later rabbinic sources, has remained a supporter of the Essene hypothesis.[38] Though frequently lavished with media attention a Jewish-Christian identification of the individuals behind the scrolls is impossible to reconcile with the date of the material. It is no longer possible to argue for a background to the events described in the scrolls in the life of the early church in the light of the recent confirmation of F.M. Cross's palaeographical results by

36. Cf. L.H. Schiffman, 'The New Halakhic Letter (4QMMT) and the Origins of the Dead Sea Sect', *BA* 53 (1990), pp. 64-73; *idem*, 'The Sadducean Origins of the Dead Sea Scroll Sect', in H. Shanks (ed.), *Understanding the Dead Sea Scrolls* (London: SPCK, 1993), pp. 35-49. For the official edition of 4QMMT, see E. Qimron and J. Strugnell, *Qumran Cave 4. V. Miqsat Ma'ase Ha-Torah* (DJD, 10; Oxford: Clarendon Press, 1994).

37. Cf. R. North, 'The Qumran Sadducees', *CBQ* 17 (1955), pp. 164-88. For a critique of Schiffman's recent proposition, see P.R. Davies, 'Sadducees in the Dead Sea Scrolls', in *idem*, *Sects and Scrolls: Essays on Qumran and Related Topics* (South Florida Studies in the History of Judaism, 134; Atlanta: Scholars Press, 1996), pp. 127-38; J.A. Fitzmyer, 'The Qumran Community: Essene or Saddu-cean?', *HeyJ* 36 (1995), pp. 467-76; J.C. VanderKam, 'The People of the Dead Sea Scrolls: Essenes or Sadducees?', in *Understanding the Dead Sea Scrolls*, pp. 50-62; G. Vermes, *The Dead Sea Scrolls: Qumran in Perspective* (London: SCM, rev. 3rd edn, 1994), pp. 102-104.

38. Cf. J.M. Baumgarten, 'The Pharisaic–Sadducean Controversies about Purity and the Qumran Texts', *JJS* 31 (1980), pp. 157-70; *idem*, 'The Disqualifications of Priests in 4Q Fragments of the "Damascus Document", a Specimen of the Recovery of pre-Rabbinic Halakha', in J. Trebolle Barrera and L. Vegas Montaner (eds.), *The Madrid Qumran Congress: Proceedings of the International Congress on the Dead Sea Scrolls, Madrid 18–21 March 1991*, II (STDJ, 11; Leiden: E.J. Brill), pp. 503-13, esp. pp. 503-505; and *idem*, 'Sadducean Elements in Qumran Law', in E. Ulrich and J.C. VanderKam (eds.), *The Community of the Renewed Covenant: The Notre Dame Symposium on the Dead Sea Scrolls* (Notre Dame: Notre Dame University Press, 1994), pp. 27-36. An equally cautious assessment of these issues has been offered by Y. Sussman, 'The History of the Halakhah and the Dead Sea Scrolls. Preliminary Talmudic Observations on *Miqṣat Ma'aśe ha-Torah* (4QMMT)', in Qimron and Strugnell, *Qumran Cave 4*, V, pp. 179-200.

technologically improved carbon 14 tests.[39] Furthermore, N. Golb recently revived a theory suggested in the 1960s by K.H. Rengstorf by postulating that the scrolls do not go back to a particular community but originated from the library of the Jerusalem temple.[40] Neither Rengstorf nor Golb have found much support, and a number of scholars have published strong refutations of this theory.[41] Finally, M. Goodman has recently suggested that the Dead Sea Scrolls may go back to a Jewish group that was previously unknown and has not left any traces in our sources.[42]

Although the majority of Qumran scholars today favour an Essene identification of the background to the Dead Sea Scrolls a number of different variations of the Essene hypothesis are being proposed. The Essene hypothesis as it was developed by the first generation of Qumran scholars maintained that the Essenes and the Qumran community are best seen as identical entities.[43] In other words, everyone and only

39. Cf. F.M. Cross, 'The Development of Jewish Scripts', in G.E. Wright (ed.), *The Bible and the Ancient Near East* (Garden City, NY: Doubleday, 1961), pp. 133-202; G. Bonani *et al.*, 'Radiocarbon Dating of Fourteen Dead Sea Scrolls', *Radiocarbon* 34 (1992), pp. 843-49; and A.J.T. Jull *et al.*, 'Radiocarbon Dating of Scrolls and Linen Fragments from the Judaean Desert', *'Atiqot* 28 (1996), pp. 1-7. See further the following recent assessments of both methods of dating: F.M. Cross, 'Palaeography and the Dead Sea Scrolls', in P. Flint and J.C. VanderKam (eds.), *The Dead Sea Scrolls After Fifty Years: A Comprehensive Assessment*, I (Leiden: E.J. Brill, 1999), pp. 379-402, and G. Doudna, 'Dating the Scrolls on the Basis of Radiocarbon Analysis', in P. Flint and J.C. VanderKam (eds.), *The Dead Sea Scrolls After Fifty Years: A Comprehensive Assessment*, II (Leiden: E.J. Brill, 1999), pp. 430-71.

40. Cf. N. Golb, 'The Problem of Origin and Identification of the Dead Sea Scrolls', *Proceedings of the American Philosophical Society* 124 (1980), pp. 1-24; *idem, Who Wrote the Dead Sea Scrolls?* (London: O'Mara, 1995); and K.H. Rengstorf, *Ḥirbet Qumrân and the Problem of the Library of the Dead Sea Scrolls* (Leiden: E.J. Brill, 1963).

41. See O. Betz and R. Riesner, *Jesus, Qumran, and the Vatican: Clarifications* (London: SCM Press, 1994), esp. ch. 4; F. García Martínez and A.S. van der Woude, 'A "Groningen" Hypothesis of Qumran Origins and Early History', *RevQ* 14 (1990), pp. 521-41; and Stegemann, 'Qumran Essenes', pp. 96-100.

42. M.D. Goodman, 'A Note on the Qumran Sectarians, the Essenes and Josephus', *JJS* 46 (1995), pp. 161-66.

43. Cf., for instance, F.M. Cross, *The Ancient Library of Qumran* (Sheffield: Sheffield Academic Press, rev. 3rd edn, 1995); Milik, *Ten Years of Discovery*; and G. Vermes, *Les manuscrits du désert de Juda* (Tournai-Paris: Desclée, 1953).

those who were Essenes were members of the Qumran community that had its centre at the settlement at Qumran by the Dead Sea, although Essenes inhabited outlying communities in the towns and villages of Palestine. Such a view on the distribution of the Essenes is based on the information in the classical sources, which refer to a community by the shores of the Dead Sea (Pliny) as well as Essenes living in the towns and villages of Palestine (Josephus) and was already popular in the pre-Qumran phase of research on the Essenes.[44] More recently archaeologists have discovered evidence reflecting the distinctive burial practice that characterizes the Qumran cemeteries at another site in the Judaean desert as well as in Jerusalem, which seems to point to the presence of Essene communities at these sites.[45] Further evidence for the presence of an Essene community in Jerusalem is a reference to 'the gate of the Essenes' in Josephus (*War* 5.145).[46]

The view that the Essenes and the Qumran community are identical remained very influential for many years. More recent developments in Qumran studies, however, are moving away from a straightforward identification model (Essenes = Qumran community) in favour of more complex models.[47] An alternative theory known as 'the Groningen hypothesis' holds that the Essene movement and the Qumran community are two distinct though related groups. This hypothesis was developed by F. García Martínez and A.S. van der Woude, two scholars based at the Dutch University of Groningen.[48] García Martínez and

44. Cf. Friedländer, *Die religiösen Bewegungen*, p. 145; Lightley, *Jewish Sects and Parties*, pp. 282-83; and Schürer, *Geschichte des jüdischen Volkes*, II, pp. 562-63.

45. Cf. P. Bar-Adon, 'Another Settlement of the Judaean Desert Sect at 'En el-Ghuweir on the Shores of the Dead Sea', *BASOR* 227 (1977), pp. 1-25; and B. Zissu, '"Qumran Type" Graves in Jerusalem: Archaeological Evidence of an Essene Community?', *DSD* 5 (1998), pp. 158-71.

46. Cf. R. Riesner, 'Essene Gate', *ABD*, II, pp. 618-19, and further literature listed there.

47. For an overview of some recent developments, see C. Hempel, 'Qumran Communities: Beyond the Fringes of Second Temple Society', in S.E. Porter and C.A. Evans (eds.), *The Scrolls and the Scriptures: Qumran Fifty Years After* (Roehampton Institute London Papers, 3; JSPSup, 26; Sheffield: Sheffield Academic Press, 1997), pp. 43-53.

48. Cf. F. García Martínez, 'Qumran Origins and Early History: A Groningen Hypothesis', *Folia Orientalia* 25 (1988), pp. 113-36, and García Martínez and van der Woude, 'A "Groningen" Hypothesis'.

van der Woude argue that the Essene movement emanated from the Palestinian apocalyptic tradition whereas the Qumran community emerged after a split within the wider Essene movement, which resulted in the withdrawal of a group loyal to the Teacher of Righteousness, a prominent individual associated with the early history of the community in a number of scrolls, to Qumran. An important corollary of this hypothesis is that the Qumran library contains works authored by both the Essene parent movement and the Qumran community. Finally, the German Qumran specialist H. Stegemann has recently revised his own earlier views on the nature of the Essenes.[49] He now argues that the Teacher of Righteousness was the founder of 'the main Jewish Union of Second Temple times', which embraced all conservative Jews of the time with the sole exception of the Maccabean high priest and the Temple establishment. On Stegemann's revised view the classical authors' term 'Essenes' refers to this union. Stegemann's revised hypothesis has not found as much support as his earlier reconstruction, to which I will now turn.

Essene Origins

Based on what is said in a number of texts from Qumran about the pivotal role played by an individual referred to as the Teacher of Righteousness during the earliest phase of the community's history and this figure's opponent, known from the biblical commentaries, especially the *Commentary on Habakkuk*, as the Wicked Priest, the origins of the Essenes are often thought of as having come about as a result of priestly conflict.[50] In particular it is frequently argued, following a suggestion by Stegemann, that the Teacher of Righteousness was a former high priest who was ousted from his office by the Hasmonaean ruler Jonathan in 152 BCE. Because Jonathan was not of Zadokite descent, the Teacher and his adherents considered Jonathan to be an illegitimate holder of the high priestly office. After the Teacher was driven out of office, Stegemann goes on to argue, he and his followers found asylum with a community of pious Jews known as the Ḥasidim. A second

49. Cf. Stegemann, 'Qumran Essenes', and *idem*, *The Library of Qumran: On the Essenes, Qumran, John the Baptist, and Jesus* (Grand Rapids, MI: Eerdmans; Leiden: E.J. Brill, 1998), pp. 139-210.

50. See, for example, G. Vermes, 'The Essenes and History', *JJS* 32 (1981), pp. 18-31.

century BCE date for the emergence of the Essenes was popular already in the pre-Qumran debate on the Essenes. Such a date was suggested primarily on the basis of Josephus's writings, where the first references to the Essenes occur in the context of events in the middle of the second century BCE.[51] Moreover, a number of writers from the first half of the twentieth century already proposed that the Essenes emerged among the Hasidim.[52] A slightly different view on Essene origins was espoused by Friedländer, who argued for seeing their roots in the pre-Maccabaean wisdom tradition.[53]

On the basis of the evidence of the scrolls Stegemann further maintains that the arrival of the Teacher led to a split within the Hasidim over the Teacher's demand of boycotting the Temple. The faction loyal to the Teacher subsequently formed the Essene Qumran community whereas the remainder came to form the Pharisees. Two aspects of Stegemann's reconstruction of the origin of the Essenes have been questioned. First, P.R. Davies and others have drawn attention to the scarcity of evidence on the Hasidim as an organized movement in the Maccabaean era.[54] Secondly, J.J. Collins has challenged Stegemann's suggestion that the Teacher of Righteousness was a former high priest rather than simply a priest held in high esteem by his followers.[55] Finally, most recent developments in Qumran studies, such as the 'Groningen hypothesis' mentioned above, are characterized by attempts

---

51. Cf. Lagrange, *Judaïsme avant Jésus-Christ*, p. 320; Schürer, *Geschichte des jüdischen Volkes*, II, p. 560.

52. See, for instance, Bousset and Gressmann, *Religion des Judentums*, p. 457, and Lightley, *Jewish Sects and Parties*, pp. 278-80.

53. Cf. Friedländer, *Die religiösen Bewegungen*, pp. 114, 119.

54. Cf. P.R. Davies, 'Hasidim in the Maccabean Period', *JJS* 28 (1977), pp. 127-40; reprinted in *idem, Sects and Scrolls: Essays on Qumran and Related Topics* (South Florida Studies in the History of Judaism, 134; Atlanta: Scholars Press, 1996), pp. 5-21.

55. J.J. Collins, 'The Origin of the Qumran Community: A Review of the Evidence', in M.P. Horgan and P.J. Kobelski (eds.), *To Touch the Text: Biblical and Related Studies in Honor of Joseph A. Fitzmyer* (New York: Crossroad, 1989), pp. 159-78. See also J.H. Charlesworth, 'The Origin and Subsequent History of the Authors of the Dead Sea Scrolls: Four Transitional Phases among the Qumran Essenes', *RevQ* 10 (1980), pp. 213-33, esp. p. 222; and M.O. Wise, 'The Teacher of Righteousness and the High Priest of the Intersacerdotium: Two Approaches', *RevQ* 14 (1990), pp. 587-613.

to distinguish between the origins of a parent group and the offshoot Qumran community.[56]

The Fate of the Essenes after 70 CE

We know nothing with certainty about the fate of the Essenes after the capture of Jerusalem by the Romans in 70 CE, although it is most unlikely that they and their heritage disappeared completely.[57] The archaeological evidence of the Qumran site indicates that it was in all likelihood overrun by the Romans in 68 CE when, according to Josephus, the Roman commander and future emperor Vespasian was in the vicinity of Jericho and the Dead Sea.[58] Already in the first half of the twentieth century it was frequently argued that many Essenes became Christians.[59] Others suggested that the heritage of the Essenes was taken up by later Christian heretics.[60] The presence of a composition such as *The Songs of the Sabbath Sacrifice* both at Qumran and at Masada may indicate that some former inhabitants of the Qumran site joined the Jewish rebels at Masada and perished there when this final stronghold of Jewish resistance fell to the Romans in 74 CE.[61] What is more, M. Broshi has tried to identify traces of anti-Qumran polemics in the Talmud that would suggest the continued promulgation of Essene halakhic traditions well beyond 70 CE.[62] Such a picture is equally suggested by the halakhic parallels between some Dead Sea Scrolls and the views attributed to the opponents of the Pharisees in the Mishnah. Finally, Goodman stresses the bias of our sources for the period after

56. Cf. C. Hempel, 'Community Origins in the *Damascus Document* in the Light of Recent Scholarship', in D.W. Parry and E. Ulrich (eds.), *The Provo International Conference on the Dead Sea Scrolls: Technological Innovations, New Texts, and Reformulated Issues* (STDJ, 30; Leiden: E.J. Brill, 1999), pp. 316-29.

57. Cf. Charlesworth, 'Origin and Subsequent History', pp. 230-32.

58. Cf. P.R. Davies, *Qumran* (Cities of the Biblical World; Guildford: Lutterworth, 1982), pp. 58-62.

59. Cf. Lightley, *Jewish Sects and Parties*, p. 322.

60. So, for example, Friedländer, *Die religiösen Bewegungen*, p. 168.

61. Cf. Y. Yadin, *Masada: Herod's Fortress and the Zealots' Last Stand* (London: Weidenfeld & Nicolson, 1966), pp. 168-91, esp. pp. 172-74.

62. M. Broshi, 'Anti-Qumranic Polemics in the Talmud', in J. Trebolle Barrera and L. Vegas Montaner (eds.), *The Madrid Qumran Congress: Proceedings of the International Congress on the Dead Sea Scrolls, Madrid 18–21 March 1991*, II (STDJ, 11; Leiden: E.J. Brill, 1992), pp. 589-600.

70 CE and argues for the continued survival of pre-70 Jewish groupings, such as Essenes and Sadducees, 'for years, perhaps centuries,
after the destruction of the Temple.'[63]

To conclude, the scholarly study of the Essenes during the last hundred years has received a great impetus with the discovery of the Dead
Sea Scrolls in the late 1940s. This library, which is commonly viewed
as reflecting an Essene background, has enormously enriched the 'database' of Essene scholarship. A new lease of life has entered the study
of the scrolls themselves since the early 1990s, when all the unpub-
lished scrolls, particularly the extensive but fragmentary contents of
Qumran cave 4, were made accessible to all qualified scholars.[64] In
sum, it is probably fair to say that at the beginning of the twenty-first
century research on the Essenes is progressing at a more vigorous pace
than ever before in the course of the last hundred years, and there is
little to indicate that the intense scholarly interest in this Jewish movement and its heritage is waning.

63. M.D. Goodman, 'Sadducees and Essenes after 70 CE', in S.E. Porter,
P. Joyce and D.E. Orton (eds.), *Crossing the Boundaries: Essays in Biblical Interpretation in Honour of Michael D. Goulder* (Leiden: E.J. Brill, 1994), pp. 347-65,
esp. p. 355.

64. For an account of these events cf. Vermes, *Qumran in Perspective*, pp. 9-10.

An Analysis of Recent 'Historical Jesus' Studies

Donald A. Hagner

The current explosion of writing on the so-called historical Jesus has recently captured the interest of journalists, particularly in the United States but elsewhere too. A group calling itself the 'Jesus Seminar' has as one of its stated purposes to gain the public's attention—this through radical and shocking pronouncements concerning the 'historical' Jesus. Particularly exasperating is the repeated claim of this group to represent the conclusions of 'scholarship', when in fact their conclusions represent only a relatively small group of radical scholars who, moreover, have largely ignored the work of mainline critical scholars.

One does not have to be very cynical to believe that other agendas drive the Jesus Seminar and other current writers on the historical Jesus as much as the quest for knowledge. The journalists show us that, as with the Athenians, the public's ears always itch to hear something new. The media are always hunting for the sensational, and the Jesus Seminar has been happy to accommodate them.

This is not, indeed, the first time we have had a flurry of writing on the supposedly 'real' Jesus. It happened also in the last century, especially with the monumental book of David Friedrich Strauss, *Das Leben Jesu, kritisch bearbeitet*, first published in 1835–36,[1] but also in the dozens of liberal 'life of Jesus' books written in the nineteenth century, and surveyed in Albert Schweitzer's famous book, *The Quest of the Historical Jesus*.[2] Strauss's book sounds amazingly modern, or, to put it the other way around, the work of the Jesus Seminar and other modern writers sounds strangely familiar to those acquainted with Strauss.

---

1. The English translation by George Eliot has often been reprinted. Recently: Mifflintown, PA: Sigler Press, 1994.

2. The German title is *Von Reimarus zu Wrede* (1906). This book in English translation has also often been reprinted, for example, with an introduction by J.M. Robinson (New York: Macmillan, 1968).

It is telling that the major book recently produced by the Jesus Seminar, entitled *The Five Gospels*,[3] is dedicated to Strauss ('who pioneered the quest of the historical Jesus'), along with Galileo ('who altered our view of the heavens forever') and Thomas Jefferson ('who took scissors and paste to the gospels').

It deserves to be emphasized that in both the nineteenth-century writing on Jesus and that of today, what seems to be wanted is not so much a *truer* view of Jesus as an *alternate* view. The traditional view of Jesus, the view held by the church, is old-fashioned, uninteresting, and thought to be unconvincing. What the world craves is a debunking of the traditional Jesus, a Jesus rescued from the dogma of the church for twenty-first century human beings. What will sell books and bring fame or notoriety are new explanations of Jesus—explanations acceptable to the proclivities and sensitivities of the modern world.

In what follows, I will first look at the methodology of contemporary historical Jesus studies, then review some of the recent work that has been done, and finally make some observations.

1. *Method*

A problem exists from the very start—and the problem is of absolute importance in the whole question before us—in the juxtaposition of the two words 'historical Jesus'. These two words are incompatible to the extent that they nearly cancel each other out. The reason is that the word 'historical', as used here, means very explicitly that which can be established by the historical method per se. That method, it is argued, can only deal with natural causation—that is, with a closed system of cause and effect that can allow no interruption from outside the system. This is, in effect, to espouse a naturalistic world view that prohibits the possibility of God acting in history. But even the name Jesus (Mt. 1.21; Lk. 1.31), as every reader of the New Testament knows, refers to the unique Son of God, sent by the Father. That is, according to the New Testament, Jesus comes to us from God, from eternity, from outside the present system. Yet this is precisely what cannot have happened, given the way in which the word 'historical' is commonly used.

The result of this lamentable perspective follows automatically: if historical, not Jesus (i.e. not the Jesus of the Gospels); if Jesus, not

3.   R.W. Funk and R.W. Hoover (eds.), *The Five Gospels: The Search for the Authentic Words of Jesus* (New York: Macmillan, 1993).

historical (i.e. not according to the canons of historiography). And we are thus put in a position where the only acceptable alternative is to depart from the New Testament's understanding of Jesus. That is, *out of a perceived necessity* Jesus cannot historically have been what the New Testament and the church portray him as. The historical Jesus *must* be other than the Jesus of the Gospels.

For the roots of this viewpoint expressed most sharply, we may go back to the positivistic historical method articulated by Ernst Troeltsch in 1898.[4] Troeltsch set forth three main criteria upon which to decide positively that something is historical. He insisted upon (1) the application of *critical judgment* to every tradition and interpretation; (2) the necessity of *analogy* with what is known from experience; and (3) the necessity of *correlation*, that is, the interrelatedness of events, including, of course, causation.

This historicism, it will easily be seen, is the result of the scientific thinking that began with the Enlightenment, when the autonomy of human reason was established against all forms of authority, including especially that of the church. With the emergence of the Newtonian worldview, the tight web of cause and effect that is so apparent in the physical world and so necessary to the growth of science was extended to include all of reality. The result was the declared impossibility of metaphysical knowledge. In this way, the very notion of a supernatural causation—a causation from outside the system—was ruled out from the start. There could be, furthermore, no such thing as revelation, and the Bible could be no more than a collection of human writings. The full humanity of the biblical writings emerged with stark clarity as their divine inspiration evaporated.

Theology had to be based on the model of science, it was argued, and thus theology—with no room for God—became, in effect, reduced to anthropology. In the last analysis we are dealing with solely human phenomena and human opinion. The theology of the historicists cannot take us beyond ourselves.

---

4.   The classic German essay 'Über historische und dogmatische Methode in der Theologie' (On historical and dogmatic method in theology) is available in *Gesammelte Schriften*, II (Aalen: Scientia Verlag, 1962 [1922]), pp. 729-53. See too *Ernst Troeltsch, Writings on Theology and Religion* (trans. and ed. R. Morgan and M. Pye; Atlanta, GA: John Knox Press, 1977).

a. *The Old Quest*

The results of this rationalistic perspective naturally had a striking impact on the study of Jesus. Already in the eighteenth century Lessing published the writings of Reimarus posthumously (and anonymously) as the famous *Wolfenbüttel Fragments*.[5] Reimarus, it deserves to be pointed out, was heavily dependent on the conclusions of the English deists before him (e.g. he cites Toland, Shaftesbury, Collins, Tindal, Morgan and Middleton).[6] Here is a Jesus radically different from the New Testament and the church's understanding of him. In Reimarus's view, Jesus was a revolutionary who had hoped to be influential in the overturning of Roman rule and the setting up of a new Jewish nation. Altogether gone is the transcendent, the supernatural, the entering of God into human affairs. The claim concerning the resurrection of Jesus is merely the lie of the first Christians, who in fact had stolen the body. Although not many have shared Reimarus's understanding of Jesus as a political revolutionary, those who quest after the 'historical' Jesus today would agree with his naturalism.

The nineteenth century saw the appearance of numerous accounts of Jesus written from a naturalistic point of view. We have already mentioned the landmark work of Strauss, *Das Leben Jesu*. Strauss, who was only 27 years old when the book was first published, tried to make sense of the miraculous stories of the New Testament by regarding them not as actual historical accounts, but rather as myths that were intended to convey spiritual truth of some kind. The book became extremely popular, going through numerous printings and editions. Within five years 60 replies to Strauss appeared.[7] The public of 1835, no less than that of today, was eager to see the doctrines of the church debunked by what was thought to be a more scholarly, and thus more adequate, reading of the Gospels.

Strauss was only one of many writers—though clearly the most

---

5.   English translation: *Reimarus: Fragments* (ed. C.H. Talbert; Philadelphia: Fortress Press, 1970). See too the discussion of Reimarus in R.A. Harrisville and W. Sundberg, *The Bible in Modern Culture: Theology and Historical-Critical Method from Spinoza to Käsemann* (Grand Rapids: Eerdmans, 1995), pp. 49-65.

6.   Thus Colin Brown, 'Historical Jesus, Quest of', in J.B. Green, S. McKnight and I.H. Marshall (eds.), *Dictionary of Jesus and the Gospels* (Leicester: Inter-Varsity Press, 1992), pp. 326-41. See too Brown's excellent *Jesus in European Protestant Thought* (Grand Rapids: Baker Book House, 2nd edn, 1988).

7.   Brown, 'Historical Jesus, Quest of', p. 328.

impressive—to attempt to make sense of a Jesus from within a naturalistic perspective. Albert Schweitzer's well-known book, *The Quest of the Historical Jesus*,[8] reviewed the stream of nineteenth-century lives of Jesus and showed how fruitless their efforts were. Schweitzer's conclusion was that, rather than having found the historical Jesus, these writers had simply made Jesus over into their own image. At the bottom of the well from which they drank they saw not Jesus as he actually was, but their own reflection (thus George Tyrrell).[9] Hence Jesus was portrayed as a gentlemanly, nineteenth-century moralist, quite acceptable to polite, liberal European society. Schweitzer[10] (like J. Weiss[11] before him) argued, on the contrary, that the historical Jesus was a radical apocalyptic preacher, more like an unkempt man standing on the corner with a long beard and with a sign saying 'Repent for the end of the world is near'. In his expectation Jesus was sadly mistaken and he died in disillusionment. Neither Weiss nor Schweitzer departed, however, from naturalistic presuppositions in their portrayal of Jesus. They have no room for the supernatural in their understanding of Jesus. Their view is finally not much different from that of Reimarus, if one but substitutes apocalyptic denouement for political revolution.

The impact of Schweitzer slowed down the books and research on Jesus (but did not stop it completely—the 'no-quest' period is a misnomer).[12] The work of W. Wrede[13] and R. Bultmann in particular,[14] claiming that the Gospels reflect more the theology of the early Christian community rather than the actual history of Jesus, had an equally negative effect. Bultmann, however, was able actually to write a book on Jesus, which he entitled *Jesus and the Word*.[15] Despite the book itself, Bultmann wrote the following often quoted words:

8.   See n. 2.

9.   G. Tyrrell, *Christianity at the Cross-roads* (London: Longmans, 1909), p. 49.

10. *Historical Jesus*, pp. 361-97.

11. *Jesus' Proclamation of the Kingdom of God* (ET; Philadelphia: Fortress Press, 1971 [German, 1892]).

12. Thus rightly, M.J. Borg, *Jesus in Contemporary Scholarship* (Valley Forge, PA: Trinity Press International, 1994), pp. 3-4.

13. *The Messianic Secret* (Cambridge: James Clark, 1971 [German, 1901]).

14. *The History of the Synoptic Tradition* (New York: Harper & Row, 1963 [German, 1921]).

15. (New York: Charles Scribner's Sons, 1958 [German, 1926]).

> I do indeed think that we can now know almost nothing concerning the life and personality of Jesus, since the early Christian sources show no interest in either, are moreover fragmentary and often legendary; and other sources about Jesus do not exist.[16]

For Bultmann, as is well known, the kerygma of the early church needed no continuity with Jesus as he actually was in history; the mere thatness (the *Dass*) of Jesus was sufficient.[17] The historical Jesus was of no real significance for the Christian faith.

b. *The New Quest*

Bultmann's own students eventually reacted to the danger of the docetism posed by their master's perspective. Ernst Käsemann presented a highly influential lecture in 1953,[18] in which he indicated the importance of at least some degree of continuity between the Christ of the kerygma and the Jesus of history. The possibility of *some* knowledge of the historical Jesus was not to be so quickly abandoned. Thus was inaugurated the so-called new quest of the historical Jesus.[19]

The scholars who took up the challenge of the new quest had more modest goals than the writers of the nineteenth-century lives of Jesus. With somewhat less historical skepticism, they worked through the materials looking for what they could discover about Jesus that might be regarded as historically true. Scholars such as Fuchs,[20] Ebeling,[21] Bornkamm,[22] and Conzelmann[23] examined such things as Jesus' table fellowship with sinners, the content and authority of his teaching and his death as martyrdom.

---

16. *Jesus and the Word*, p. 14.

17. R. Bultmann, 'The Primitive Christian Kerygma and the Historical Jesus', in *The Historical Jesus and the Kerygmatic Christ* (ed. and trans. C.E. Braaten and R.A. Harrisville; New York: Abingdon Press, 1964), pp. 15-42 (25).

18. E. Käsemann, 'The Problem of the Historical Jesus', in *Essays on New Testament Themes* (SBT, 41; London: SCM Press, 1964), pp. 15-47 (first published in *ZTK* 51 [1954], pp. 125-33).

19. See J.M. Robinson's useful book *A New Quest of the Historical Jesus* (SBT, 25; London: SCM Press, 1959).

20. E. Fuchs, *Studies in the Historical Jesus* (SBT, 42; London: SCM Press, 1964).

21. G. Ebeling, *Word and Faith* (Philadelphia: Fortress Press, 1963).

22. G. Bornkamm, *Jesus of Nazareth* (New York: Harper & Row, 1960).

23. H. Conzelmann, *Jesus* (ed. J. Reumann; Philadelphia: Fortress Press, 3rd edn, 1973) (reprint of article in *RGG*, III [1959], pp. 97-116).

The new quest was new in the sense that new and earnest attempts were made to extract historical knowledge from the Gospels, and then through existentialist interpretation to build a bridge between Jesus and the kerygma. Nevertheless, the new quest was dominated by the same presuppositions and methods as the old quest. In that sense it was not new. Borg's assessment is apropos: 'its methods and results remained largely the same' as in the putative 'no-quest' period.[24] The same naturalism rules over the new quest. In short, it remains a fact that nothing can be regarded as historical that depends upon a break in the closed system of cause and effect. There is no room for the transcendent in the sense of God truly acting in the historical process.

c. *The Third Quest*

Developments in the study of the historical Jesus, beginning approximately in the 1980s have been designated as the beginning of a 'third quest' (thus N.T. Wright),[25] and it is this more recent literature that will be our focus below. According to Wright, the 'third quest' is characterized by a new attention directed to the historical context of Jesus in all its various aspects, but above all to Second Temple Judaism. It is largely owing to the increasing research in these areas that new efforts in relating Jesus to his context have gained their stimulation. Wright frankly admits that among the increasingly large number of publications devoted to the historical Jesus (sometimes now called 'Life of Jesus Research'), there is 'a bewildering range of competing hypotheses' and that 'there is no unifying theological agenda; no final agreement about method; certainly no common set of results.'[26]

The attention to the Jewish background of Jesus has long been the focus of Jewish scholars bent on the bringing home of Jesus to Judaism.[27] Now, in a book generally regarded as part of the third quest, the Jewish scholar Geza Vermes has drawn a 'historical' portrait of Jesus that places him fully within the context of first-century Judaism.[28] In this book the Jewish writing about Jesus reaches a high point.

24. *Jesus in Contemporary Scholarship*, p. 5.
25. S. Neill and T. Wright, *The Interpretation of the New Testament, 1861–1986* (Oxford: Oxford University Press, 1988), pp. 379-403.
26. N.T. Wright, 'Jesus, Quest for the Historical', *ABD*, III, pp. 796-802 (800).
27. For twentieth-century Jewish scholars on Jesus, see D.A. Hagner, *The Jewish Reclamation of Jesus* (Grand Rapids: Zondervan, 1984).
28. *Jesus the Jew: A Historian's Reading of the Gospels* (London: Collins,

What is new about the so-called third quest? In his review of recent trends, W.R. Telford[29] mentions a number of new aspects, some more convincing, in my opinion, than others. Less convincing are the claims that the new quest offers a more strict historical (and less theological) orientation and that it gives attention to broader questions. To my mind the ideological commitments of these authors are hardly less conspicuous than in the earlier quests. More convincing are the claims that the third quest criticizes over-emphasis on tradition-critical analysis and form criticism, including the criterion of dissimilarity. Most significant, however, is the wider source base employed together with the concern to place Jesus in broader contexts, openness to new, interdisciplinary methods and a new confidence that a comprehensive account of the historical Jesus is possible.

Telford himself rightly questions the extent to which the 'third' quest really is new. Thus he writes, 'Despite the differences already noted, it can also be argued that recent developments are broadly in continuity with the New Quest.'[30] Indeed, Telford agrees with S. Fowl[31] that the old and new quests were not fundamentally different, and with H. Koester[32] that the new life of Jesus research has decided similarities with even the old quest. L. Keck, in reviewing the work of Crossan and Borg, key representatives of the latest writing on Jesus, concludes that here no less than in the original quest, we again encounter modern ideas and values superimposed on the historical Jesus.[33]

Certainly, none of the new aspects of the present life of Jesus research represents a going back on the naturalism of Reimarus or Strauss. On the contrary, it is admitted even by N.T. Wright that the third quest has yet to deal with such crucial issues as the personal claims of Jesus (i.e. Christology, a point made also by Telford), his

1973); *The Religion of Jesus the Jew* (Philadelphia: Fortress Press, 1993). On Vermes, see further below, p. 100.

29. 'Major Trends and Interpretive Issues in the Study of Jesus', in C.A. Evans and B. Chilton (eds.), *Studying the Historical Jesus: Evaluation of the State of Current Research* (Leiden: E.J. Brill, 1994), pp. 33-74.

30. Telford, 'Major Trends', p. 60.

31. 'Reconstructing and Deconstructing the Quest of the Historical Jesus', *SJT* 42 (1989), pp. 319-33.

32. 'Jesus the Victim', *JBL* 111 (1992), pp. 3-15 (5).

33. 'The Second Coming of the Liberal Jesus?', *Christian Century* 111 (1994), pp. 784-87.

miraculous deeds, or of course the resurrection itself.[34] Indeed, the focus of recent Jesus research continues to be more on the background, that is the social situation of the first century, than upon Jesus himself, in the (unjustified) belief that this context contains the key to understanding Jesus. Symptomatic of most Jesus research today is the attitude reflected by the Jesus Seminar, some of whose members are key authors of the third quest. The first of what they call 'the seven pillars of scholarly wisdom' (discussed below) that support 'the edifice of contemporary gospel scholarship' is the following: '...the distinction between the historical Jesus, to be uncovered by historical excavation, and the Christ of faith encapsulated in the first creeds.'

In the face of this, however, claims have been made that the new life of Jesus research *is* in fact open to the miraculous. Craig A. Evans, somewhat euphorically, it seems to me, writes that 'the miracle stories are now treated seriously and are widely accepted by Jesus scholars as deriving from Jesus' ministry'.[35] 'The miracle tradition,' he concludes, 'is no longer the stumbling block that it once was.' And thus, he continues, 'I believe that it is not an exaggeration to describe the current scholarly mood as representing a substantial break with the past.'[36] Even the Jesus Seminar, now having established which deeds of Jesus are to be regarded as historical (after concluding that only 18 per cent of the sayings may claim a degree of authenticity), announces with pride that they accept that Jesus performed miracles.

One must note immediately, however, what is and what is not meant by 'miracle' in such a statement. What is meant are healings and exorcisms capable of being explained psychosomatically; what is *not* meant is anything that transcends or breaks the web of natural causation. David Aune's analysis of the situation is correct: 'Since most of the healings and exorcisms found in the tradition can be construed as psychosomatic cures, their occurrence is not an a priori historical impossibility.'[37] Such miracles as the raising of the dead by Jesus, the so-called nature miracles, such as the feeding of the multitudes, the

---

34. S. Neill and T. Wright, *New Testament 1861–1986*, p. 400. Cf. Wright's article in *ABD*, where he describes unfinished agendas of the third quest ('Jesus, Quest for the Historical', III, p. 801).

35. 'Life-of-Jesus Research and the Eclipse of Mythology', *TS* 54 (1993), pp. 3-26 (19).

36. Evans, 'Life-of-Jesus Research', p. 36.

37. 'Magic in Early Christianity', *ANRW*, II, pp. 1507-57.

calming of the sea, and walking on the water, not to mention of course the resurrection of Jesus himself—these things continue to be excluded from consideration.

Now the reason I am giving so much attention to this question is not so much for the sake of the individual miracles in question, but rather because of its fundamental importance methodologically. The refusal to allow the possibility of the truly supernatural in concrete history takes away the entire interpretive framework that makes possible an adequate understanding of Jesus. To my mind it is this that accounts for the wide variety of competing theories produced by those currently questing after the historical Jesus. Having cut away the essence of the narratives concerning One uniquely sent by God to bring the dawning of a new age and salvation to the world (and salvation by the death of God's Son is outside the realm of the historian qua historian), the new generation of Jesus scholars is forced to use their imagination to construct new understandings of Jesus. While they do not quite spin their hypotheses out of thin air, since they draw on the rich contextual materials provided by the contemporary sources, their quest must nevertheless be said to lack a coherent methodology.[38] Without the interpretive framework provided by the Gospels, which are the only significant sources about Jesus, the discrete data become too fragmentary and too capable of various construals. It is as though one were confronted with a large number of dots to be connected together to form a picture but lacked the numbers that indicated which way the lines were to be drawn. What happens is that each person connects the dots in his or her own way. The resultant reconstructions often become little more than brilliant exercises in subjectivity. Carl E. Braaten correctly concludes:

> All three quests have failed for the same fundamental reason. They have fallen into a chasm that separates Jesus from the church. Their approach to the historical Jesus suspends or brackets out the living reality of the church as the necessary condition of affirming the essential identity of the earthly Jesus and the risen Christ.[39]

There is no binding reason, on the other hand, why the Jesus of the Gospels may not provide a reliable portrait of Jesus as he was in history. And this is what we are interested in: not the artificial and inadequate construct known as 'the historical Jesus', but the Jesus of history.

38. Thus, too, Telford, 'Major Trends', p. 58.
39. 'Jesus and the Church', *Ex Auditu* 10 (1994), pp. 59-71.

Presuppositions against the supernatural are no more convincing in themselves than presuppositions in favor of the supernatural. What is wanted above all is an open mind on the subject—which is the only humble stance to take. We simply do not know enough to be able to rule out a priori the possibility of God acting in the historical process and the transcending of natural causation. It is my opinion, and that of many others, that the most *historically* satisfying explanation of the resurrection is the one held by the church. It is also the case that the Gospels make the most *historical* sense when *their* interpretation of Jesus is taken seriously. A coherent and convincing picture of Jesus emerges, and it is one that is compatible with what we have come to know of the historical context in which Jesus lived and worked. Those whose presuppositions are antithetical to what the Gospels describe, however, are forced to make alternate reconstructions that are simply not satisfying, even from a strictly *historical* point of view, as we shall see below.

Since the Jesus Seminar is in a way typical of the new Jesus research—indeed, several of the more conspicuous recent Jesus books are from authors who are members of the Seminar—it is important in considering the methodology of recent Jesus research to look at what they call 'the seven pillars of scholarly wisdom' that support what is called 'the edifice of contemporary gospel scholarship'.[40] The Jesus Seminar, which consists mainly of American scholars, was formed by Robert W. Funk in 1985 and has met twice a year, co-chaired by J.D. Crossan, to attempt to establish the authenticity of the words of Jesus in the Gospels (recently they have done similar work on the deeds of Jesus). The comparatively large number of seminar members at the beginning declined significantly when the bias of the seminar and its method of voting[41] on authenticity became clear. Their perspective—typical of much, but not all Jesus research nowadays—is well revealed in their methodological presuppositions

The first of these, and programmatic for the Jesus Seminar, we have already mentioned, namely the need to distinguish 'between the historical Jesus...and the Christ of faith encapsulated in the first

40. These are outlined in the introduction to Funk and Hoover (eds.), *The Five Gospels*, pp. 2-5.

41. The use of colored beads—red, pink, gray and black, in descending order of probable authenticity—has become the laughing-stock of many. The averaging together of the votes reflects the pseudo-scientific character of the seminar's work.

creeds'. This, as we have noted, indicates their a priori naturalism, and assumes that what the followers of Jesus said about him in the New Testament cannot be true to history. It accordingly forces the search for other paradigms by which to understand Jesus. With the next three 'pillars' few would quarrel, namely that 'the synoptic gospels are much closer to the historical Jesus than the Fourth Gospel' (yet this is pushed to the extreme conclusion that 'the two pictures painted by John and the synoptic gospels cannot both be historically accurate'); that Mark is prior to Matthew and Luke, and the basis for them both; and that the hypothetical source Q is the explanation of the double tradition in Matthew and Luke, against Mark (more, however, on their excessive theories concerning Q below).

The last three 'pillars', however, are much more dubious. The fifth is especially problematic. It calls for 'the liberation of the non-eschatological Jesus of the aphorisms and parables from Schweitzer's eschatological Jesus'. Most of the new proposals concerning the historical Jesus begin with the assumption that Jesus did *not* preach an eschatological message. It is nothing less than remarkable—after the corrective work of Weiss and Schweitzer directed against the nineteenth-century liberal lives of Jesus—to find such strong advocacy of a non-eschatological Jesus. This would appear to me to be more of a conclusion that is in serious need of substantiation than a beginning methodological pillar. It is something that needs to be proved rather than simply assumed, and there is a wealth of material in the Synoptics that points in the direction of an eschatological message in the mouth of Jesus, even in the parables and aphorisms.

The sixth pillar calls for 'the recognition of the fundamental contrast between the oral culture (in which Jesus was at home) and a print culture (like our own)'. This is true enough, except for the conclusion that the Seminar wants to draw from it, namely that material cannot be accurately handed on in oral tradition. What is forgotten here is that the effectiveness of oral transmission of material of the first century must not be judged by that of our day. As Birger Gerhardsson[42] above all has shown, the first-century context is one in which memories were exceedingly well trained and where the practice of the handing on of a sacred

---

42. *Memory and Manuscript: Oral Tradition and Written Transmission in Rabbinic Judaism and Early Christianity* (1961), now reissued with his *Tradition and Transmission in Early Christianity* (Grand Rapids: Eerdmans, 1998).

tradition was well established (so too, now, Rainer Riesner[43] and Samuel Byrskog).[44] Thus the point made here cannot be used to undercut the reliability of the sayings tradition in the Synoptic Gospels.

The seventh and final pillar is a particularly revealing one. It concerns

> the reversal that has taken place regarding who bears the burden of proof. It was once assumed [the Seminar states] that scholars had to prove the details in the synoptic gospels were *not* historical...the gospels are now assumed to be narratives in which the memory of Jesus is embellished by the mythic elements that express the church's faith in him, and by plausible fictions that enhance the telling of the gospel story for first-century listeners... Supposedly historical elements in these narratives must therefore be demonstrated to be so.[45]

This avowedly negative bias towards the gospel material is unique in the historical study of antiquity. No other historical sources are subjected to such a demanding burden of proof. Indeed, were this required of all historical sources, the possibility of any historical knowledge would all but disappear. It is, quite simply put, a totally unreasonable demand that furthermore fails to allow that all historical knowledge is at best probable knowledge.

Of course, the Jesus Seminar, like other present-day Jesus research, relies heavily on the earlier conceived 'criteria of authenticity'. The first and most important of these is the criterion of dissimilarity, that is, that the only trustworthy material in the Gospels is that which finds no parallel in either first-century Judaism or early Christianity. How unreasonable this criterion is should be self-evident. It effectively cuts Jesus off from both his Jewish background and from those who followed him and made him the subject of their proclamation. While some eccentricities of Jesus in relation to those around him, before and after, may emerge through the use of this criterion, the so-called resultant critically assured minimum of knowledge can hardly arrive at what is *characteristic* of him—indeed, the risk of a seriously distorted picture

43. *Jesus als Lehrer: eine Untersuchungen zum Ursprung der Evangelien-Überlieferung* (WUNT, 2.7; Tübingen: J.C.B. Mohr, 3rd edn, 1988).

44. *Jesus the Only Teacher: Didactic Authority and Transmission in Ancient Israel, Ancient Judaism and the Matthean Community* (ConBNT, 24; Stockholm: Almqvist & Wiksell, 1994).

45. This view was articulated forcefully by Norman Perrin over 30 years ago in *Rediscovering the Teaching of Jesus* (New York: Harper & Row, 1967), p. 39.

of Jesus is enormously increased when one is limited to such data.[46] Other criteria that were used in earlier quests for the historical Jesus, such as multiple attestation (in independent strata) and coherence (with an emerging picture), also find place in the method of the Jesus Seminar. Again, in my judgment these are far too constraining when it comes to knowledge about the Jesus of history.

One further word is necessary, so far as distinctives of the Jesus Seminar and much of the recent Jesus research is concerned, namely the high value accorded to Q and the non-canonical gospels, especially Thomas (included in *The Five Gospels*) and Peter. Since Q and Thomas consist only (or largely) of sayings material, and have no birth/infancy narratives or resurrection narratives, it is concluded that the earliest Christian community or communities (in any event, we are dealing with the highly speculative here) did not believe in or placed no value upon these matters; Christology was the concern only of a much later community. From the aphoristic teaching of Thomas and Q, it is possible to understand Jesus as merely a teacher of wisdom. Since this understanding of Jesus appeals to the Jesus Seminar, these sources are given the highest priority for access to the historical Jesus. In fact, however, the Q that we can construct from Matthew and Luke contains apocalyptic content (not to mention content reflecting a high Christology) that does not fit the presupposition of a non-apocalyptic Jesus. Not to be hindered by this, however, the speculation is conveniently extended to an even more nebulous document—produced like a rabbit from a hat—that purportedly lay behind Q, namely Q^1, containing no apocalyptic teaching from Jesus and, of course, no Christology. It is then concluded that earliest Christianity had no Christology or apocalyptic hope.[47] With this imagination of document upon document in mind, one may wonder about the suitability of the term 'scholarship' so flaunted by the Jesus Seminar.

While it is certainly true that Q must predate at least Matthew and Luke, Q can just conceivably have been not a document, but instead

---

46. For a critique of the criteria as commonly used, see C.A. Evans, 'Authenticity Criteria in Life of Jesus Research', *CSR* 19 (1989), pp. 6-31; C.L. Blomberg and S.C. Goetz, 'The Burden of Proof', *JSNT* 11 (1981), pp. 39-63; R.H. Stein, 'The "Criteria" for Authenticity', in R.T. France and D. Wenham (eds.), *Gospel Perspectives*, I (Sheffield: JSOT Press, 1980), pp. 255-63.

47. See especially B.L. Mack, *The Lost Gospel: The Book of Q and Christian Origins* (San Francisco: Harper, 1993).

reflect collections of oral tradition. Much more problematic is the esteem given to the so-called Gospel of Thomas (discovered at Nag Hammadi in 1945, in a fourth-century Coptic MS), which is regarded by the Jesus Seminar scholars as frequently offering a more reliable account of the sayings of Jesus than that found in the Synoptic Gospels. The majority of those who have studied Thomas, however, have concluded that Thomas depends on the Synoptics rather than vice versa, as the Jesus Seminar claims.[48] Its clear gnostic orientation also supports an early second-century date. The idea of Thomas being given priority over even Mark seems ludicrous to most critical scholars.

2. *A Survey of Recent Historical Jesus Studies*

This is not the place to go into a detailed examination of the various and vying hypotheses that are currently being set forth concerning the historical Jesus, nor would this be rewarding for our purposes. But it is worth indicating broadly some of the major proposals,[49] while at the same time noting some of their inadequacies.

Such is the volume of publishing on Jesus currently taking place that it is helpful to divide the books into four categories: (1) official books of the Jesus Seminar (so readily identifiable and prominent that I put its work in a category by itself); (2) books by authors reflecting a similar orientation; (3) books reflecting an independent orientation; and (4) more popular, sensationalist books. Some of these categories can be regarded as overlapping, but I think the distinction is still useful.

1. The main works of the Jesus Seminar to date are the translation cum commentary entitled *The Five Gospels: The Search for the Authentic Words of Jesus* (1993), and *The Acts of Jesus* (1998)[50] reporting the work of the Seminar on the deeds of Jesus, and perhaps later by one on

---

48. See C.M. Tuckett, *Nag Hammadi and the Gospel Tradition: Synoptic Tradition in the Nag Hammadi Library* (Edinburgh: T. & T. Clark, 1986). The same is true for the Gospel of Peter. See C. Maurer, 'Gospel of Peter', in E. Hennecke and W. Schneemelcher, *New Testament Apocrypha*, I (London: Lutterworth, 1963), pp. 179-83.

49. For a helpful survey, see B. Witherington III, *The Jesus Quest: The Third Search for the Jew of Nazareth* (Downers Grove, IL: InterVarsity Press, 2nd edn, 1997). See too N.T. Wright, *Jesus and the Victory of God* (Philadelphia: Fortress Press, 1996), pp. 3-124.

50. Ed. R.W. Funk; San Francisco: Harper SanFrancisco.

the canon. The Seminar continues to seek and receive exceptional publicity. Its final estimate of Jesus is that he was a 'laconic sage', a kind of secular iconoclast, who travelled about teaching a proverbial wisdom that often disturbed the religious establishment. Now the founder and co-chair of the Seminar, Robert W. Funk, has his own book out on Jesus entitled *Honest to Jesus: Jesus for a New Millennium*,[51] in which he fleshes out the Seminar's conclusions, describing Jesus as a secular sage and social critic who through satire and humor opposed the religious authorities in favor of the marginalized of society, especially the poor. Also to be noted is the apparent interest of well-known film director Paul Verhoeven, who has attended some of the Seminar's sessions, in producing a Hollywood movie about Jesus based on the results of the Seminar's work.

I cannot resist quoting Birger Pearson's devastating assessment of the work of the Jesus Seminar:

> A group of secularized theologians and secular academics went seeking a secular Jesus, and they found him! They think they found him, but, in fact, they created him. Jesus the 'party animal' whose zany wit and caustic humor would enliven an otherwise dull cocktail party—this is the product of the Jesus Seminar's six years' research. In a sense the Jesus Seminar, with its ideology of secularization, represents a 'shadow image' of the old 'New Quest'—and its ultimate bankruptcy.[52]

2. In the second category are books by scholars of a persuasion similar to that of the Jesus Seminar, and some of whom are indeed themselves members of the Seminar. The book here that has made the biggest impact in the United States is that of John Dominic Crossan,

51. San Francisco: Harper, 1996. The play on the title of J.A.T. Robinson's 1963 bombshell *Honest to God* (Philadelphia: Westminster Press, 1963) is of course deliberate.

52. 'The Gospel according to the Jesus Seminar', *Rel* 25 (1995), pp. 317-38, now in expanded form as chapter of Pearson's *The Emergence of the Christian Religion: Essays on Early Christianity* (Harrisburg, PA: Trinity Press International, 1997). See too his 'An Exposé of the Jesus Seminar', *Dialog* 37 (1998), pp. 28-35. For other critiques of the Jesus Seminar, see L.T. Johnson, *The Real Jesus: The Misguided Quest for the Historical Jesus and the Truth of the Traditional Gospels* (San Francisco: Harper, 1995); N.T. Wright, 'Five Gospels but No Gospel: Jesus and the Seminar', in W.R. Farmer (ed.), *Crisis in Christology: Essays in Quest of Resolution* (Livonia, MI: Dove, 1995), pp. 115-57; B. Witherington III, 'The Promise of History: Jesus and his Cultural Admirers', *Lexington Theological Quarterly* 31 (1996), pp. 155-66.

who has been closely associated with the work of the Jesus Seminar from the beginning: *The Historical Jesus: The Life of a Mediterranean Jewish Peasant.*[53] The one key word missing from the subtitle to the book is the word 'cynic', which points to the the critical attitude of Jesus to his society. For Crossan, Jesus proclaims a 'brokerless' and 'egalitarian' kingdom, and a kingdom that does away with the traditional purity taboos. That is, a kingdom without mediators, a kingdom without hierarchy, a kingdom without prejudice against sinners. Thus Jesus offers his healing miracles to all, and he sits at table without discriminating against any class of 'sinners'. At bottom, Jesus is a radical, anti-establishment, countercultural social reformer. Crossan's book is filled with speculation, as he admits, but he nevertheless sets it forth as plausible history. Crossan's impact is due, perhaps, more to his charm and eloquence, as well as the popular appeal of his Jesus, than to the strength of his arguments.

Burton L. Mack's view of Jesus is similar to that of Crossan, but he points to Hellenism rather than Judaism as the primary background for Jesus' activity. In his book *A Myth of Innocence: Mark and Christian Origins*[54] and now more recently *The Lost Gospel: The Book of Q and Christian Origins,*[55] he presents Jesus as an itinerant social reformer, very much resembling a Cynic sage, whose wisdom was directed against conventional beliefs. Like a Jewish Socrates, he was a gadfly who scoffed at and ridiculed the traditional constraints under which people suffered.

Also to be mentioned here, although he is not associated with the Jesus Seminar, is the work of F. Gerald Downing, who as early as 1982, but especially in his 1988 book, *Christ and the Cynics: Jesus and Other Radical Preachers in First Century Tradition,*[56] similarly concluded that Jesus was a Cynic sage.

Clearly belonging in this category, however, is the work of Marcus Borg, one of the more prominent representatives of the Jesus Seminar. The view of Jesus promoted in his several books (e.g. *Jesus: A New Vision*[57] and *Meeting Jesus Again for the First Time*[58]) is that of a

53. J.D. Crossan (and now in a short, popular version of the same, *Jesus: A Revolutionary Biography* [San Francisco: Harper, 1994]).

54. Philadelphia: Fortress Press, 1988.

55. San Francisco: Harper, 1993.

56. Sheffield: Sheffield Academic Press, 1988.

57. San Francisco: Harper, 1987.

mystic or 'Spirit person', that is, one in touch with the transcendent reality of another world. Jesus was, however, at the same time, a social revolutionary and the teacher of a subversive wisdom, with the goal of transforming Judaism by his critique of the religious system of his day. His was a politics of holiness wherein traditional notions of purity were to be displaced by compassion.

3. Moving to the third category, we may quickly indicate some of the more independent directions that have been taken. A number of these are similar to aspects pursued in the preceding category. Thus, Gerd Theissen (*Sociology of Early Palestinian Christianity*;[59] *The Shadow of the Galilean: The Quest of the Historical Jesus in Narrative Form*[60]), a pioneer in the sociological study of the New Testament, also sees Jesus as a social prophet/reformer, this despite the fact that he holds to an eschatological Jesus who expected the end of the world within that generation. For Theissen, Jesus was a radical charismatic itinerant preacher who called disciples to follow him in this calling. His ethical teaching was radical, although his reform movement was not zealotic, but a movement of peace.

Richard A. Horsley (*Bandits, Prophets and Messiahs: Popular Movements of the Time of Jesus*[61] [with J.S. Hanson]; *Jesus and the Spiral of Violence*;[62] *Sociology and the Jesus Movement*[63]) builds on the work of Theissen but takes it much further. For him, Jesus was decidedly a social reformer standing with the vast majority of the population who were the poor and oppressed. Like the prophets of old, Jesus preached against social injustice, and with his radical ethical teaching attempted to set up a new societal order that was radically egalitarian, abolishing all hierarchy and patriarchy. This call to social transformation was the kingdom Jesus preached, accompanied by the eschatological expectation that God would overthrow the power structures of this world.

E.P. Sanders's work on the historical Jesus (*Jesus and Judaism*;[64]

58. San Francisco: Harper, 1994. See too his *Jesus in Contemporary Scholarship*.
59. Philadelphia: Fortress Press, 1978.
60. Philadelphia: Fortress Press, 1987.
61. Minneapolis: Winston, 1985.
62. San Francisco: Harper, 1987.
63. New York: Crossroad, 1989.
64. Philadelphia: Fortress Press, 1985.

The Historical Figure of Jesus[65]) stands rather alone in its perspective among recent Jesus research. Beginning with acts that Jesus did, especially the episode in the Temple, Sanders pieces together a picture of Jesus as an eschatological prophet with the expectation of an imminent apocalyptic end of the world and the restoration of the 12 tribes of Israel. Jesus was far from being a social reformer, but rather a preacher of the unqualified acceptance of sinners. He perhaps thought of himself in very high terms as the last of God's messengers and his eschatological representative. Sanders's view of Jesus is thus firmly against the non-eschatological Jesus of the Jesus Seminar.

The title of the still-emerging multi-volume work of the Catholic scholar John P. Meier, *A Marginal Jew* (vol. I, *Rethinking the Historical Jesus*;[66] vol. II, *Mentor, Message, Miracle*[67]) may lead one to believe that he will present a strictly sociological explanation of the historical Jesus. This is not so. Meier explains that he uses the word 'marginal' to describe Jesus because it describes the location of Jesus in the first century as on the edge of things rather than at the center of power, authority, success, etc. Indeed, Meier's approach to the historical Jesus is the most sane and balanced of the lot—which is to say the least speculative and the least upsetting to an orthodox understanding of Jesus. Although we await Meier's third volume for his final assessment of Jesus, already it is clear that Meier regards the historical Jesus as a number of things: proclaimer of the eschatological kingdom, charismatic healer, teacher, prophet, restorer of Israel, and presumably one who thought of himself as the Messiah. Meier's work shows how fruitful a reasoned and reasonable approach to the subject of the historical Jesus can be, when one puts a limit on speculation and when one makes judicious use of the sources and avoids special agendas.

There are, of course, many more books that qualify for this third category that deserve consideration. We can here only mention a few titles. Among the more idiosyncratic discussions, we may note the

---

65. London: Allen Lane; Penguin Press, 1993.

66. New York: Doubleday, 1991.

67. New York: Doubleday, 1994. See Meier's informative article 'Dividing Lines in Jesus Research Today: Through Dialectical Negation to a Positive Sketch', *Int* 50 (1996), pp. 355-72. Meier discusses six major areas of disagreement: the question of sources; the Q document; the eschatology of Jesus' proclamation; the miracles of Jesus; Jesus as Messiah; and institutional elements from the historical Jesus.

book of Elisabeth Schüssler Fiorenza, *Jesus: Miriam's Child, Sophia's Prophet: Critical Issues in Feminist Christology*,[68] where it is argued that Jesus was an eschatological prophet of God, known by Jesus as Sophia (Wisdom) and not Father. Indeed, Jesus was the leader of a social revolution that involved the overthrow of traditional patriarchalism in favor of an egalitarian society where female and male had full equality. We also note the book of Geza Vermes, *Jesus the Jew: A Historian's Reading of the Gospel*,[69] where Jesus is portrayed as a charismatic hasid, a Galilean holy man with the gift of healing and exorcism, analogous to such Talmudic figures as Hanina ben Dosa and Honi the Circle Drawer. Further classifications of Jesus could be mentioned: Jesus as magician (Morton Smith);[70] Jesus as rabbi (P. Lapide);[71] Jesus as Zealot (S.G.F. Brandon);[72] Jesus as Pharisee (H. Falk);[73] Jesus as Qumran Essene (C.F. Potter).[74]

We have by no means catalogued the totality of important historical Jesus books. One wants at least to mention the more constructive titles that often do not receive the publicity (just for that reason!) other volumes get. For example, Markus Bockmuehl, *This Jesus: Martyr, Lord, Messiah*;[75] J.D.G. Dunn, *The Evidence for Jesus*;[76] A.E. Harvey, *Jesus and the Constraints of History*;[77] Marinus de Jonge, *Jesus, the Servant Messiah*;[78] Ben F. Meyer, *The Aims of Jesus*;[79] Peter Stuhlmacher,

68. New York: Continuum, 1994.

69. New York: Macmillan, 2nd edn, 1983. See too his *Jesus and the World of Judaism* (Philadelphia: Fortress Press, 1984) and *The Religion of Jesus the Jew* (Minneapolis: Augsburg–Fortress Press, 1984).

70. *Jesus the Magician* (San Francisco: Harper, 1978).

71. 'Two Famous Rabbis', *Annual of the Swedish Theological Institute* 10 (1976), pp. 97-109. The second is the eighteenth-century Rabbi Israel of Mezibezh.

72. *Jesus and the Zealots* (Manchester: University of Manchester Press, 1967).

73. *Jesus the Pharisee: A New Look at the Jewishness of Jesus* (New York: Paulist Press, 1985). Among several others: M. Buber, *Two Types of Faith* (London: Routledge & Kegan Paul, 1951); H. Maccoby, *Revelation in Judea: Jesus and the Jewish Resistance* (London: Orbach & Chambers, 1973); W.E. Phipps, 'Jesus the Prophetic Pharisee', *JES* 14 (1977), pp. 17-31.

74. *The Lost Years of Jesus* (New Hyde Park, NY: University Books, 1963).

75. Edinburgh: T. & T. Clark, 1994.

76. Philadelphia: Westminster Press, 1985.

77. London: Gerald Duckworth, 1982.

78. New Haven, CN: Yale University Press, 1991.

79. London: SCM Press, 1979.

Jesus of Nazareth—Christ of Faith;[80] B. Witherington III, *The Christology of Jesus*;[81] idem, *Jesus the Sage: The Pilgrimage of Wisdom*;[82] and N.T. Wright, *Jesus and the Victory of God*;[83] idem, *The Original Jesus: The Life and Vision of a Revolutionary.*[84]

4. Then there is always the sensationalist, pop literature, which has little time for the truth but panders to the public's lust for the sensational. We limit ourselves to three:[85] A.N. Wilson, *Jesus*:[86] Jesus was a Galilean holy man teaching a simplified form of Judaism, without its moralism and sectarianism; J. Spong (bishop of the Episcopal church and member of the Jesus Seminar), *Born of a Woman: A Bishop Rethinks the Birth of Jesus*:[87] Jesus' mother had been raped, the birth and resurrection narratives are Christian midrash based on mythological speculation; and Barbara Thiering, *Jesus the Man: A New Interpretation from the Dead Sea Scrolls*:[88] Jesus was a member of the Qumran community who married Mary Magdalene, had two sons and a daughter, divorced Mary for another woman, and died some time in the sixties! It must be admitted, however, that even the respectable scholarly literature, with its often unrestrained speculation presented as fact, does not often provide the best model.

3. Analytical Observations

First, an assessment of contemporary historical Jesus studies. Despite the enthusiasm of some, to my mind the results of the recent historical Jesus studies are not very encouraging. When the overall framework provided by the Gospels is done away with, the pieces remain too fragmentary to reconstruct Jesus as he actually was, with the result that

80. Peabody, MA: Hendrickson, 1993.
81. Philadelphia: Fortress Press, 1990.
82. Minneapolis: Augsburg–Fortress Press, 1994.
83. Minneapolis: Fortress Press, 1996.
84. Grand Rapids: Eerdmans, 1996.
85. For discussion of these three books, see N.T. Wright, *Who Was Jesus?* (London: SPCK, 1992).
86. London: Sinclair–Atkinson, 1992.
87. San Francisco: Harper, 1992.
88. New York: Doubleday, 1992. See too her *Jesus and the Riddle of the Dead Sea Scrolls: Unlocking the Secret of his Life Story* (San Francisco: Harper, 1992). For a sane perspective on the subject, see O. Betz and R. Reisner, *Jesus, Qumran and the Vatican: Clarifications* (London: SCM Press, 1994).

many different reconstructions become possible.[89] Paul Johnson has rightly concluded: 'Using the same texts and scholarly apparatus, dozens, perhaps hundreds of different Jesuses can be constructed.'[90] Telford, from whom I have borrowed the quotation, concludes: 'In a nutshell, he has perhaps captured the problem and challenge of Jesus Studies today!'[91]

Some important choices do emerge, however. One of the most important is whether Jesus is to be understood primarily as a social prophet or an eschatological prophet. Only a minority presently opt for the latter. The question is a difficult one, for Jesus came with an eschatological message that has clear social implications, and yet the latter is not at the heart of his purpose.

A major problem with most of the Jesus research being done today is that it is *reductionistic*. That is, it seems that every author attempts to force the extensive and complex variety of the data under a single heading that excludes other analyses. On the contrary, however, it might fairly be said that there is perhaps a modicum of truth in every analysis, which is then taken and blown entirely out of proportion and made to explain everything about the historical Jesus.

A further point to be made here, is the rather obvious way in which each of the reconstructions inevitably reflects the ideological convictions of the author—indeed, precisely as in the old quest. These author see what they want to see. I suppose, as reader response theory is showing us, that this is true of all of us. But whereas one might expect this in people of faith, that is, people of the church, it is somewhat surprising in these authors, who often claim scholarly objectivity. There is, however, no neutrality, just as there is no viewpoint without its presuppositions.[92]

89. Sharyn Dowd rightly asks, 'When the variety of "historical" reconstructions of Jesus is so great that they cannot be made to refer to the same person, in what sense can historical findings serve as a norm?' ('Which Jesus? A Survey of the Controversy over "The Historical Jesus" ', *Lexington Theological Quarterly* 31 [1996], pp. 87-186 [101-102].)

90. Review of B. Thiering's book *Jesus the Man* in the *Sunday Telegraph*, 13 Sept. 1992.

91. 'Major Trends', pp. 46-47.

92. This is pointed out very effectively by A.G. Padgett, 'Advice for Religious Historians: On the Myth of a Purely Historical Jesus', in S.T. Davis, D. Kendall and G. O'Collins (eds.), *The Resurrection: An Interdisciplinary Symposium on the Resurrection of Jesus* (Oxford: Oxford University Press, 1997), pp. 287-307.

Secondly, a comment on the legitimacy of the quest of the historical Jesus. It is a part of orthodox faith that Jesus was *fully* human. It is part of New Testament Christology that the appearance of Jesus in history involved a *kenosis*, or 'emptying', of some kind (Phil. 2.6-11)—the content of the emptying is not specified, but presumably it was of the divine glory and certain divine prerogatives. We have to do with a mystery here, in short, the great mystery of the incarnation. It may, of course, be interesting to study Jesus simply as a human being. But the real story of Jesus is not in the humanity to the exclusion of the transcendent, but in the humanity that uniquely manifests deity and uniquely accomplishes the will of God. To limit ourselves to one side (either side) is inevitably to distort. Such is the interconnection attested to by our sources that the humanity cannot really be understood apart from the transcendent, and the transcendent apart from the humanity. We will not make sense of the Jesus of the Gospels if we strictly limit ourselves to the level of his humanity and exclude the rest.

Thirdly, a comment on the historical method. What are its limitations? What may we expect of it? As we saw at the beginning, the historical method has a self-imposed limitation that prohibits it from considering the transcendent or supernatural causation. In light of what we have just been saying, it will be unable finally to do justice to the Jesus of the Gospels. We cannot therefore expect the historical-critical method to produce a complete picture of Jesus. Starting with the raw data of the available sources (of every kind), it cannot construct *de novo* a historical Jesus that is fully adequate.

What Jesus research *can* do—and this its best exponents have been doing—is to demonstrate that there is a substantial continuity between the Jesus of history, considered just at that level, and the Jesus of faith. I say continuity, and not identity, because there *is*, of course, a difference between the Jesus of history—how he actually was—and the Jesus the church confesses. This difference is due to the fact that the picture of Jesus in the Gospel accounts is the result of retrospective, post-resurrection knowledge. But how did Jesus think of himself and how did the disciples think of Jesus *during the actual ministry* of Jesus? God from God, light from light, true God from true God? Of one substance with the Father? The incarnation of the Logos? But all of this is interpretation long after the fact.

We do not have the information we need to penetrate the self-consciousness of Jesus, or indeed to know how the disciples regarded him during the ministry. Had the disciples any inkling that they were frater-nizing with the second person of the Trinity, they would have been paralysed with fear. Peter's confession of Jesus as the Messiah, the Son of the living God in Matthew 16, does not prevent him a few moments later from sternly rebuking Jesus for the idea of his being put to death. One does not rebuke God, knowingly.

If I were to write a historical Jesus book by the rules, it would run like this (and it is as important to note what is *not* said, as to note what *is* said): Jesus of Nazareth came proclaiming that the kingdom (i.e. the reign) of God was *uniquely* dawning in and through his person and ministry. In this capacity he was conscious of being uniquely *the Son* of the Father. That kingdom was beginning in the ministry of Jesus, but was also future. In both present and future Jesus knew himself to be the supreme *Agent* of God's redemptive purposes. Although Jesus never spoke of himself as such, he admitted that he was the *Messiah* (Mk 14.62), accepting the confession and acclaim as Messiah. He went to his death, in obedience to the will of God, conscious that his death was an atoning sacrifice for the sins of the world, on the model of the suf-fering *Servant* of Isaiah 53. A portrait such as this is not adequate in itself, but it is in continuity with what the early church confessed about Jesus. The Christology of the early church, under the catalyst of the resurrection, drew out the implications in the above material for the understanding of the person of Jesus. The Gospels, reflecting the post-resurrection, post-Pentecost interpretation of Jesus, present us with a fully adequate understanding of Jesus, which is to say that the inter-preted Jesus is the truest understanding of Jesus. Inspired paintings can be more useful and informative than photographs—indeed, more *truth*ful.

Fourthly, a comment on the importance of historical research itself, even for the church. There are many, who like Bultmann and the liberal Lutherans, believe that the work of the historian is at best irrelevant to the believer. The need to justify one's position by argument is said to reflect a lack of faith. We cannot, it is sometimes said, make the histo-rian a kind of high priest of the Christian faith, by whose 'authoritative' conclusions we must shape our faith. There are those who openly advocate a division that I personally find intolerable: namely, that our faith is one thing and our scholarship something quite other, and there need be no congruence between the two. One of the most significant names in present-day Jesus research, the Catholic John P. Meier, takes this point of view. Another Roman Catholic scholar, Luke Timothy Johnson, author of a blistering attack on the Jesus Seminar,[93] also shies away from the importance of historical evidence for the truthfulness of Christianty. He argues that the real Jesus is experienced by the believing community as risen Lord altogether aside from—indeed, safe from—the results of historical scholarship. To be sure, historical scholarship can never prove the truth of Christianity. Nevertheless, Christian scholars must take up the challenge of historical study of Jesus that seems to disprove traditional Christian beliefs. Answers must be given to irresponsible claims and to wild speculations set forth as truth. It is especially ironic that Meier and Johnson take this position since their understanding of the historical Jesus is, to my mind, in a sufficient degree of continuity with the church as not to threaten its view of Christ.[94] This may be all that historical study can do, but it is not unimportant.

Fifthly, we come full circle by returning to the problem of the naturalistic presuppostions of the historical method. The unfortunate implication of this is that all reality can be covered by the method, and indeed, that anything not subject to its scrutiny cannot be real. But should it not be possible to modify the method with an openness to the possibility of supernatural causation? (I do not call for an uncritical acceptance of every claim to the supernatural! Historical criticism can and should be applied to an evaluation of the evidence of such claims.) We have, after all, entered a post-Newtonian era, where the phenomena of quantum physics have relativized the Newtonian system so that it may no longer be regarded as comprehensive of all reality. The system is not entirely closed. Alongside necessity we have contingency, as Harald Riesenfeld points out.[95] We simply do not know enough to be able to exclude the possibility of God's direct intervention in history. Reality, as scientists readily admit, is at bottom filled with the mysterious. The implications, furthermore, of post-modernism for epistemology and the newer understanding of history as necessarily more than

93. Johnson, *The Real Jesus*.

94. The same cannot be said of Borg, whose 'pre-Easter' Jesus has little continuity with the 'post-Easter' (canonical, creedal) Jesus. See M. Borg, 'Jesus and the Revisioning of Theology', *Dialog* 37 (1998), pp. 9-14. For insightful analysis, see E.M. Boring, 'The "Third Quest" and the Apostolic Faith', *Int* 50 (1996), pp. 341-54.

95. 'Kristologi och kontingens', *SEÅ* 58 (1993), pp. 33-50.

brute facts, but as data inescapably interpreted, must now be allowed to affect our thinking and talking about historical reality. It is well time to take notice of the limitations and the relativity of the historical method as hitherto practiced, and to begin to modify the method so as to make it more useful in coming to terms with a universe bigger and more mysterious than Newton's.[96]

4. *Conclusion*

The current flood of books on the historical Jesus, or at least the vast majority of them, ask us to believe that those who were closest to Jesus, the disciples and earliest believers in him, either fundamentally misunderstood him or misrepresented him in the most culpable manner. We are asked to believe, instead, that a relatively small group of scholars in the twentieth century, working with a set of presuppositions totally alien to the first century, and with ideological commitments no less than those of Christian faith, know him better!

We are asked furthermore to believe in the truth of hypothetical reconstructions of Jesus that are totally inadequate to explain the origin of Christianity and the growth of the church, while being asked to reject the understanding of Jesus that alone can provide such an explanation.

In short, the conclusions of the radical historical Jesus scholars require too much of us. Their claims hardly constitute a devastating blow to the church's view of Jesus. At the same time, the character and frequently the tone of their claims, especially those of the Jesus Seminar, invite a polemical response. The issues at stake are of the greatest importance.

96. See now the fine work of philosopher C.A. Evans, *The Historical Christ and the Jesus of Faith: The Incarnational Narrative as History* (Oxford: Clarendon Press, 1996).

DIVERSITY IN PAUL

James D.G. Dunn

1. *Introduction*

Strategically, Paul is one of the most fascinating figures in all mid-dle-eastern and western history. According to the Acts of the Apostles (Acts 22.3) he was a Diaspora Jew, born and brought up in Tarsus, a centre of Hellenistic influence in what is now south-east Turkey, and a Roman citizen to boot. At the same time, however, he was brought up as a strongly traditionalist Jew—not just a 'Hebrew' (2 Cor. 11.22), itself a traditionalist title, but a 'Hebrew of the Hebrews' indeed (Phil. 3.5)—and he evidently chose to return to Jerusalem to train as a Pharisee (where else would an aspiring Pharisee complete his educa-tion?). So fierce was his 'zeal' for the ancestral customs that he per-secuted those of his fellow Jews who proclaimed Jesus of Nazareth to be the Jewish Messiah (Gal. 1.13-14; Phil. 3.6), because, it would appear, they took the message of this Messiah Jesus to Gentiles, offer-ing them a share in Israel's heritage. But then in a classic turn-about, he was converted to this very same 'sect of the Nazarene' (Acts 24.5), turned his back on what he had previously counted so precious (Phil. 3.7-8), and became, for the rest of his life, a missionary for that sect among the Gentile nations.

If one was looking for a study in diversity one might think that the bare outlines of this story were alone sufficient to provide it—Saul, traditionalist Jew, become Paul the Christian, or should we say Paul the apostate?—the Diaspora Jew become Pharisee become apostle to the nations. But the outline indicates nothing of the richness (or should we say confusion?) of the diversity that was Paul's work and teaching. The fuller picture is best analysed in three sections.

2. *Paul, Troubler of Israel*

Paul is remembered as one who stretched the diversity that was Second Temple Judaism to breaking point. It was not simply that he believed in and preached Jesus as Messiah. There were a good many other of his Jewish contemporaries who believed and taught the same. But they remained fully within the boundaries of a Second Temple Judaism, whose own diversity has become more widely appreciated since the Dead Sea Scrolls were first discovered half a century ago. To name another Jew as 'Messiah' was no offence to Jews; most looked for the coming of one such, and the descent of Jesus from David does not seem to have been controversial (Rom. 1.3). To name a *crucified* Jew as 'Messiah' was certainly more difficult for many/most(?) Jews to stomach (1 Cor. 1.23; Gal. 3.13). Even so, however, the bulk of Jerusalem/Judaean believers in Jesus seem to have been able to practise their new belief without too much disturbance from their fellows, if Acts 21.20 is anything to go by. And, as we shall see below, Paul's own fiercest opponents seem to have been fellow Jewish *believers* who presumably were also well regarded in many Jewish circles.

Where Paul began to stretch the diversity of Second Temple Judaism was much more in relation to the Gentiles. Consequent upon his conversion, Paul began to preach the faith he once tried to destroy (Gal. 1.23), the gospel to Gentiles. Here too we need to be clear on what was at issue. Traditionally, Israel was not particularly antagonistic to other nations. Devout Jews saw it as incumbent on them to maintain their set-apartness to God by keeping themselves apart from the defilements of the (other) nations (Lev. 20.22-26 indicates the rationale of such purity concerns). But that did not make them unfriendly to foreigners as such. On the contrary, the legislation of Israel is notable for its concern for the 'resident alien' (e.g. Exod. 22.21; 23.12; Deut. 24.17-21). In the Diaspora synagogues there were often to be found a sometimes quite substantial penumbra of interested or sympathetic Gentiles (usually known as 'God-fearers'). Gentiles ready to convert to Judaism ('proselytes') were generally welcomed in Jewish synagogues. Quite a strong strand of Jewish expectation looked for an 'eschatological pilgrimage' of Gentiles to Mount Zion (e.g. Isa. 2.2-4; 56.6-8; Zech. 2.11; Tob. 14.6-7), and there were even those who were willing to allow that Gentiles might find a place in the world to come without becoming proselytes ('righteous Gentiles').

So Paul's pushing out the boundaries of his ancestral faith was not simply that he was open to Gentiles finding acceptance with God. It was the way he went about it, and the way he understood the Christian gospel in relation to membership of Israel. That's what stretched the identity of Israel to breaking point for most of his fellow Jews.

1. The stretching of the diversity can be seen in the fact that the sect of the Nazarene was probably the first and only Jewish sect of the time to understand itself as committed to the task of evangelism. Contrast traditional Judaism. Traditional Judaism did not regard itself as a missionary religion. Why should it? It was the religion of the Jews, of the Judaeans. That is, it was an ethnic, a national religion. Why should a non-Jew, the native of one country, want to adopt the religion of another country (Judaea)? As we have seen, Second Temple Judaism was generally hospitable to Gentile sympathizers and welcoming of proselytes. But they did not set out to convert Gentiles. To be fair, the point is widely, though not unanimously accepted. But those who affirm a missionary motivation among first-century Jews are probably mistaking as evangelistic what was actually apologetic literature (to help Diaspora Jews to maintain self-respect among intellectual Gentiles). In contrast, Christianity from very early days understood itself as a missionary religion (cf. Mt. 28.19-20; Acts 1.8). And Paul was at the forefront of the drive to take the gospel of Jesus Messiah among Gentiles. Paul begins to stretch the diversity of Second Temple Judaism by his claim to be 'apostle (missionary) to the Gentiles' (Rom. 11.13).

Again we need to be more precise. One or two passages do suggest that there were Jewish missionaries active at or around the time of Paul's missionary work. There is Paul's own testimony (particularly Galatians; 2 Cor. 10–13; Phil. 3.2-10) that other Jewish missionaries were interfering with Paul's Gentile converts ('Are they Hebrews? So am I. Are they Israelites? So am I'—2 Cor. 11.22; cf. Phil. 3.4-5). And there is the famous denunciation of the Pharisees in Mt. 23.15—'You cross sea and land to make one proselyte, and when you succeed you make him a son of hell twice as bad as you are.' The best way to understand these allusions, however, is provided by the also famous story, told by Josephus, the Jewish historian from the generation after Paul, of the conversion of King Izates of Adiabene. A Jewish merchant (Ananias) had persuaded Izates that he could become a proselyte without undergoing the painful and potentially embarrassing rite of circumcision. But when Eleazar, a strict Jew from Galilee arrived, he convinced Izates that circumcision was unavoidable for a proselyte. Izates was then circumcised (the story is told by Josephus in his *Jewish Antiquities* 20). The parallel with the references in the Pauline letters suggests that this is what all the above texts had in mind. That is to say, what is in view in them all was not initial evangelization of Gentiles but the concern to ensure that they were properly converted. Probably, therefore, Mt. 23.15 refers to Pharisees, or their successors (Matthew being written after 70 CE), intent on ensuring that all would-be proselytes truly were proselytes (not simply God-fearers).

2. If so, we begin to see more clearly what was the point of tension occasioned for many of Paul's fellow Jews by his evangelization of Gentiles. It was not so much the evangelizing itself. Rather, it was that Paul's evangelization did not go far enough; his converts had not converted fully enough. For most Jews, and particularly strict Jews, conversion without circumcision was simply inconceivable. And Paul seems to have made, early on, a point of insisting that Gentile converts to the new movement growing round the name of Jesus the Christ (Christians) did not need to be circumcised (Gal. 2.1-10). So far as Paul was concerned, insistence on circumcision undermined and even contradicted the gospel (Gal. 2.16).

Where this began to impact on Judaism and to stretch its diversity was in the effect Paul's understanding of the gospel had on his fellow Jewish members of the new sect. If Gentiles did not need to go all the way, to Judaize completely, then where did that leave Jewish believers in Jesus? Should they in turn abandon their characteristic and traditional Jewish practices? In order to have fellowship with the weakly Judaizing Gentile Christians, should the Jewish believers sit equally light to such Jewish distinctives as avoidance of unclean foods and observance of the sabbath? This was precisely the issue that arose in the church in Syrian Antioch, following the Jerusalem resolution that, after all, Gentile believers need not be circumcised (Acts 2.11-14), and again among the Galatian churches (Gal. 4.10; 5.2-6). And the accusation levelled against Paul later on in Jerusalem indicates that Paul was widely suspected of having abandoned his ancestral religion altogether: the thousands of Jewish believers 'have been told about you that you teach all the Jews living among the Gentiles to forsake Moses, and that you tell them not to circumcise their children or observe the customs' (Acts 21.21).

This was where the diversity promulgated by Paul began to become too much for many of Paul's fellow Jews; indeed, many/most of his fellow Jewish Christians. In sum, the issue revolved round Paul's attitude to the law, the Torah. Was the Torah, in every part, equally binding on Jews? And was the Torah binding on Gentile converts to this Jewish sect?

3. Underlying this issue was the more profound question that Paul's missionary work and gospel posed for Jewish diversity. For at stake was not simply a matter of certain laws, crucial as the question even in that form was. At stake was actually Israel's self-understanding, Israel's identity.

The problem, if that is the appropriate word, is that Paul was not simply offering Gentiles forgiveness of sins, or in his preferred language, justification by faith, through the gospel. He was offering them a share in the inheritance of Abraham, offering them status as Abraham's offspring (Rom. 4; Gal. 3). Whether the issue of 'who are Abraham's offspring' was first raised by Paul himself, or by other Jewish missionaries using it against Paul (as the argument of Gal. 3–4 may well suggest), the fact remains that Paul seized the challenge and made the affirmation of Gentile participation in Abraham's offspring central to his theology. It is something of a puzzle why Paul did not remain content for Gentiles simply to believe in Jesus as God's agent/Messiah, and to offer them the prospect of final salvation on that basis. Why should the issue of quasi-Jewish status (offspring of Abraham, but without circumcision) be a factor at all? Why not simply an affirmation that the one God, God of Gentile as well as Jew (Rom. 3.29-30), was willing to accept Gentiles as Gentiles?

The answer puts us right into the heart of the enigma of Paul the Jew become Christian apostle. For Paul evidently counted it as of first importance that his gospel was in complete continuity with God's purpose for and through Israel, was indeed the eschatological fulfilment of Israel's law and prophets (e.g. Rom. 1.2; 3.21). It was fundamental to him that Gentiles were being asked to believe in the Messiah of Israel (e.g. Rom. 1.3-4; 9.4-5; 15.8-9). It was fundamental to the identity of the Gentile believers that they should be understood and should understand themselves as full partners in the inheritance of Abraham, despite their lack of circumcision. The trouble was, that to put forward such a proposition on such terms was not simply to assert an 'Abrahamic' identity for believing Gentiles; it was also to threaten the traditional identity of more or less all Jews. If Gentiles could be seed of Abraham without circumcision and without such 'works of the law', how could Jews continue to assert that membership of Israel was bound up with and inseparable from just such works of the Torah? Thus did Paul strain the diversity of Second Temple Judaism to breaking point.

4. Yet Paul did make this claim (that Gentiles could participate in Israel without becoming proselytes). But he did not do so in a reckless or thoughtless manner, far less in a deliberately destructive or apostate manner. On the contrary, he did so as an Israelite (Rom. 11.1; 2 Cor. 11.22). He did so because he saw this expansion to embrace Gentiles as Gentiles as part of *Israel's* destiny, as part of the hidden mystery of God's purpose that he had been privileged to have revealed to him (Rom. 11.25-32) and privileged to bring to consummation (Rom. 11.13-15). This was the real heart of the challenge that Paul's diversity brought to Judaism: as a Jew, as an Israelite, he challenges Israel, he challenges Second Temple Judaism to recognize and respond to this calling as its destiny.

The point is evident from the beginning of Paul's life and work as a Christian. When he recalls his conversion, he does so deliberately in terms of a prophetic commission. In Gal. 1.15-16 he deliberately echoes the language of Jer. 1.5 and Isa. 49.1-6. Jeremiah had been commissioned with the words: 'Before I formed you *in the womb...I* consecrated you; I appointed you a prophet *to the nations*' (Jer. 1.5). The Servant of Yahweh (Israel himself) had been commissioned likewise: 'The Lord called me before I was born, while I was in *my mother's womb* he named me... (The Lord says) "...I will give you as a light *to the nations*, that my salvation may reach to the end of the earth" ' (Isa. 49.1, 6). Paul bears testimony in similar terms: 'When God, who had set me apart from my *mother's womb* and called my through his grace, was pleased to reveal his Son in me, in order that 1 might preach him *among the Gentiles...*' (Gal. 1.15-16). In other words, Paul saw himself not just as apostle to the Gentiles, but as *Israel's* apostle to the Gentiles, as called to continue/ carry out Israel's mission to be a light to the Gentiles (cf. Acts 13.47 = Isa. 49.6; Acts 26.17-18—cf. Jer. 1.8; Isa. 42.7).

Again worth noting is the play Paul makes on the promise to Abraham—in this case, not just the promise of seed (or land), but the third strand of promise, that in Abraham all the nations of the earth would be blessed (Gal. 3.8, referring particularly to Gen. 12.3 and 18.18). What is so striking in this reference of Paul is that he describes this promise as the gospel: 'The scripture, foreseeing that God would justify the Gentiles from faith, preached the gospel beforehand to Abraham, "In you shall all the nations be blessed" ' (Gal. 3.8). In so doing, Paul both affirms that the Abrahamic promise is integral to the gospel, and recalls Israel/Second Temple Judaism to this dimension of its heritage and commission. Paul claims that the gospel to Gentiles is the fulfilment of God's covenant with Israel. Of course, in so doing Paul interprets that strand of the promise (blessing of the nations) in a controversial way. But the challenge he poses to his people, and still poses to his people, is whether this interpretation is not a legitimate interpretation, and so whether Paul's claim should not remain on the table as part of Israel's/ Judaism's own ongoing debate about its obligation to the (other) nations under the covenant.

And if this was not enough, Paul even challenges his people to accept a redefinition of Israel, or, as Paul himself would presumably prefer to put it, to accept a recall to the primary definition of Israel. The argument is put in Rom. 9.6-12 and through the difficult 9.13-23 to its climax in 9.24: that Israel is not to be defined in terms of physical descent or ethnic identity (9.7-9); that Israel is not to be defined in terms of Torah obedience or religious distinctives (9.10-12); but that Israel is and always has been and always should be defined in terms of God's call (9.7, 12, 24-26). That is, Israel so defined can and does include 'us whom he has called, not only from Jews but also from Gentiles' (9.24).

Now, that was a bridge too far: how many (how few!) Jews could accept a definition of Israel that did not identify 'Israel' with 'Jew' in straightforward terms? And yet one could still say that Paul has not been the first Jew to raise the question, Who is a Jew? What does it take for a non-Jew to be recognized as a proselyte to Israel? And if he was not the first, he certainly has not been the last. No one aware of the political and religious realities of Israel and Judaism today can fail to recognize how vigorous the very same debate is today. The point is that Paul still claims a voice in that debate, and that he does so as himself a Jew and Israelite. As a Jew, fully within the heritage of Israel, Paul offers a still controversial reconfiguration of Israel and of Israel's heritage. That is to say, he still claims a place within the diversity of Judaism. Until his voice is fully heard afresh within Judaism his claim to speak for Israel and within the diversity of Israel will remain without adequate scrutiny.

3. *Paul, Second Founder of Christianity?*

If Paul is remembered as a stormy petrel within late Second Temple Judaism, the picture is scarcely different within emerging Christianity. The picture can be filled out with several features.

1. The historical situation is fairly clear. More or less overnight Saul, the persecutor of the Nazarene movement, became Paul the apostle, one of the new movement's most active, and latterly, most successful evangelists. That immediately brought a new tension into the young movement. For at the beginning the new movement lay wholly within the diversity of Second Temple Judaism. So the stretching of Judaism's diversity that Paul's apostolic work occasioned also meant a stretching of infant Christianity in a multi-ethnic, or perhaps better, non-ethnic direction.

It was perhaps inevitable, therefore, that Paul soon found himself regarded with suspicion by those who continued to prize their ethnic identity as members of the people of Israel marked out by the familiar Jewish distinctives (circumcision, observance of food laws and sabbath, focus on the Jerusalem Temple, etc.). This point, of course, is just a repetition of the previous main point (section 2). Here, however, it needs to be stressed that most of the fiercest opposition to Paul on such issues came not from Jews at large, but from *Christian* Jews, Jews who like himself had come to believe in Jesus as Messiah, but who had not taken the same step of opening the gospel of this Jesus to Gentiles without requiring them to become proselytes.

This is certainly the testimony of Paul's own letters. Those who attacked Paul most energetically and who tried to convert again (convert properly) his converts were fellow Jews, but more to the point, fellow Jewish missionaries on behalf of Jesus. The implication is clear in the key passages. Those who were 'troubling' the Galatians were certainly calling for circumcision, but were also preaching the 'gospel' (Gal. 1.6-9). Those who were causing such confusion among the Corinthians were fellow 'Hebrews' and 'Israelites' (2 Cor. 11.22), but were also 'apostles', indeed, 'apostles of Christ', 'ministers of Christ' (2 Cor. 11.13, 23). The picture is borne out by Acts 21—the opposition to Paul was coming from 'myriads of the Jews' who believed (Acts 21.20-21).

Not least of significance is the fact that at least some degree of opposition to Paul came from the leadership in Jerusalem itself. This is implied in the same two letters. The tone used by Paul in Galatians 2 in relation to the 'pillar apostles' (Peter, James and John) indicates a distinct coolness on Paul's part towards them at the time of writing ('what they once were makes no difference to me'—Gal. 2.6). And in 2 Cor. 11.5 it is quite possible that the 'super apostles' alluded to include the Jerusalem leadership. In the same way, earlier in 2 Corinthians, Paul disparages the letters of recommendation, very likely from the Jerusalem leadership, by means of which Paul's opponents sought to bolster their authority in the eyes of the Corinthian believers (2 Cor. 3.1-3).

Here then it is evident that Paul's missionary vocation stretched the diversity of infant Christianity almost to breaking point. Paul himself attempted to hold the spectrum together—partly by appealing regularly to the way things are done in 'all the churches' (1 Cor. 4.17; 7.17; 14.33), and particularly by the collection that he made among his (Gentile) churches for the poor among the Jerusalem church (Rom. 15.25-31; 1 Cor. 16.1-3; 2 Cor. 8-9). Yet surprisingly, Luke at best alludes only in passing to what was the primary reason for Paul's undertaking the dangerous final journey to Jerusalem (Acts 24.17). Why should this be? Paul's own misgivings about the possible outcome perhaps suggests the reason (Rom. 15.31). The fact may be that the collection was not accepted—hence Luke's embarrassed silence; for the Jewish believers to accept a gift at the hands of such an apostate would have been too dangerous for the Jerusalem church itself. If so, we have to conclude that Paul's missionary endeavours resulted in something approaching a schism within Christianity—the effective rejection of Paul implying a continuing breach with the growing Gentile churches. This last, of course, is speculation. But the fact that our sources give it as much credibility as they do is itself indicative of Paul's impact on the Nazarene sect.

2. The other side of the same stretching process is what has often been referred to as the 'Hellenizing' of Christianity. Paul is the man most associated in Christian history and consciousness with the transition from Middle East to Europe, from Galilean village to Hellenistic city, from Jewish categories and modes to those of Greek language and thought. There is certainly truth in all this. According to Acts (16.6-12) Paul it was who made the transition from Asia to Europe—though, to be fair, the significance of this move across the north-east Aegean is almost entirely the perspective of hindsight. Again, the different patterns of ministry, as between Jesus (in the Synoptic Gospels) and Paul

(in Acts and by implication in Paul's letters) can hardly be denied. The transition to a more characteristically Graeco-Roman world would inevitably have involved social transformation in forms of organization and ministry anyway. And Paul introduced several features into his theology and teaching that can only have come from more distinctively Graeco-Roman thought. We need only think of his use of a concept like 'nature' (as in Rom. 1.26 and 2.14), or 'conscience' (e.g. Rom. 2.15; 1 Cor. 10.25-29), or 'adoption' (as in Rom. 8.15, 23), or the body used as an image for different groups living together in harmony in the same city (Rom. 12.4-8; 1 Cor. 12.12-27), or the appeal to 'virtue' as praiseworthy (Phil. 4.8-9). Paul's indebtedness to Greek rhetoric is indicated in 1 Cor. 1.18–2.5 at the very time he gives warning against measuring the gospel in its terms. His argument in Romans is characterized by use of the 'diatribe', that is, the development of his case by arguing its points with an imagined interlocutor (especially Rom. 2.1–3.8). Later on Paul and his school introduce the use of household codes (rules for good household management) into Christian paraenesis (Col. 3.18–4.1; Eph. 5.22–6.9), possibly indicating a further stage in accommodation with the everyday morality of the ancient city-state (the household as the basic unit of orderly society).

If Paul can be described as 'Hellenizing' Christianity, there are those who think he was responsible for the 'acute Hellenization' of Christianity. The reference is to the fact that the gnostics of the second and subsequent centuries regarded Paul with considerable favour; Paul himself has indeed been called 'the greatest of all the Gnostics'. Marcion, generally regarded in mainline Christian tradition as the greatest of Christian heretics, regarded Paul as *the* Apostle and his own system (the God of the Old Testament as the evil creator, the Old Testament and the law to be totally rejected) as simply the outworking of Paul's gospel.

Paul must have done at least something to encourage such attitudes. The evidence has usually been found in such as his talk of spiritual people and spiritual body (1 Cor. 2.13-15; 15.44-46; Gal. 6.1) and his seeming hostility to the law (2 Cor. 3; Gal. 2.19; 5.4), although pushing down that line would generally be regarded as over-interpretation today. Some have tried to press the point by arguing that Paul derived his understanding of baptism or Lord's Supper from mystery religions, and his Christology from a gnostic myth of a heavenly redeemer myth. But the evidence has proved far too insubstantial to support such claims. Nevertheless it can be seen that Paul generated a dynamic which broadened out the infant Christian movement and which in some degree opened the door for emphases and teachings that the later Church, and probably Paul himself, could not accept as expressions of Christianity.

3. The title of this section is itself a reminder that for most of the nineteenth century Paul was indeed regarded as the principal shaper of Christianity, possibly even as the real founder, or at least most influential formative influence on Christianity. This was the period when Jesus was often regarded primarily as a teacher of morality (love God and your neighbour). So the emergence of Christianity as a religion, with emphasis on Jesus' death as sacrificial and on sacramental rituals, was regularly regarded as something of a departure not to say decline from the purer, simpler gospel that Jesus had preached. And who else could be credited or blamed with that development other than Paul?

Such views have long since ceased to command much credence in scholarly circles. Nevertheless, the fact remains that Paul can be credited with inserting a far stronger theological backbone into Christianity. It is his exposition of the significance of Jesus' death and resurrection that placed these two features so much at the heart of the Christian gospel. His letter to the Romans became in effect the first attempt at a systematic Christian theology. His teaching on 'justification by faith' has been the foundation stone on which the Protestant Reformation was built. No one can really engage with historic Christian theology without engaging with Paul.

The significance of Paul for Christian diversity at this point can be illustrated simply by reference to the New Testament itself. The two most obvious features of the New Testament are the Gospels and the letters. It was indeed this feature that first suggested the divide between Jesus and Paul. For the Gospels speak solely of Jesus. And when one considers the Letters, it is Paul who dominates the scene. It is this very feature that prevents Christianity from lapsing into a Jesus Society, a sentimental remembrance of a charismatic leader. For it is the letters that introduce a harder edge of thinking *about* Jesus. And it is Paul whose voice speaks much the loudest in this enterprise. If Christianity commends itself as a coherent system of thought, it is primarily Paul we have to credit for that.

At the same time, we should at least just recall that the corpus of Paul's letters is usually taken to include several that were written not by Paul himself, but probably in the following generation, by close disciples anxious to preserve a Pauline counsel into the subsequent generations. The point is that the diversity of Christianity that began to be marked out by Paul himself continued to be stretched, though not so much in diversifying theology or praxis. On the contrary, the second generation of Paulinism, marked out particularly by the Pastoral Epistles, seems rather to represent a consolidation of much of the Pauline heritage, if not, indeed, a solidification of it. In the Pastorals 'the faith' seems to have become more fixed, and the structures of ministry more set (e.g. 1 Tim. 3.1-13; 4.14; 2 Tim. 1.12-14; 2.1-2). In so doing the Pastorals probably established the direction for the Great Church of the following generations, helping it to form a more coherent and durable structure of faith and organization, a development that confirmed Christianity in its break away from its Jewish matrix and commitment to continuing existence in the Graeco-Roman world. Though one could perhaps ask whether Paul has been thus preserved for the subsequent centuries of Christianity at some cost to the diversity that he both embodied and stood for.

4. *Was Paul a Consistent Thinker?*

The last sentence of the penultimate paragraph would raise eyebrows in some quarters. For it is less obvious to quite a number of Pauline scholars that Paul was a coherent or consistent thinker. In considering diversity in connection with Paul, therefore, we cannot avoid considering what at the very least has to be called the diversity *in* Paul. In this connection it is worth considering, for example, the diversity, or should we rather say tensions within the various sections of Paul's theology and practice. Here we will look in particular at his Christology, his ideas of salvation, his concept of the church and his principles of praxis.

1. Paul's understanding of Christ. The main feature here is the fact that Paul evidently found it necessary to stretch his language in different ways and different directions in order to express what he saw to be the significance of Jesus Christ.

In relation to God, Paul did not hesitate to associate Christ with God as the joint source of 'grace and peace' in his epistolary greetings (e.g. Rom. 1.7; 1 Cor. 1.3; Phil. 1.2; Phlm. 3). His most regular title for Christ is 'Lord' (*kyrios*), and the Lordship seems to reflect and share in

God's (e.g. Rom. 14.9; 2 Cor. 5.10). Most striking in this connection is the fact that Paul seems quite comfortable in applying to Jesus *kyrios* scriptural texts that referred originally to Yahweh (most striking in Rom. 10.9-13, citing Joel 2.32; and Phil. 2.9-11, echoing Isa. 45.23). In 1 Cor. 8.6 it is almost as though he splits the *Shema* (Deut. 6.4) between 'one God, the Father' and 'one Lord Jesus Christ'. And in Rom. 9.5 many scholars, perhaps the majority, conclude that Paul 'doxologizes' Jesus as 'G/god'.

At the same time Paul also speaks of Jesus as one whose status was wholly transformed by his resurrection. He had been 'appointed Son of God in power as from the resurrection of the dead' (Rom. 1.4). At his resurrection he became the 'last Adam', 'life-giving Spirit' (1 Cor. 15.45). Like Adam, he (the risen, exalted Christ) is the image of God (2 Cor. 4.4), the first-born of a new family of the resurrected (Rom. 8.29), so that the process of salvation can be understood as a process of being conformed to that image (2 Cor. 3.18; 1 Cor. 15.49). 'Image' language can also be used to evoke for Christ the role of divine wisdom, 'through whom all things were made' (1 Cor. 8.6; Col. 1.15), a classic way of referring to God's way of interacting with his creation (Prov. 8.22-31; Sir. 24.1-22; Wis. 9-11).

Paul can also envisage Christ as a sort of place or context wherein Christians are located—'in Christ', a phrase that occurs no less than 83 times in the Pauline corpus: for example, 'no condemnation for those in Christ' (Rom. 8.1); 'in Christ shall all be made alive' (1 Cor. 15.22); 'you are all one in Christ Jesus' (Gal. 3.28). Add to the 'in Christ' motif parallel and complementary phrases, such as 'in the Lord', 'through Christ' and 'with Christ', and the portrayal of Christ begins to become somewhat confusing. Not to forget the concept of the church as 'the body of Christ', to which we shall return.

And lest we begin to think that the understanding of Jesus as a single, recognizable individual has become lost behind a diversifying conceptuality, we need to recall that Paul also envisages Christ coming again on clouds from heaven (e.g. 1 Thess. 4.16-17; Phil. 3.20-21). This hope was preserved from the Aramaic-speaking churches (1 Cor. 16.22) and remained a constant element in the Lord's Supper as celebrated in the Pauline churches (1 Cor. 11.26).

This range of conceptuality could be extended. But sufficient has been said to indicate how wide and diverse the range is. We might well ask how it was that Paul could hold all of these images together. Did

Paul have a single mental picture of Jesus in mind? Or was his thinking simply confused, inconsistent on the point? Presumably he did not feel the different portrayals pulling against each other in the way that the bare catalogue of the preceding paragraphs might seem to imply. Or are his diverse formulations designed to prevent any single conception either gaining overall dominance or reducing the conception of Christ to a single figure? Whatever the case, and whatever the reason, the fact of christological diversity in Paul can hardly be denied.

2. *Paul's ideas of salvation.* Here we may simply note the kaleido-scope of images Paul draws upon to bring out the richness of the salvation process into which he called his converts.

He draws metaphors from the customs of his time: 'justification' (acquittal) from the law courts (e.g. Rom. 3.21-26); 'redemption', the buying back of a slave or a war captive (e.g. Rom. 3.24); 'liberation' and 'freedom' (e.g. Gal. 5.1, 13); 'reconciliation' (2 Cor. 5.18-20); new citizenship (Phil. 3.20).

He draws metaphors from everyday life: 'salvation' (wholeness of health, rescue, preservation) (e.g. Rom. 1.16; 5.9-10); 'inheritance' (Rom. 4.13-14; 8.17); waking up (Rom. 13.11); putting off/on clothes (e.g. Rom. 13.12, 14); receiving an invitation (e.g. Rom. 8.30; Gal. 1.6); writing a letter (2 Cor. 3.3).

Paul looked equally to agriculture for his images of salvation: sow-ing and watering (1 Cor. 3.6-8); irrigation (1 Cor. 12.13c); a pitcher of water poured out (Rom. 5.5); grafting (Rom. 11.17-24); harvest (Rom. 8.23).

Likewise from commerce: the 'seal' as a stamp of visible ownership (2 Cor. 1.22); the 'first instalment and guarantee' (*arrabōn*) (2 Cor. 1.22; 5.5); 'into the name of' as the formula for transfer of ownership (1 Cor. 1.13-15); 'confirm' (from conveyancing) (1 Cor. 1.6); 'tested and approved' from the process of refining (e.g. Rom. 14.18); building (1 Cor. 3.10-12).

Finally we might note metaphors drawn from the major events of life: 'abortion' (1 Cor. 15.8), birth (1 Cor. 4.15; Gal. 4.19, 29); adop-tion (Rom. 8.15, 23); engagement (2 Cor. 11.2); marriage (1 Cor. 6.17); death, even crucifixion (Rom. 6.3-6; Gal. 6.14).

Here too the range of images could be extended. And here too we have to note the obvious corollaries. For one thing, it is evident that Paul was ransacking the language and imagery of his day to find appropriate metaphors for the wonder of the new experiences and relationships he and his converts were enjoying. There was no single image that dominated, no single metaphor adequate to capture the richness of these experiences and relationships. Any attempt to standardize the experience of salvation, its ritual expression or its theological statement would surely have been resisted by Paul. Alternatively put, it would surely be too pedantic and nit-picking to conclude from the range of metaphors reviewed above that Paul's thought was incoherent or inconsistent. Such diversity is only inconsistent for the small of mind or the short of experience.

3. *Paul's concept of church.* Two features are particularly worthy of note here.

One is the way Paul uses the term 'church'. The word (*ekklēsia*) is the normal term for a popular assembly of citizens entitled to vote in a Greek city (as in Acts 19.39). At the same time, Paul's talk of 'the church of God' (1 Cor. 1.1; 10.32; etc.) almost certainly echoes the regular LXX talk of 'the assembly of the Lord' (e.g. Num. 16.3; Deut. 23.1-3, 8; Neh. 13.1). In other words, Paul saw the new Christian churches as on a par with the properly constituted gatherings of the citizen body of the city where these churches were now being established, and as in continuation with the Israelite assembly of Yahweh.

It is all the more striking, then, that Paul could use the term (church) so diversely. In particular, he hardly, if at all, uses it of what we today would call the universal church. His typical use is for the gathered body of believers in a particular place or region (e.g. Rom. 16.1, 23; 1 Cor. 1.2). So he can speak, at one end of his usage, of the churches (plural) of a region, Judaea, Galatia, Asia or Macedonia (1 Cor. 16.1, 19; 2 Cor. 8.1; Gal. 1.2, 22; 1 Thess. 2.14). And at the other end, he can speak of the church (which met) in someone's house—of Priscilla and Aquila, of Nympha and of Philemon (Rom. 16.5; 1 Cor. 16.19; Col. 4.15; Phlm. 2).

Such diversity of usage again indicates a remarkable breadth and flexibility of conception. It should perhaps be recalled that this was a time long before church buildings were constructed, a development that resulted in 'church' becoming so much identified with a building; these first 'churches' were small groups of people meeting in private homes. It was the ability to hold together the bold claim made for these small groups and the flexibility of their form that was probably one of the secrets of their success.

The other notable feature of Paul's ecclesiology is the way he took over the familiar metaphor of the corporate body of a city or state (the body politic) and applied it also to the same little groups in the cities of the north-eastern Mediterranean (Rom. 12.4-8; 1 Cor. 12.12-27) as the 'body of Christ'—'the body of Christ (in Corinth)' (1 Cor. 12.27). The point is that the metaphor was used in Graeco-Roman political philosophy as a way of stressing the need for the different factions (ethnic groups, trade guilds, etc.) of a city to cooperate for the sake of the city's safety and prosperity. Paul takes it over to the same effect: the unity of the body is a peculiar one, made up of many different members (limbs and organs), and dependent on the different functions and ministries working together for the common good. In other words, the body is the prime image for unity in diversity, a unity that consists in, grows out of and depends on the diversity functioning as such. If the whole body were an eye, or the sense of hearing, where would the body be (1 Cor. 12.17-19)?

4. Paul's principles of praxis. There is one other area within Paul's thought and activity that we should not neglect. That is the passage where he states most explicitly his own principles of adaptability, of principled diversity of conduct (1 Cor. 9.19-22).

> For though I am free with regard to all, I have made myself a slave to all, in order that I might win more of them. To the Jews I became as a Jew, in order that I might win Jews. To those under the law I became as one under the law...in order that I might win those under the law. To those outside the law I became as one outside the law...in order that I might win those outside the law. To those who are weak I became weak, in order that might win those who are weak. I have become all things to all people, in order that I might by all means save some.

This can be understood as a missionary principle, but in its context it clearly also functions as a pastoral principle. As such it is to be understood precisely as an affirmation of the need for diversity, or here, adaptability, in dealing with diverse people and situations.

Paul was in no sense a rigid thinker or practitioner. He drew firm lines at certain points, particularly warning against his converts conforming to or relapsing into the sexual laxity of much Greek life (1 Cor. 6.9-13), or of forgetting the dangers of idolatry (1 Cor. 10.20-22). But in other sensitive matters of personal and social relationships, Paul's flexibility of mind and practice is striking. The unsympathetic can readily portray it as manipulative. But Paul's dealings, for example, with marital problems in 1 Corinthians 7 and with the relationship between slave and master in his letter to Philemon, when read with care and with an ear for the nuances, are better heard as the open-mindedness of an exceptional pastor alert to the diversities of people and problems.

5. *Conclusion*

The diversity associated with Paul is therefore very striking and of immense significance for a proper grasp of first-century Mediterranean history, particularly the history of Christianity's beginnings, and particularly in its interaction with early Judaism.

Paul stretched the diversity in late Second Temple Judaism to the limit and beyond, and yet both remains a characteristically Jewish voice within Christanity and a disturbing Jewish voice within the history of Judaism. He stretched the diversity of infant Christianity, preventing it from falling back into a Jewish sect, and leaving developing Christianity the challenge of addressing wider cultures in meaningful language.

As the first voice of structured Christian theology, the diversity of his theological assertions helps prevent his successors succumbing to a narrowly consistent Christology, a monochrome concept of salvation or a uniform concept of community. And his vision of principled adaptability remains a model for sensitive and flexible pastoral practice.

In a word, Paul the apostle is the apostle of Christian diversity.

THE EARLY CHURCH

Thomas O'Loughlin

1. *Confessional Histories*

Our perceptions of the past, what I shall refer to as 'history', change through two distinct processes. The first process is discovery, and occurs when evidence hitherto unknown comes to the attention of scholars. A papyrus document is found in the sands of Egypt, a parchment manuscript is found in some dusty library where it has lain unread for centuries, or an archaeologist uncovers ruins with inscriptions or magnificent mosaics. Such events fire the imagination and sometimes even hit the headlines, for such discoveries can shed light on a part of the past that was previously obscure, and in the light of the new discovery the whole of a past world seems different. In the area of early church studies there have been several such discoveries during the past century and not only have they changed the way we view the period, but they have brought a certain excitement to the whole discipline: old impressions fade away while new details of the lives of the first Christians come into view.

However, for all its excitement, the process of discovery is the lesser of the two processes by which our historical picture changes. The other process is the re-evaluation of our sources in the light of the changed intellectual world in which we, as students of the past, live. If investigators approach the evidence with one set of assumptions and questions they get one set of answers and one image of the early church, but if they approach the past from a different angle and attitude to the sources of information, then the emerging picture will be totally different. Since these shifts in historical perception are more significant in changing the picture of the early church than much publicized—but serendipitous—discoveries, it is worthwhile looking at an example of this process.

In 1870, the Revd Joseph Bingham published a massive study of the early church entitled *The Antiquities of the Christian Church*. It was to remain a staple element in courses for undergraduates until well into the twentieth century.[1] Anyone reading it today would be struck, most of all, by its confidence: he knew in detail what had happened and the whole story fitted together with few gaps or question marks. This confidence took several forms.

First, Bingham was in no doubt as to his time-frame. The life of the church was that which took place after the time of Jesus—so questions about Jesus and the Gospels belonged to the period before 29–33 CE (the time range is due to the recognition that the calculation of 1 CE might be four years too late, but that Jesus was 33 when he was crucified was not questioned). Then the church began, and its earliest days were described in vivid detail in the Acts of the Apostles and the epistles in the New Testament for they were contemporary eye-witness accounts. Then one entered a time at once glorious (an 'Age of Saints' when there were not yet any 'corruptions') and painful (the persecutions). These led up to the 'Great Persecution' of the Emperor Diocletian (245–313) and to the eventual victory of the church with the 'Edict of Milan'[2] (313). Then came the age of the great 'oecumenical' councils up to Chalcedon in 451. However, the shadows had already begun to gather in 313 when links with the empire had introduced temptations and impurities into the church. It was no longer a pure vessel of gold but had become an alloy incorporating base elements. This process of corruption—summed up with one pejorative word: 'syncretism'—was going to continue until it reached the dire level of superstition and lack of true Christian faith that Bingham associated with the 'dark ages' of Roman Catholicism.[3] That perceived period of corruption was the deep gulf that bounded the 'early church', separating it from later history, and made it a time to be looked back upon

1.   J. Bingham, *Origines Ecclesiasticae: The Antiquities of the Christian Church* (2 vols.; London: Henry G. Bohn, 1870).

2.   Since 1891 it has been recognized that this action by Constantine was not technically the issuing of an 'edict'; however, it is still commonly known by this term and would be out of place here to depart from such terms in the interests of precise terminology. I shall use this as my rule of thumb throughout this paper.

3.   For an account of anti-Catholic agenda of Bingham, and many other historians of the early church until well into the twentieth century, see J.Z. Smith, *Drudgery Divine: On the Comparison of Early Christianities and the Religions of Antiquity* (Jordan Lectures in Comparative Religion, 14; London: School of Oriental and African Studies, 1990), pp. 36-53, 58.

with longing as to a golden age, which set a standard for imitation, and which could act as a guarantee of one's identity in the present: if we are like them, we are perfect Christians.

Secondly, Bingham was confident that he had enough information to accurately describe antiquity. The writings of the earliest Christians were all to be found in the New Testament, and not only could they be trusted to tell the truth, but their inherent accuracy was only questioned by those who were antagonistic to religion as such. Thus a little careful scholarship would be able to date all the events mentioned in Acts, and anything which looked liked a contradiction between Acts and a Pauline letter (e.g. with Gal. 2.11-21 on the 'Council of Jerusalem') was solved by the confident application of the Law of Non-Contradiction: they *must* be only different aspects of a single event, for each account is true. Moving into the later first century one met the 'Apostolic Fathers', and again a succession of saints guaranteed the positions taken: so long as the writings were genuine (e.g. the letters of Bishop Ignatius of Antioch, c. 110), then the accounts were direct statements of the facts.

Thirdly, Bingham was doctrinally confident: 'the faith which was once delivered to the saints'[4] was that of himself and his ideal reader. He was not going to discover a different religion in the earliest times to that which he professed—that would be, for him, tantamount to saying that his Christianity was not true—and both the early church and he shared exactly the same Scriptures, and both could access its meaning more or less directly. This doctrinal confidence provided him with a whole pattern of church life and belief against which he could situate every detail he found in early sources, for he knew what it should have looked like. In turn, this knowledge allowed him to fill in blanks in his information from his own experience of Christianity. So, for example, he imagined that they had a minimum emphasis on the liturgical aspects of cult, and a maximum emphasis on preaching 'based on the Scriptures'. This doctrinal confidence was openly denominational, for history was the background of one's own brand of Christianity. Since the Reformation it was agreed on all sides that history was the place where one 'proved' one's position: either 'they were what we are' or 'we can show that we are a legitimate growth from that time'.[5] And so if they

---

4.   The quotation from Jude 3 follows the Authorized Version of 1611.
5.   I have examined some of these attitudes in so far as they affect mediaeval

acted or believed in a way that was at variance from the way one acted, then one was no longer in the 'faith of the apostles'. This meant that any show of uncertainty about the past was equivalent to doctrinal uncertainty in the present and an actual lack of commitment, even disloyalty, to one's group.

Lastly, Bingham was confident that he could understand the past in a manner very similar to the way he understood his own society. The past was simply an earlier version of the present and the historian collected evidence, facts, in the manner of a policeman gathering information after a traffic accident. Once one had 'the facts' one simply arranged them and described the overall picture. History was not *a presentation* of the past, but an encyclopaedic discipline that collected information and 'told the story'. History was a simple affair, and only became complicated in that one had to be trained in such things as ancient languages, reading inscriptions and manuscripts, and to learn other technical tricks, such as how to establish a chronology. This confidence reached every area of history whether it concerned the early church or republican Rome, and the only difference that entered the scene in the case of religious history was the attempt to discern 'the hand of Providence' in the whole narrative of events. Just as there was a tendency to link the beliefs of the early church with one's denomination, so there was a tendency to identify the 'plan' in history with one's religion. In this perspective—and it was a commonplace in history writing by Christians going back to Eusebius of Caesarea (c. 260–c. 340), if not to Luke writing Acts—when one studied the early church and how it spread over the Mediterranean world one was observing the work of the Holy Spirit. In watching the growth of the early church Bingham was not watching a religious movement grow and change due to factors that could operate within any similar organization at the time, rather he was looking at parts of a vast plan within the Providence of God unfolding on the earth.

Bingham's vast work (1,261 large pages, each of two columns) is not without erudition—the amount of detail he amassed is truly amazing and still repays careful reading—but it is now no more than a quarry of such snippets. Indeed, it is itself a historical document providing evidence for how the nineteenth century viewed early (or as he would

church history in T. O'Loughlin, 'Medieval Church History: Beyond Apologetics, after Development, the Awkward Memories', *The Way* 38 (1998), pp. 65-76.

have said 'primitive': literally, 'the first age') Christianity. So how have our views changed?

2. *Discoveries*

The most obvious change has come through discoveries of new documents, older fragments of documents we already possessed, and the testimony of the spade.

a. *The Didache*
In 1873 Philotheus Bryennius came across a short text in a much later manuscript, then housed in the Patriarch's Library in Constantinople (Istanbul).[6] He recognized this as a very ancient document, and its title (*The Teaching* [*didache*] *of the Twelve Apostles*) alerted him to the fact that it was a work that Christian writers, such as Jerome (c. 347–419), had referred to as being important in the early preaching of the church. Here was the first document that could be as old as the first communities, but which was not considered 'Scripture' and which, more importantly for the historian, was a document that dealt with the everyday concerns of an actual community. Its picture of such a community was startling in many ways, but its most surprising feature was that the community had such strong internal cohesion, with structures for prayer, fasting, administration and liturgy. This seemed so far from the romantic image of the early Christians as structure-free charismatics for whom an administration was as unnecessary as it would have been cumbersome that many scholars simply could not believe that it came from the first century. Concerns about such matters as fasting and the Eucharist *must* be much later, they argued,[7] but the weight of the evidence was against them. The question was virtually sealed in the early 1950s with the discovery of the Qumran material, which brought to light many literary affinities that showed that the *Didache* had to

6.   For more information on any of these topics, the best place to start is A. Di Berardino and W.H.C. Frend (eds.), *The Encyclopedia of the Early Church* (Cambridge: James Clarke & Co., 1991) for not only is a summary of each topic provided, but a very focused bibliography (the entry of the *Didache* is by W. Rordorf, I, pp. 234-35).

7.   A proponent of a much later date who was influential in the English-speaking world was F.E. Vokes, *The Riddle of the Didache: Fact or Fiction, Heresy or Catholicism?* (London: SPCK, 1938).

come from a time when Christianity and Judaism had not drawn far apart.[8] Today we date it to the period between 50 and 70 CE, and instead of seeing it as providing incidental information to what is contained in the writings in the New Testament, we recognize that it is the primary witness to the life of the early church—coming from a period before the writings that made it into the canon of the New Testament.[9]

b. *The Nag Hammadi Library*
In December 1945, in the Egyptian town of Nag Hammadi, not far from Luxor, occurred the largest single find of ancient books that can throw light on early Christianity.[10] The place was once, in the late fourth and fifth centuries, the site of the great monastery of Chenoboskion, and these books (found in 12 codices)[11] contained 46 different literary works (and there were duplicates of some of these), but we had copies of only 6 of these writings prior to the discovery. All the writings were in Coptic—the ancient language of Egypt outside Alexandria, the language of the early desert monasteries, and still that of the Egyptian Church.

The discovery—especially of works such as the *Gospel of Thomas* of which we had only a few scraps until then—caused a sensation, not helped by those who started to use tabloid labels to draw more attention to these otherwise rather boring, and obscure, manuscripts. Thus it became a 'secret library', 'the writings they do not want you to read', and 'forgotten ancient wisdom'. The central plank in the argument of

8. See J.P. Audet, *La Didachè: Instruction des apôtres* (Paris: Lecoffre, 1958)—this is still a basic study for all modern work on the *Didache*, but unfortunately it has not been translated into English.

9. For a survey of the state of the question on the *Didache*, see C.N. Jefford (ed.), *The* Didache *in Context: Essays on its Text, History and Transmission* (Leiden: E.J. Brill, 1995). For an overview of work on the *Didache*, see K. Niederwimmer, *The Didache: A Commentary* (Minneapolis: Fortress Press, 1998).

10. See G. Filoramo, 'Nag Hammadi Writings', in A. Di Berardino and W.H.C. Frend (eds.), *The Encyclopedia of the Early Church*, II, p. 579.

11. The word *codex* (plural: *codices*) describes one of the ways books were produced in the ancient world—it contains pages lying on top of one another and bound on the left margin (the book you are now reading is a codex). The other ancient method of producing a book is the *scroll* where the pages are attached to one another at each side, and then it is rolled up, and has to be unrolled as one reads it.

those wishing to gain the attention of those interested in the esoteric was to say that it was 'gnostic'.[12] The basis of this claim is that, philosophical writings apart, some of the Christian texts could be given a gnostic interpretation—but Gnosticism is one of those movements that if one sets out to find it in some writing, then one usually succeeds.[13] Equally, the fact that the library contained another writing, the *Gospel of Thomas*, claiming to give sayings by Jesus, many of which were not paralleled in the canonical gospels, made many conservative Christians very leery about Nag Hammadi. So they too wished to put as much distance as they could between 'Christianity' and what might disturb their views of the early church: their method was to join the chorus labelling these writings as 'gnostic'.

The exact nature of the library, why it was buried, the role it played in the life of the monastery that produced it, are all matters of ongoing investigation, as is the question of just how much gnostic influence can be seen in some of the writings. But what is beyond dispute is that it alters how we view the early church and our view of the range of opinions that were to be found within the church long before these writings were gathered together in Chenoboskion. The best example of this is the *Gospel of Thomas*. It was put together by Christians around the end of the first century CE out of the traditions of sayings of Jesus—Luke writing at more or less the same time says (at the beginning of his gospel [1.1-3], which did make it into the canon) that many were doing this—and so it has a great many overlaps with the other gospels, and contributes to our understanding of how earlier traditions (probably some were written, some oral) were formed into the books we now possess. The form of the *Gospel of Thomas* is that of a collection of statements without the narrative structure of the life story of Jesus with which we are familiar from the other gospels. Possibly its compiler wished to present the words of Jesus as a series of challenges to his hearers.[14] Alas, he failed to reckon with human nature, for if ever

---

12. This advertising ploy can still be seen in the cover of the paperback edition of the sober and reliable English translation by J.M Robinson *et al.* (*The Nag Hammadi Library in English* [New York: HarperCollins, 1990] [the original hardback was published in Leiden, 1978], which reads: 'The definitive new translation of the Gnostic scriptures, complete in one volume.')

13. It is not so long since many scholars could hardly open the Gospel of John without finding Gnostic elements!

14. This is a theme developed by R. Valantasis in what is the most accessible,

there is a choice between a book with a strong story-line (e.g. Matthew or Luke) and one that is just words of wisdom (e.g. 'Q' [the collection of sayings used by both Matthew and Luke] or Thomas), then it will be the one with the story-line that will be popular, copied and disseminated, and which will survive and so stand a much better chance of being canonized.

Nag Hammadi has shown us that we must be very careful of thinking about the early church in neat, highly defined categories, an early version of the neat religious world in which many scholars wish to live! There were many currents of thought in the early church, differences from region to region, and many endeavours—most no longer extant—to commit the Christian message to papyrus or parchment. Only some of these efforts were successful or survived, and we are disposed towards seeing these as the seeds of what later became central features in the Christian edifice: this is the 'history is written by the victors' phenomenon. Documents like the *Didache* and those from Nag Hammadi remind us that we know far less about the beliefs of the earliest Christians than scholars a century ago imagined.

c. *The Dead Sea Scrolls*

The discoveries that were made in the Judaean desert in the later 1940s have changed our views of Judaism in the first century CE, and so also our views of Jewish figures from the period, such as Jesus of Nazareth, and they have also influenced our views of the early church. Prior to their discovery, the only comparison that could be made for structures, customs, and beliefs found among the Jesus movement was with writings representing a Judaism from several centuries later, or else with documents whose own date and context were obscure. The appearance of the Qumran material has given those studying early Christianity a firm base for comparison—and many features of early Christianity that seemed to appear from nowhere can now be seen to have parallels in Palestinian Judaism at the time. We have already noted how the Qumran discoveries were a decisive factor in proving the early date of the *Didache*, but that is just an instance of how they are contributing to the study of the early church. However, we should note that there are still psychological barriers for many scholars when it come to using this

and balanced, introduction to this gospel I know: *The Gospel of Thomas* (London: Routledge, 1997).

material. Specialists on the early church often still come from a classics background and view antiquity in terms of the Mediterranean world and see its *lingua franca*, Greek, as their main scholarly language. The Qumran material is then felt to belong to the world of the Old Testament/Hebrew Bible specialists whose languages are Hebrew and Aramaic. Such divisions are the lingering result of the now outmoded Christian theological division that put a gulf between what was Holy Writ (studied by scripture scholars) and 'history' (a lesser discipline that told what happened to mere human institutions). One of the key tasks facing those who work in the study of the early church in the future is to remove the remaining barriers that put materials about Judaism in the last century BCE and the first centuries CE into a different category of sources to those which they see as their 'own'.[15]

d. *Other Documents*

Spectacular finds always attract us—I call it the 'hidden treasure syndrome'—but there are also the umpteen little discoveries that are only heard about by a handful of specialists but which gradually change the way that the past is viewed. A century ago the standard text of the New Testament in Greek was based on parchment manuscripts of the fourth and fifth centuries. Then gradually more and more bits of papyrus came to light: they were older than the parchments and often contained variants on the text that help us to clear up obscurities or which tell us how the Scriptures were used in the early church.[16] This process is rarely mentioned, yet its effects reach large numbers of Christians through new, and more accurate, translations of the Bible (e.g. the *New Revised Standard Version*).

This process of discovery goes on quietly day by day; sometimes the new piece completes a whole section of the historical jigsaw, other times it just shows us that there are parts of the jigsaw we never

---

15. There is an excellent example of a more integrated approach in the 'New Schürer' (*History of the Jewish People*), but this work is still more likely to be found on the shelves of those who see themselves as 'scripture scholars' than historians of the early church.

16. I know of no up-to-date general introduction to this field of investigation, but, for a learned summary, see E.J. Epp, 'The Papyrus Manuscripts of the New Testament', in B.D. Ehrman and M.W. Holmes, *The Text of the New Testament in Contemporary Research: Essays on the Status Quaestionis* (Grand Rapids: Eerdmans, 1995), pp. 3-21.

thought of before. But it should remind us, always, that our picture of the early church is not static—and those who imagine that it is, ignore the nature of our evidence.

e. *Archaeology*

A century ago archaeology was just beginning to emerge from being a gentleman's pastime to being a branch of academic study, but it was still dominated by the desire to find famous places or items worthy of display in museums.[17] Since then it has been transformed both technically—it has become the science of excavation analogous to forensic science—and in perspective, with an emphasis on discovering the culture of antiquity: how people lived, worked and traded. In the process, the living conditions of the earliest communities have come to light.

A good example of this is Corinth. Corinth is a name well known to every Christian from hearing sections read to them from Paul's letters to the Christian community in that city. To this was added what is said about Corinth in Acts,[18] and references to the city from classical writers. Now archaeologists have carried out a series of excavations not of great palaces, fortifications or sacred building, but of the houses and workshops of the ordinary people who would have made up the Jewish and Christian communities there in the first century CE. We now know what sort of house, and its size, in which an early community would have met for the Eucharist, and from a study of the economy that would have been needed to sustain such a house, we can glimpse the whole social world of the early Christians.[19]

Archaeologists still make spectacular finds, such as the inscription bearing the name of Pontius Pilate,[20] but most of their work is far less glamorous. However, in uncovering the living conditions of the earliest Christians, details of their places of work, places of worship, and their

17. The indispensable guide to this topic is W.H.C. Frend, *The Archaeology of Early Christianity* (London: Geoffrey Chapman, 1996) which not only provides an overview of the evidence, but sets the development of early Christian archaeology in its various modern contexts.

18. For example, it mentions Paul's arrival there from Athens at Acts 18.1.

19. See W.A. Meeks, *The First Urban Christians: The Social World of the Apostle Paul* (New Haven: Yale University Press, 1983) both for a more detailed account of Corinth, and for an example of how the social context of Christianity can be revealed by archaeology.

20. See H.K. Bond, *Pontius Pilate in History and Interpretation* (Cambridge: Cambridge University Press, 1998), pp. 11-12.

connectedness to one another by roads and through trade, they gradually create the social scene in which we can interpret texts and evaluate
our historical constructions. The overall effect of this work is that historians today can describe the environment in which the early church
lived with a precision unimaginable only a few decades ago.[21]

3. New Perspectives

I began this chapter by saying that history is our perceptions of the
past: it tells us as much about our world, our view of life, our concerns,
hopes and fears, as it does about the times past upon which it focuses.
So when we read historians from a hundred years ago, we learn at least
as much about the concerns and aspirations of the writers as we do
about the early church.

a. *The Past is a Foreign Country*[22]

Most historians of the early church a century ago not only were
Christians, but were very conscious that they shared the 'same faith as
the apostles' and so wrote about a world that did not seem foreign to
them in terms of its beliefs and assumptions. The early church was their
own church—time created distance, not difference. Gradually, as the
twentieth century progressed, such notions of familiarity disappeared.
Just as we no longer expect other contemporary cultures to share our
views of what is important, how individuals and families perceive
themselves and how they construct a religious worldview, so we recognize the distinctiveness of the past and that we have a duty not to
project our values backwards. Anachronism (reading the past as if it
were the present) is not only a methodological fault producing a false

21. For examples of this creative use of archaeology in describing the early
church one should look at many of the publications originating from the École
Biblique in Jerusalem, for instance, E. Nodet and J. Taylor, *The Origins of Christianity: An Exploration* (Collegeville: Liturgical Press, 1998).

22. The powerful phrase is from L.P. Hartley's novel *The Go-Between*, but it
has become a stock phrase among historians to indicate that there is a conceptual
gulf between their world (the time and society in which they live) and the world
they seek to study. The whole theme has been studied, in a book that has become a
classic among modern historians, by D. Lowenthal, *The Past Is a Foreign Country*
(Cambridge: Cambridge University Press, 1985). For an exploration of how the
theme affects the history of the early church in particular, see R. Bultmann, *Primitive Christianity in its Contemporary Setting* (London: Thames & Hudson, 1956).

picture, but is the same as colonizing a foreign culture. It is equivalent to saying, 'There is only one right way to view the world, the way we modern people do it!'

A good example of this can be seen in the way that historians react to accounts of the miraculous. I, like most historians today, do not expect miracles to happen, and when something wonderful and unexpected happens I usually attribute it simply to chance. Underlying this attitude is the notion that events in the physical world can be explained rationally in terms of the processes of this world. This is a very modern belief (two centuries old) and one radically different to the beliefs of all early Christians who expected God to intervene in the world in wonderful ways, and who believed that a rationally satisfying explanation required not just an explanation of *how* something happens, but *who* ultimately *caused it* to happen. We see this, in some way, in virtually every early Christian writing: for example, Acts 5.19 where an angel opened prison doors. Both systems are equally rational, but the beliefs and expectations of each are poles apart. Earlier historians sought to 'explain away' such miracles for they feared that such stories made Christianity look ridiculous: angels simply do not open prison doors. Either this was some sort of illusion, or else it was a story to amuse the simple, or it showed that Luke could not understand what happened and his miracle story was a cover for this lack of understanding. Today, we are aware that what one sees is not just what happens 'out there', but involves one's world view and one's beliefs: they expected God to intervene and so saw many cases where that belief was seen to be justified. Now the question for the historian becomes far more subtle: when I read an account of a miracle, given that the writer is sincere, what does it tell me about that author and his audience that they can expect such happenings? So miracles stories need no longer be seen as embarrassments, but rather pointers to how they viewed the physical world, their questions of time and space, and their theology of the interaction of the deity and nature, and the place of the believer within history. To recognize that the past is foreign country initially makes one feel uneasy—here I am a stranger in a different place—but it also makes one more aware: one starts to notice things that people who are familiar with a place never see.

It is a starting point of most modern studies of the early church that, while there is a legacy and chain of continuity between then and now, the historian's task is to see what the early church believed about themselves, their society, the world around them, the deity, and the bonds between all of these. This is producing a very different style of history that asks new questions and sees older debates—for instance, that favourite old chestnut about what sort of ministers, and their powers, were appointed by Jesus—as simply irrelevant to the scene in the early church. However, if this has been a theme in most books written in recent decades, this does not mean that it is a prevalent view. On the whole, Christian clergy continue to propagate the older view in sermons and popular presentations that their group and the first Christians share virtually an identical worldview. Indeed, when faced with the foreignness of the past many believers find the experience uncomfortable, but this disturbance may at least alert them to the fact that they are not the centre of the universe.

b. *The Search for Context*
That we should always try to situate a set of beliefs in the context of the group that hold them, and that in turn we should set that group within its historical context, might seem little more than common sense. However, until quite recently there was tendency to treat the evolution of religious ideas apart from their social context. It was felt that, if religious topics were examined using the methodologies of social history, it would constitute a reduction of those ideas to being consequences of their contexts. As recently as the 1970s, the Portuguese scholar Fernando Belo caused a controversy with a book entitled *A Materialist Reading of the Gospel of Mark*,[23] which sought to examine Mark, and so the early church in which it was written, in terms of its economic, social and cultural circumstances. The term 'materialist' is here contrasted with 'idealist' and argues that one should look at the early church and its doctrines as closely related to the material conditions in which those Christians lived and believed. This movement has led to a major re-evaluation of writings that have come down to us, and has revealed details of the lives of ordinary Christians in a manner parallel to the way archaeology has opened up their lives to our gaze through the excavation of ordinary houses. This approach to the past is part of a much wider movement in historical studies in general, and is often referred to as 'social-scientific criticism' when it is used

23. *Lecture matérialist de l'évangile de Marc: Récit pratique–idéologie* (Paris: Cerf, 1974) (ET New York: Orbis Books, 1981).

for the early church, as if it were simply a movement within the exegesis of texts.[24]

This increased sensitivity to the social factors that affect religion has shown that there was not one 'early church' as a social unit, but many. While those early Christians had a very strong sense that to join them was to join a 'people' and was not the same as becoming followers of a philosophical message; what it meant to be that people varied greatly depending on the cultural situation in which those Christians were located. So we see some groups who had the mentality of a people under siege, others who thought that time was about to end, while among others there were disputes about wealth, administration and the nature of Christianity as a system of ideas.[25] It was this variety of social contexts that, in part, gave rise to the variety of concerns, beliefs, and arguments we see represented in early Christian documents.[26]

c. *There Are No 'Raw Facts'*

At the beginning of the twentieth century, the great historian Lord Acton dreamed of a time when all historical facts would be recorded accurately in such a way that the interests and perspectives of historians would be invisible: it would be a record of facts such as one would get if, at the time of the events, one looked down on the scene from a great height with a camcorder. Such views as Acton's did lead to a recognition of how easy is it for the historian to be biased, and highlighted the tendency for history to be 'our' narrative (e.g. it is 'dark period' when 'we were persecuted' or it is 'progress' when 'we had a success')—and this afflicted historians of the early church since there was such a religious commitment to the notion that one belonged to 'the apostolic church'. The 'scientific' approach also led to a greater emphasis on history as a scholarly profession for which one needed

24. J. Elliott, *Social-Scientific Criticism of the New Testament: An Introduction* (London: SPCK, 1995).

25. A good example of this would be G. Theissen, *Essays on Corinth: The Social Setting of Pauline Christianity* (Edinburgh: T. & T. Clark, 1982).

26. The rise of this methodology—and it is still fiercely resisted in many quarters—sounded the death knell for the myth of the early church as 'the golden age of Christian perfection', for long after that theme disappeared from the surface arguments in books, it still appeared in the form of a longing on the parts of authors to show all the richness of this period by means of an unspoken comparison with later, duller, times.

proper training and which must be approached with methodological rigour, and for this we can all be grateful. However, the weakness of Acton's love of 'facts' was that it ignored the manner in which humans know, observe, learn and remember—it was a wonderful dream of detachment, but not one that took account of human nature. We know, after a century dominated by mass propaganda, that there is no 'neutral observer': even when the camcorder is running, it must have something in its focus, and that means it is always selective![27]

In terms of the early church this has meant that the desire for 'a grand narrative' (where what is intended is more than a convenient summary for students) has been replaced with many different histories, each approaching the evidence from a distinct perspective. So we have studies of the traditional areas of interest, such as liturgy and community organization in the early church, but also studies of areas that were formerly ignored, such as early Christian attitudes to women, the place of women in their church structures and attitudes to slavery. Moreover, many historians would hold that one must approach ancient sources with a 'hermeneutic of suspicion' whereby one asks who was intended to be the beneficiary, in practical terms of power and influence, of a particular text, practice or statement: once one knows this one realizes that one does not have 'facts' but the bias of that original group of Christians, and one can ask who were they ignoring and at whose expense were they gaining their power.

4. *History and Scripture Studies*

Libraries, academic departments and curricula still make a distinction between 'New Testament studies' and 'early church history'. In this they reflect the position of the disciplines at the beginning of the twentieth century, rather than at its close. Within this view, Scripture is an elevated study dealing with the revealed Word of God, while history is a worldly concern that only deals with incidental matters, such as whether or not the organization was administered by bishops. In fact, as it was actually practised, the church historians only interested themselves in the period after that of the composition of the New Testament, and most would have been happy with the notion that all its

27. For a critique of Acton's views of the relationship between the historian and the 'facts', see E.H. Carr, *What Is History?* (repr.; Harmondsworth: Penguin Books, 1964).

documents were written (by divinely inspired authors who were preserved from error by a special grace) by the last quarter of the first
century.

The massive shift that has come over New Testament studies, and
studies of Jesus in particular, has had one unforeseen result: the New
Testament exegete has, in many ways, become indistinguishable from
the early church historian. The Gospels, and all the other writings, are
the products of the community, the church and its life and concerns,
and so to study the meanings of these texts is to study that community.
While those in quest of the historical Jesus might express their frus-
tration that they could not get back 'behind the time of composition'
and 'the concerns of the early church', there was no regret whatsoever
for those who were historians of that church: they had been given a
larger addition to their corpus of evidence for the history of the early
church—the whole of the New Testament—than that provided in all
the discoveries put together.

There is still the tension between those who see the focus of their
work as the text—and understanding the text—and those whose focus
is on the community the text reveals, but that tension is found everywhere in pre-modern historical studies, and the study of the New
Testament and the early history of the church are, in essence, one. This
transition has not been a smooth one. There have been reactions to the
process that aimed to save either a biography of Jesus or the sacrality
of the texts that make up the New Testament as 'revealed' documents,
but they have been in vain. Once the exegetes abandoned their perspective on Scripture as a sacred written revelation, they were destined to
become historians, while for the historians those same writings were
always (at least) human documents that could be tackled using their
techniques, except their labours were no longer looked down upon by
'exegetes' as peripheral.

5. *History and Doctrine*

The possible overlaps between the work of the Christian Scripture
scholar and the historian are plain to see: both deal with the products of
the first two centuries of the Common Era. The relationship between
the history of the early church and systematic theology is far less visible, but arguably it has exercised until recently an even greater influence on historians.

a. *History as Doctrine*

Variants on the theme 'history is morality teaching by example' have been part of western rhetoric for centuries, but it has also had a more refined form for many theologians: if one could really get a grip on the history of the early church, then one would be able to solve present-day doctrinal disputes definitively. The underlying idea was that the history of the early church was theology in the form of praxis. The resulting history read not so much as an account of human beings as a lesson in theology with named character parts. There was also a more developed form of this supposed direct link between sanctity, orthodoxy, and the early church: the evidence was viewed not in terms of what it might tell us of the beliefs of the first or second centuries CE, but as the anticipation of the positions of Aquinas, Luther or Calvin. Moreover, any statement from the early period that conflicted with later orthodox-ies was either ignored or seen as irrelevant to the larger scheme. This was not a case of dishonest obfuscation, but an attitude based on the religious/doctrinal conviction that such variations must have been aberrations—which would be justly ignored—for their beliefs were vouched for by the Spirit who protected the apostolic faith. Orthodoxy was an embracing unity that did not admit of exceptions, and this meant that many scholars automatically assumed they knew the opinion (note, not 'the opinions') of the early church before they ever looked at the extent of the evidence.

Shifts during the last century in how the theological enterprise is perceived have therefore freed historians from the need to rescue every detail from the suspicion of heresy, and allowed for a history that notes the trails that eventually disappeared, as well as those that became dominant within the church. In turn, there has been a slow recognition that theological frameworks are themselves historical realities shifting with time. This has meant a reversal of roles within the academy. In an earlier time the doctrinal agenda was often set for the historian by the systematician who claimed a more lofty vantage point towards truth than that enjoyed by the student of shifting human realities. However, once it is recognized by the theologian that his or her formulae are shaped within the historical processes of the church, then to continue using those formulations requires the theologian to listen to the his-torian who can unlock their meanings and establish their context. So historians of the early church may be as embroiled in doctrinal controversy as ever; but today they act as a source for theologians rather than as systematicians' puppets.

b. *History as Apologetic*

One specific use of the history of the early church was in inter-denominational apologetics. Here the whole focus of the investigation was not on what happened 'back then', but on 'a proof from antiquity' that one's denomination was the one in line with the apostles. So there were studies of infant baptism in the early church, or the absence of it; studies of the authority of Peter, or the lack of it; studies of attitudes to sin and forgiveness; and the list can be multiplied. Here we are not dealing with shifts in historical interest—it is a phenomenon in the study of history that some area generates great interest for years, and then almost overnight the topic evaporates from the field of interesting questions—but of denominations wishing to use history as their title deeds.

While the more crass forms of doctrine dictating to historians the shape of the story have, on the whole, disappeared, the more subtle influence of denominational interests highlighting areas of special concern is still a factor to be reckoned with. To an extent this is inevitable: very few historians engage with questions about the past that are without interest for them in the present, and if a historian is engaging as either a human being or a Christian with a question in the present, then it seems natural that that should identify areas for his or her historical research. Scholarship is a human endeavour; and the notion of a view of the past that is without a stamp of a living person who hold views and opinions is part of the illusion of detachment pursued by Acton. However, to hold that historical precedents can solve doctrinal questions for today is to take a theological position—and that action is distinct from the activity of being an historian.

6. *Extending the Canvas*

So far I have tried to show how history has been affected by (1) discovery and (2) shifts in historical consciousness, but this leaves out of account the more gradual change that occurs in every discipline just as a result of more and more work.[28] However, to attempt a list of such

28. In recent years many historians, myself included, have used the notion of

changes would be impossible, but this example may indicate the sorts of changes that have taken place.

Until after the Second World War, most history of the early church worked with a map of the area of the early church that focused for the first decade or so on Palestine, then the scene shifted to Asia Minor and the cities of Greece visited by Paul, then by the early second century the interest had shifted firmly to the west and the focus was on the centre of the empire: Rome, with a few outliers, such as Alexandria, Antioch and, later, Constantinople. The area of the early church was, in effect, the areas that were perceived as the background to the modern western denominations. You can verify this interest by looking at the areas covered by the maps placed in church history books or even at the backs of Bibles. You will not see detailed maps of the eastward spread of Christianity into Syria and beyond the Tigris and Euphrates, nor south along the Nile into Ethiopia, nor later northwards into places like Armenia or among the Goths.

Today, there is a greater realization that Christianity from the beginning took on a variety of expressions and spread not just around the Mediterranean, but also to places that are not part of the western memory. In a way this shift in focus is symptomatic of the changes that have come across the whole of the discipline: we are learning that we cannot make ourselves the centre of the universe and make the past in our image.

'paradigm shifts' as developed by T.S. Kuhn, *The Structure of Scientific Revolutions* (Chicago: University of Chicago Press, 2nd edn, 1970) to mark off significant periods in the history of ideas. However, a paradigm can shift without a discernible 'eureka' moment: more and more work is done—the practitioners still imagining that they are engaged on the task laid out long before, but the cumulative effect is greater than the sum of the parts, and eventually the new *Gestalt* is intellectually a new world, and a paradigm shift, in Kuhn's terms, has occured. The abandonment of the notions of inerrancy, literal inspiration and direct inspiration in favour of a notion of documents reflecting a tradition of belief within a community is, to me, an example of such a paradigm shift without a dramatic realization that the older frames of reference could no longer contain the evidence.

GREEK RELIGION IN THE ROMAN EMPIRE:
DIVERSITIES, CONVERGENCES, UNCERTAINTIES

Graham Anderson

The term 'Greek religion' is at any period in classical antiquity an uncomfortably wide one;[1] for the period of the Roman Empire we can only hope to understand the immense variety of religious experience, geographically, socially and culturally within the Greek-speaking half of the empire in the first four centuries CE, and pick out some points of convergence that appear on closer examination. I shall also emphasize the difficulty of generalizing with any certainty about the experience of later antique paganism[2] or the reasons for its decline. I have not hesitated to press into service some literary narrative sources where possible, even where the latter are fictional or fictionalized: in the study of religious activity it is of great importance to see any religious action through to the end rather than catch a glimpse of part of it at random, as is so frustratingly often the case where we rely on epigraphic or papyrus evidence alone.

I begin with an arresting example: the gods themselves are debating the problem of illegal immigrants to their ranks; ambrosia and nectar are in limited supply and there are now many more mouths to feed, as foreign deities rub shoulders with the traditional Olympians, and Fate and Chance can be objects of worship, as indeed can the stars themselves. Under pressure Zeus proposes countermeasures, including the

1.   For an overview of the whole subject, Burkert (1985); and most recently Kearns (1995). Reports on the materials for paganism in the early empire alone occupy a daunting space in *ANRW*, II, 16-18. Many studies entitled 'Greek Religion' tend to deal principally with the Greek mainland, or with Athens before Alexander: for the latter Mikalson (1983); Parker (1995).

2.   For a healthy scepticism on the limitations of our evidence and the dangers of generalization, Macmullen (1981: esp. 62-73).

registration of new deities in the future (we know that he will somehow never get round to carrying it out):

> Since many of the strangers, not only Greeks but barbarians also, being in no wise worthy to share in our polity, but having falsely registered by some means and masquerading as gods have filled heaven so that our drinking-parties are full of a riotous rabble of many tongues and a motley crew... Be it resolved...that in the case of all those who have been considered worthy of temples or sacrifices, their statues be torn down and there be substituted those of Zeus or Hera or Apollo or some other (legitimate) god (Lucian, *Deorum Concilium* 14, 18).

This amusing sketch by Lucian from the latter half of the second century CE underlines in some respects the sense of multi-ethnic religious pluralism so characteristic of the age. The same kind of picture is presented from an entirely different viewpoint in Lucian's contemporary Maximus of Tyre.[3] Everyone has a different view of god:

> The Celts worship Zeus, but their image of him is a tall oak-tree. The Paeonians worship the Sun, but the Paeonian image of it is a tiny disk on top of a long pole. The Arabs worship a god, but which one I do not know; I have seen their image, a square stone. The Paphians worship Aphrodite; but their image of her you would compare most accurately to a white pyramid of an unknown substance. To the Lycians their mount Olympus sends forth fire, not like the fire of Etna, but unthreatening and under control; and this fire serves both as their temple and image. The Phrygians around Celaenae honour two rivers, the Marsyas and the Meander... What a profusion, what a variety of images! (*Oration* 2.8, 9).

But Maximus goes on to accept a common understanding of the divine under such diverse manifestations, and already we have a perspective of convergence; Maximus is as ready as Herodotus had been to accept the integration or equivalence of Greek and foreign deities. He also has fashionable Platonizing sympathies, and his master alternates readily between *theos* and *theoi* in the description of the divine.

Both Lucian and Maximus are literary conservatives who all too often trade in stereotypes, but we can look at the diversity implied by both these pictures in practice. It will be useful to look at the levels of activity in a brief sample of urban populations, and contrast it with some of our pictures of rural religious belief and practice, before

---

3. For the character of this rarely used author, see now M.B. Trapp (1997: xiii-lv).

raising the question of intellectual approach to religion; though we shall have occasion to blur such categorizations in due course.

1. *The Cities*

The Roman Empire was still an agglomeration of city-states[4] of very diverse historical backgrounds, with Roman laissez-faire much in evidence in religious matters. The religious life of Ephesus in western Asia Minor offers a good example of intense local pride in a deity who might take responsibility for the life of the city itself. It is inevitable to begin with the celebrated New Testament vignette in Acts 19.23-41. The inroads made by Pauline missionary activity resulted in a riot of silversmiths dependent on the goddess for their livelihood: the urban population naturally supports them with a public demonstration in the theatre where 'Great is Diana of the Ephesians' is affirmed for around two hours on end. For the Acts author the point is of course the spectacular inroads of the missionary church; but for the more objective viewer it also illustrates the resilience of the cult and its identification with the economic and social health of the city. We should of course feel entitled to assume that no such demonstration would have occurred if the sudden intrusion of an exclusive new cult had not been perceived as a material threat to the local goddess or her servants. Like Lucian's traditional gods, the Ephesians are suspicious of interlopers.

As it was, tactful action defused the situation, and we hear nothing from secular historians about the incident. Much less well publicized is a more bizarre disturbance (to our eyes), when the quasi-Pythagorean sage Apollonius of Tyana denounced a beggar as the source of a plague at Ephesus at some indefinite date in the same century (Philostratus, *Life of Apollonius* 4.10-11). The sage invited the mob to stone his opponent, which they did, at the foot of a statue of Heracles *alexikakos* (warder-off of ills).[5]

Against both these instances of disturbance (in both cases occasioned by outsiders), we can set two instances of civic harmony and concord. We have an immense inscription of the year 104 CE detailing the benefaction of Gaius Vibius Salutaris for the city of Ephesus: it set

---

4. For the nature of religion in the *polis* during the classical period itself, Sourvinou-Inwood (1990: 295-322). A slightly more flexible formulation is needed during the current period.

5. For possible explanations, Anderson (1994: 105-106).

up a pageant commemorating the birth of Artemis herself and other foundation legends relating to the city, and would have set out to use the power of the past as an affirmation of the self-confident (and un-Roman) identity of the present—and of course the status of the benefactor himself.[6] And the festival habit within such a community had an evidently increasing appeal: further epigraphic evidence from the second century shows the extension of a festival period of the goddess for the whole of the month Artemision.[7]

Nor need we confine our attention to purely official manifestations of public religious activity. We do as it happens have a romantic novel, the *Ephesiaca* of Xenophon of Ephesus, in which two teenage lovers have their first romantic encounter through the festival of Artemis, with indeed the girl Anthia herself got up in the guise of the goddess: as the course of the novel unfolds Artemis plays her part in the protection of the couple's chastity against the traditional threats. Of course there would have been few means of access to the sight of nubile aristocratic women outside such a context: but that only underlines how readily the goddess will be credited for her services.

We might be tempted to step back and ask what such a random collection of disparate evidence can tell us about religious life in one place in one era. It leaves unanswered such questions as the following: Did the silversmiths manipulate religious fears for their own ends? Was the Salutaris endowment merely an excuse for the personal aggrandizement of Salutaris? Did Xenophon merely use the festival as a clumsy way to get the lovers' eyes to meet? These sorts of questions are a reminder of the limitations of our evidence; but set in a larger framework of similar experience elsewhere, and indeed of the physical remains of the public buildings of Ephesus itself, the city and its cult provide a strong sense of the gods alive and well and living in Ephesus, and with supporters capable of strong reaction.

The religious activities of Ephesus can be readily set against those of Athens during the same period: again we can pinpoint another evidently unsuccessful encounter of Paul at the Areopagus in Acts 17.22-34 and a general refusal to allow his identification of an altar probably

---

6. For detailed interpretation, Rogers (1991).

7. L. Vidman (ed.), *Sylloge inscriptionum religionis Isiacae et Serapiacae* (Berlin: W. de Gruyter, 1969), no. 867.

dedicated to a plurality of unknown gods with an altar to Yahweh.[8] The Acts author himself observes the religious fervour of the Athenians: the whole implication of the story is that be that as it may, the Athenians were not indiscriminately enthusiastic, for reasons which are not hard to guess: the cultural ethos of Athens did not readily accommodate itself overnight to the sudden claims of an unknown tentmaker from Tarsus. And we have a very vivid picture from Pausanias in the next century of the richness of the local heritage of divinity, particularly after the sympathetic support of the philhellene Emperor Hadrian.[9] We can also match the pomp of Salutaris' benefaction with a vivid picture in the Athenian Philostratus of the benefactions by the local magnate Herodes Atticus in the annual festival of renewing the *peplos* to the goddess Athena.[10]

Here too we have religious-related controversy, when the enemies of this same Herodes are able to trigger an intervention by that redoubtable magnate's close friend, the emperor Marcus Aurelius in person, over the religious politics of sacred offices in the city and breaches in their traditional rules of allocation. We are unable on present evidence to sort out the full ramifications of the quarrel; but we are not entitled to dismiss it as 'pure politics': we are dealing with a society small enough for it to matter whose son performed the traditional office of Sacred Herald that had been in their family for generations.[11]

2. Religion in the Countryside

We might multiply such examples from cities large and small all over the eastern half of the empire. Outside their walls, however, lesser deities could go about their business of regulating human life untainted by the passions of personal politics. Perhaps our most telling glimpse of popular religion in a continuous narrative context is to be gleaned from a text that is actually fictitious, but which shows a thorough understanding of how deities and their devotees were expected to behave.

8. Detailed commentary in Haenchen (ET of the 14th German edn; Oxford: Basil Blackwell, 1971) on vv. 16-34, pp. 515-31.

9. On Pausanias's presentation, Habicht (1985); Arafat (1996); on trees and groves, Birge (1994: 231-45).

10. Philostratus, *Lives of the Sophists* 550.

11. The evidence is based on *EM* 13366 from the Roman Market-Place: see J.H. Oliver (1970).

In Longus's novel from the late second or early third century CE the foundlings Daphnis and Chloe are sustained by the nymphs whose local rustic cult they maintain: in return the nymphs regulate the essential aspects of their lives, along with Pan and Eros. If the whole picture of peasant life in Lesbos is idealized, the mechanics of village life and religion has still to be at least plausibly authentic. Accordingly we find that the nymphs protect the two foundling children in return for the simple piety of honouring their shrine with garlands and pipes; Pan is on call (at the advice of the nymphs) in the case of a kidnapping from the neighbouring town of Methymna; and the nymphs even tip off the penniless bridegroom as to where he can find a substantial dowry. They do not teach him the facts of life, which he has been unable to acquire; but the predatory older woman who instructs him, partly for her own pleasure, is careful to introduce herself as having been sent by them. They still regulate human life, by a combination of intervention and reputed intervention. Much of Longus has been regarded as a mannered imitation of no less mannered pastoral poetry of an already bygone age: but the religious dynamics of the piece are not in any sense out of date. On the basis of services rendered to Daphnis and Chloe (and their elderly mentor Philetas before them) Eros in return receives an altar to Eros *Poimen*: Daphnis has found his own good shepherd.[12]

The picture can again be extended in a totally different area from coastal Lesbos: in central Asia Minor a profusion of gods great and small, and looking at least partly Hellenic, obviously serve peasant votaries through cults shared perhaps by several villages at a time; indeed the local gods may themselves be 'the law' (sometimes even with such titles as Dikaiosyne or Hosion and Dikaion ('Justice'; 'Holy and Just'), which proclaim the fact; and which emphasize that local divine justice is less complicated than that involving distant officials.[13]

In the countryside as well as the town we must expect innovation as well as continuity. We have a relatively little-known testimony emanating from Herodes Atticus about his encounter with a rustic child of nature in the Athenian hinterland who comes to be regarded as a Heracles or Marathon-style hero to whom offerings may be made (and who detects impure ones by means of his supernatural powers). The oddity

12. On degrees of religious initiation in Longus, Chalk (1960) remains the most plausible presentation: Merkelbach's revised position (1988) still seems to overstate the case for mystery elements.

13. See now Mitchell (1993: I.11.V, II.16.II).

about this second-century Robin Goodfellow is that Lucian wrote favourably about him as well, on his own admission: rare praise indeed from so iconoclastic an observer of religious matters.[14] The existence of such a character may help us to solve a strange curiosity of long standing: the odd passage in Plutarch where a report is passed on of the alleged announcement of the death of Pan[15]. This is advanced by Plutarch as evidence that demigods are really long-lived but not immortal *daimones*. If such a figure as the Boeotian Heracles reported by Herodes and Lucian could be accorded some kind of divine status and then actually die, then so could some slightly earlier counterpart.

Plutarch's Pan had to be mourned in the vicinity of the island of Paxi; it is often crucial to emphasize the relationship between locality and cult. We can now learn a great deal from so apparently incidental an aspect as the study of sacred trees:[16] On the evidence of Pausanias, 'single landmark trees and groups of trees at hero shrines maintain a stronger connection with the distant, intangible past than with the contemporary cities' visible territory, in which they grow' (while the temple *alsos* is felt as part of the present). We might confirm their role from a famous tale in Dio Chrysostom's first oration: when the wandering Dio gives an account of his meeting with a wise woman between Heraea and Pisa in the western Peloponnese, he finds her in the vicinity of 'a clump of oak-trees on high ground, like a sacred grove' (*Or.* 1.52-56). The literary instinct is to see this as a highly contrived imitation of the pastoral setting of Plato's *Phaedrus*,[17] where Socrates finds inspiration beside the plane-tree at the Ilissus; but it also emphasizes the sacred environment in which the wise woman will foretell Dio's current encounter with the emperor Trajan. The grove is sacred to Heracles, and the cue is given for an updated version of the 'Choice of Heracles' myth—a contemporary warning for princes now set in a deliberately numinous and timeless setting.

---

14. For this curiously neglected episode, Anderson (1994: 128-29). Herodes' report is paraphrased in Philostratus, *Lives of the Sophists* 552-54; for Lucian's view, *Vita Demonactis* 1, referring to a lost *Sostratus*.

15. *Moralia* 419B: for convenient overview of religious themes in Plutarch, Russell (1972: 63-83); F. Brenk (1977).

16. D. Birge in Alcock and Osborne (1994: 231-45 [at 245]).

17. See now M.B. Trapp in Russell (1990: 141-44).

3. *Greek and Barbarian*

The Greek world in the larger sense bore witness to a multitude of deities and cults from a variety of cultures: it has been a great service of Fergus Millar's *The Roman Near East* (1993: 229-532 *passim*) to draw attention to the cultural mix that takes place all over the Greek East under Roman administration throughout the period of the pre-Constantinian empire. We are able, for example, to puzzle over the foot of an alleged Zeus of Heliopolis apparently also presented as a deity of Mt Carmel by one G. Ioul(ios) Eutychas of the colonia of Caesarea; the foot was found on Carmel itself, when we should normally regard the site like Hermon as a Semitic High Place that would attract worship but without a cult-image.[18] Or we should ask what religious amalgam would have been expressed at the Actia Dusaria of the colonia metropolis of the Bostreni, before the advent of a Christian bishop. Dusares himself was a Nabatean deity (Millar 1993: 399-400), whose festival was some-how expressed by Graeco-Roman games. If we move north, there are similar opportunities for cultural and religious diversity in Anatolia in central Asia Minor, where the no less magisterial survey by Stephen Mitchell emphasizes the difficulty of classifying cults (Mitchell 1993: II, 19). It also makes a key contribution in seeing crucial religious change in an area where cults are particularly subject to limiting environmental factors: where, in other words, sheer physical isolation could preserve local differences for longer. But the case of Anatolia also emphasizes time and again one factor that does render pagan cults uniquely vulnerable: their sheer receptivity, through which the inhabitants of Lystra in Acts are all too ready to take Paul and Barnabas for Hermes and Zeus respectively.[19]

The new religious development of the imperial cult operates from Augustus onwards both east and west, in the first instance as a focus of loyalty to the emperor's already deceased and deified family, and less directly to the emperor himself, except in the cases where he allows himself to be felt as a living deity. But it is an easy matter to add the cult to the kind of blend we have just noticed. We might note the letter

---

18. Millar (1993: 269-70), with his comment: 'Once again it is futile to ask what an ancient deity "really was": for he was whatever his worshipper said he was.'

19. For discussion, see Lane Fox (1986: 99-100).

of the hierophant Marcus Aurelius Apollonius to the canephor at Neis-memis: the latter is asked to sacrifice for our lords the emperors and their victory, for the rise of the Nile and increase of crops, and for favourable conditions of climate, and to do this in the temple of Demeter.[20] The users, or as we might say, the consumers of religion may be much less sensitive to religious distinctions than we take for granted; any available combination of religious forces will do, so long as it works.

Such syncretizing situations must eventually have contributed to the monotheizing tendencies of the later empire. We do not actually find Jesus Christ saying 'I am Hermes and Apollo', or the Virgin Mary claiming to be Artemis and Aphrodite; but the pagan vision of Constantine preceding by two years the victory at the Milvian bridge could indeed suggest just such an equation: well might Constantine feel the need to pray to the god who sent him a vision before the battle to identify who he actually was.[21]

4. *Dreams, Magic, Oracles*

The identity of gods apart, established means or supposed means of discerning divine will or motivating divine intervention have to be related to cults of any kind, Christian or pagan. Dreams and oracles in particular are essential engines of religious cults in antiquity. It is through dreams in particular, whether spontaneous or induced, that any individual can be felt to be seeing his god(s); and through oracles that he can gain access to their public pronouncements. Throughout later antiquity it is increasingly difficult to distinguish between pagan and Christian forms of perception. Both might experience dreams and visions; a pagan magician may claim a magic that can coerce the gods, whereas a Christian miracle-worker might be convinced of the efficacy of prayer. The contrary claims over the Rain Miracle under Marcus Aurelius illustrate diversity and convergence alike.

We have as it happens for the second century CE a particularly rich haul of dreams and dreamers. We have Aelius Aristides' self-portrait through his dreams in the later second century; and an almost exactly contemporary view from the perspective of a professional peddler of

20. The implications of proxy prayers of this kind have still to be assessed. Do they point to a quasi-magical view of the efficacy of prayer?

21. Eusebius, *Vita Constantini* 1.28.1.

dream interpretations, Artemidorus of Daldis. The two collections complement each other: Aristides' dreams and visions are those of a satisfied customer, convinced of the loyalty of Asclepius to his own physical well-being and career fulfilment; while Artemidorus has his own
arbitrary system, which, though claimed to be tested against actual
cases, is patently mechanistic, but has sufficiently flexible parameters
to enable him to serve the interests of clients of comparable eminence
to Aristides himself.[22] The prestige of oracles in the first three centuries
CE rises upwards: one notes the celebrated inventory of Oxyrynchus
questions as symptoms of anxiety:[23] such questions would in due course
be easy to Christianize, as suggested by sixth-century Christian papyri.
And the *Sortes Astrampsychi*, with a second-century basis that can be
reconstructed from a later version, offers a sense of lottery gaming to
numbered lists of basic concerns, and duly attracted Christian inter-
polation.[24] The function of oracles has been well explored as an instru-
ment of social regulation and control:[25] it is certainly very clear from
Lucian's picture of the late second-century oracle-monger Alexander at
Abonouteichos.[26] His oracle could point the finger at offenders or find
lost property; it could glorify itself to its fellow-oracles, or it could
point the finger of blame at others. And its oracle-giving god Glycon is
related to the success of his entrepreneurial priest and mystagogue
Alexander. The fact that most (but not all) of our information comes
from the bitterly hostile Lucian[27] only serves to underline the profusion
of finely observed detail in his portrait, and the plausibility of his
insight. Above all it shows the ability of an obscure local cult at an
inaccessible site on the north coast of Pontus to gain rapid international
significance. Nor would the case of Alexander have been entirely
isolated; what is unique is simply the level of documentation. But what
can a phenomenon like this prove for paganism in general? Are we
entitled to postulate the idea of decadent paganism finding room for a
petty criminal charlatan as a symptom of decline, or of health and
vitality? The speed and success of the cult, as of Manichaeism in the

22. For dreams in later antiquity, Miller (1994) (on Artemidorus, 77-91).
23. E.g. *P. Oxy.* 1477 (among much).
24. See now W. Hansen (1998: 285-324).
25. Cf. Evans-Pritchard's still classic study (1976).
26. For detailed study, see still the commentary by Caster (1938); L. Robert
(1980); Jones (1986: 133-48).
27. For the bibliography, n. 31 below.

next century,[28] should tell us something about the rapid adaptability of pluralist religion.

Moreover the needs catered for by Alexander can be demonstrated from sub-literary materials widely spread through the empire at large. One conveniently contemporary example will suffice from Lydia, dating from the end of the fifties of the second century CE. The complex circumstances have to be discerned from the tablet itself:

> Because Ioukoundos fell into a condition of insanity and it was noised abroad by all that he had been put under a spell by his mother-in-law Tatia, she set a up a scepter and placed curses in the temple in order to defend herself against what was being said about her, having suffered such a state of conscience. The gods sent punishment on her which she did not escape. Likewise also her son Socrates was passing the entrance that leads down to the sacred grove and carrying a vine-dressing sickle and it dropped on his foot and thus destruction came upon him in a single day's punishment. Therefore great are the gods of Axiottenos (Gager 1992: no. 137, editor's translation).

(The inscription goes on to record that the family of Iucundus and Tatia now worship the powerful gods who had been able to override Tatia's precautions against them). Here we have a succinct illustration of the kind of forces that could keep pagan cults going at a level of cultic magic, and exercise a hold on a local population. The situation implies no level of education, though it does presuppose the level of wealth to enable other members of the ill-fated family to afford the inscription in the first place. The gods have apparently been involved in what we should call 'a domestic'. Mental illness, rumours generated by family tensions, extreme countermeasures involving the gods through magic, and family misfortune, have all been inevitably linked together in a nexus of belief. Alexander the oracle-monger could have done a roaring trade in precisely such situations as this. However we disentangle the individual details, the inscription shows clearly enough that mental illness and accident alike are attributable by a community to impiety, compounded no doubt by recourse to magic.

5. *Intellectual Religion*

Not only can we attempt to make rudimentary distinctions between city and countryside, but we can also attempt to make a distinction between

28. On which see Brown (1969); Lieu (1985).

upper-class intellectuals and the rest of mankind. Concern for religious matters, personal religion and piety are inevitably to be seen through the rich documentation in the literary sources, however distorting that might be. Plutarch of Chaeronea in particular offers a wealth of information about intellectual perception of the gods through a conservative, traditionalist prism; as well as raising a whole host of matters of minutely antiquarian interest, he continues a Hellenistic effort to give demonology an intellectual basis: Middle Platonism saw demons as superhuman forces, as intermediate between gods and men, to the point of their actually managing the day-to-day business of oracles on the god's behalf; and such issues as the slowness of divine punishment could accordingly be given a convenient explanation. But sometimes philosophical and religious enquiry are ill-matched, as when the Platonist Plutarch reels off explanation after explanation for the mysterious symbol E at Delphi. I am less sure than some that Plutarch took these explanations lightly:[29] the (to us) nonsensical idea that the letter symbolized five philosophic first principles is in uncomfortable harmony with the Christian Irenaeus's 'demonstration' late in the second century that there are four Gospels because there are four winds, and other fantasies of the kind.[30] We have a useful means of contrast within intellectual circles if we contrast Plutarch's presentation of Isis and Osiris with that of the devotee Apuleius in *The Golden Ass*: both authors have strong Platonist connexions, and Plutarch's piously Platonizing erudition shows through, whether he is dismissing the tales of Osiris and his enemy Typhon as equivalent to Middle Platonic *daimones*, or simply enumerating the ingredients for the *kuphi* burned as incense.[31] But amid the precise details of the cult of Isis Apuleius betrays his carnavalesque perception of its processions and his satisfaction with how Osiris has advanced his own career.[32]

It is also useful to outline the diversity of outlook of some educated

---

29. Despite Russell (1972: 64): 'There have been ages in which this kind of interpretation of a religious symbol would have been taken in earnest; but it can hardly be so with Plutarch.' It is difficult to place Plutarch and Irenaeus in different ages, and allegorism is a recurrent intellectual disease throughout Graeco-Roman antiquity and well beyond.

30. Irenaeus 3.11.11.

31. Plutarch, *Moralia* 360D-F; 383E–384C.

32. Apuleius, *Metamorphoses* 11.8, 28.

men contemporary with Apuleius, who write very differently about the religious phenomenology of the later second century: throughout the *Meditations* the emperor Marcus Aurelius is tastefully cautious and restrained, whether the topic is healing dreams, *deisidaimonia* or magic.[33] Aelius Aristides might be advanced as an almost opposite case: as often as Marcus is self-effacing, this tendentious sophist is living in a fantasy world of self-advertisement, in which dream, miracle or theurgy alike explain a very profitable partnership with Asclepius:

> And so when we arrived at Smyrna, (the god) appeared to me in some such form as this: he was at the same time Asclepius and Apollo, both the Apollo of Claros and the Apollo known in Pergamum as Kallitechnos, to whom the first of the three temples is dedicated. He stood before my bed in this form, and when he had extended his fingers and calculated times, he said, 'You have ten years from me and three from Sarapis', and as he spoke the three and the ten appeared by the position of his fingers as seventeen. This he said was not a dream but a waking state, and that I too would know it. And at the same time he told me to go down to the river which flows in front of the city and bathe. He said that a young boy would lead the way, and he pointed out the boy... [Aristides duly fulfils the instruction, and so] there was an inexplicable sense of contentment, which made everything also less important than the present moment, so that even when I was seeing other things, I seemed not to see them. Thus was I wholly with the god (*Hieroi Logoi* 2 = *Or.* 48.18, 23).

So short a passage underlines a number of themes from late antique religious experience. The divine image that Aristides reports is ambiguous: one thinks again of Constantine's request for clarification in his crucial vision of the god subsequently interpreted as that of the Christians. It also suggests one of the most basic and obvious possibilities for syncretism: if one can dream that two gods share the same pedestal, it is a short step to allowing them to do so. The understandable interest in how long a life the gods have granted the subject is reminiscent of Trimalchio's proclamation that he has over 30 years to live on the authority of a travelling soothsayer (Petronius, *Satyrica* 77.2); the calculation confided by an itinerant fortune-teller is reminiscent of the scenario where the astrologer Regulus keeps a dying patient on tenterhooks with digital calculations (Pliny, *Ep.* 2.20). Hope and Fear, in

---

33. *Med.* 1.17.9; 1.16.3; 1.6. On the religious views of Marcus overall, Rutherford (1989: 178-220).

Lucian's perception, are writ large in Aristides' everyday actions in the service of Asclepius.[34]

As it happens, we can compare the intimate and unguarded tone of the *Hieroi Logoi* with a much more formal treatment of divine themes in Aristides' Prose Hymns.[35] Here there is ample opportunity to display the rhetorical resources and commonplaces of the professional rhetorician, but again calling and personal devotion are closely integrated, with Aristides' claim in four instances that the composition was commanded by a dream. One believes the claim of this sophist where one might suspect many another.[36] Moreover we have yet another perspective on this extraordinary, and extraordinarily unattractive figure: in the *Hieroi Logoi* we have almost the serialization of a saga of Aristides' quest for exemption from compulsory public service as a *rhetor*.[37] When dealing with this complex saga it is once again tempting to see the whole business as 'purely political'. And yet it is no less obvious that Aristides himself believes quite sincerely in the hand of the god Asclepius himself in the whole business: and unless we are prepared to deny the possibility that people do see forms in dreams that can be then or subsequently interpreted as gods, then it is really quite hard to see why Aristides should not have done so.

Again Lucian offers a useful contemporary gloss on people like Aristides, as in the setting of the last story in Lucian's *Philopseudeis*. The author sets out to make fun of the superstitious attitudes of the educated, who should know better. We might argue that this is inadmissible evidence, as the author is writing for purposes of sophisticated literary entertainment, and has a proven propensity to exaggerate, not without a backward look at Theophrastus's celebrated caricature of the *deisidaimon*. The value of his narrative is most clearly in the number of religious concerns that the narrator Eucrates subliminally combines:

> When I was spending time in Egypt in my student days—for my father had sent me there on an educational trip—I wanted to sail to Coptos and on to see the statue of Memnon to hear the famous marvel of its song to the rising sun. Now I did hear it, but not the way most people do, as

34. For the nature of the *Hieroi Logoi*, Festugière (1954: 85-104); Behr (1968).

35. For analysis, Russell (1990: 199-219).

36. Or to put it another way: 'in Aristides' heated mind vision and reality, inspiration and the pride of his skill were no doubt indissoluble' (Russell 1990: 200).

37. Cf. Bowersock (1968: 36-41).

some meaningless noise: instead Memnon himself actually opened his mouth and gave me an oracle in seven verses, and if it were not irrelevant to the story I would quote the very lines...and I refrain from mentioning that I have a certain holy ring with the image of Apollo engraved on the seal, and this Apollo speaks to me; I don't want you to think I'm only boasting. But I do want to tell you what I heard from Amphilochus in Mallus, when the hero spoke to me in my waking state and gave me advice about my personal affairs, and what I went on to see in Pergamum and what I heard in Patara... (*Philopseudeis* 33, 38).

Lucian has superbly caught the ethos of what we might call religious tourism, with the thrill of the, in this case evidently indiscriminate, believer. It would not be difficult to envision the fictitious narrator Eucrates as a victim for Artemidorus's dream interpretations; nor might we find a much different outlook on the part of the Christian Egeria 'doing the rounds' of exclusively biblical sights at the turn of the fourth/fifth centuries. This comparison is important to underline the level of education at which oracles might operate: any social class might gain access to them, and the well-to-do and those of limited horizons, the highly educated and the educationally very naïve, could share a common outlook. The sense of being chosen by any oracle delivered to one has for Eucrates almost the one-upmanship of receiving a letter from God.

The imperial cult offers a special case for the interpretation of intellectual reaction. In a highly original study of the cult's operations in Asia Minor, Simon Price (1984) has challenged the traditional view of its effect as purely political, and instead focuses on the overlap between the deification even of a living emperor and a sense of security and power. Price contends that it is a reflex of modern Christianizing opinion that forces us to assume that no thinking person could have taken seriously the idea of a living emperor as a living god. It is suggested that the few jokes to be gleaned from very careful satirists about ruler cult actually underline its importance.[38] The impact of the cult can certainly be reinforced at a literary level: Dio Chrysostom's first oration is at pains to stress the analogy between Trajan and Heracles; as the latter was a superhuman hero on earth before his transition from heroic to divine status, Trajan can be compared to him without

38. Price (1984: 115) (on the questionable authority of Freud's *Jokes and their Relation to the Unconscious*).

theological offence.[39] But the question may be one of wider scope: we might take account not only of the gibes of classical satire, but of the views of divine rulership expressed in the Near East away from the highroad of classical literature: the conclusions of the Sumero-Akkadian *Epic of Gilgamesh* and the *Alexander Romance* both underline the vulnerability of mortal kings to the foolishness of the search for or presumption of immortality. And there is always the anecdote preserved in Aelian that the Spartans passed a decree to the effect that Alexander the Great was a god on the grounds that that was how he wanted to be regarded.[40] The ironic undertone of the story is not to be missed, even for someone as naively pietistic as Aelian. Not only could intellectuals take divided attitudes, but popular attitudes to ruler cults in Near Eastern antiquity were not always favourable. But the problem serves to emphasize once more the difficulty of our penetrating beyond the immediate reactions of specific individuals.

In the case of the emperor Julian we have a belated opportunity to see an intellectual paganism under serious and unavoidable pressure from Christianity: by the mid-fourth century it is difficult to disentangle convergent monotheist tendency from the need to offer a competitive alternative to the faith of Constantinian emperors. Recent perspectives on Julian's religious mentality and its relationship to his anti-Christian policies have shown considerable variation.[41] Coherent views are necessarily circumscribed in some measure by the shortness of the reign and the hurry to put the clock back as fast as possible. Here we must be content to emphasize the instinctive conservatism of ethos: Julian is in pursuit of the good old days when the smell of sacrificial meat was a normal part of public religious experience; we should be reminded of the same sort of sentiments from the Younger Pliny when the balance between Christian and pagan had been very different. But the idea of taking a leaf out of the Christian book either in some pagan Church organization or in a search for monotheism is again part of pagan experience in general; it is part and parcel of a general willingness to change and reconstruct.

The ultimate example of convergence of intellectual and popular, Christian and pagan might be seen in an example of prophecy cited by

39. On the purpose of the speech, Jones (1978: 116-19).

40. Aelian, *Varia Historia* 2.19.

41. See, among much, Bowersock (1978: 79-93); Athanassiadi-Fowden (1981); and now Smith (1995).

Eunapius on the destruction of the Serapeum at Alexandria in 391. The historian gives a clumsy, pompous, and circuitous notice of a prophecy made by Antoninus, son of the philosopher Sosipatra:

> After crossing to Alexandria, (Antoninus) was then so lost in admiration for the Canopic mouth of the Nile that he devoted and attached himself to the gods there and their secret rites; he soon applied himself to affinity with the divine, despised the body, and renounced its pleasures; and he practised a wisdom unknown to the many…when he considered students worthy of an interview, some would put forward a logical problem, and were immediately generously fed with Platonic wisdom; but those who put forward questions more related to diviner matters encountered a statue. He would not utter a word to any of them, but he would fix his eyes and gaze at the sky; he would lie speechless and wrapt, nor did anyone see him lightly conversing with men on such weighty subjects.
>
> Not long afterwards there was a clear sign that there was some more divine quality about him. For he had no sooner departed from the world of men than the cult of the Alexandrian temples and the shrine of Sarapis was dispersed. (After they had destroyed the temples, the Christians) introduced into the sacred places the so-called monks, men in their outward appearance but like swine in their lifestyle, who openly endured and perpetrated countless unspeakable vices. And yet they considered this as an act of piety, to despise what was divine… For they collected the bones and skulls of men condemned for numerous crimes, punished by the cities' courts, and regarded them as gods, and thought themselves the better for defiling themselves at their sepulchres… This at any rate brought a great reputation for foresight to Antoninus, that he had foretold to everyone that the temples would be tombs (*Vitae Philosophorum* 471-73).

Eunapius's claims for Antoninus have an air of the tendentious about them. It is only too facile to predict that x or y will become an abomination of desolation, and either side can be prepared to claim disproportionate prestige for the fulfilment of any such claims. The text moreover once more stresses the importance of effecting ingenious transition from one orthodoxy to the next: although Eunapius might be the last to see it, there is an air of religious 'business as usual' once the transition has been made, and of new pieties for old. The text is illuminating for the polemical view of a pagan on the whole aspect of the monks and the threat to civilization they represented, a view easy to replicate from Libanius or Julian himself, but a view just as readily applied at any period of the empire by sectors of the establishment to Cynic philosophers. In any treatment of 'Greek religion' the relationship of 'the gods' to Hellenism itself has to be addressed. We might be tempted to see the Hellenism of the Roman Empire as rooted in a kind of élitist conservatism, whether of language or literature, or more generally of attitude and environment. This climate prompts as a matter of course the restoration of shrines and cults: one thinks of Hadrian's completion of the Athenian Olympieion some six and a half centuries after Peisistratus had begun the initial project; or of Apollonius of Tyana's reported communication with the ghost of Achilles at the Troad.[42] And such a climate even leads Lucian, when describing that most un-Hellenic shrine of Atargatis at Hierapolis, to do so in the Ionic Greek of Herodotus (*De Dea Syria*). And that same Hellenism is moreover central to the cultural psychology of the emperor Julian and his admirers.

6. *Some Aspects of Uncertainty*

We can see, then, how often one after another of our attempted categorizations is open to exception. The picture of upper-class rationalisms is cleverly undercut by Lucian's sketch in the *Philopseudeis* of upper-class *deisidaimonia* or the naivety of Aristides or Eunapius; and it is perhaps a little premature to claim that the lower classes have scarcely a voice in the surviving evidence when we have the evocation of Trimalchio's freedmen, with their stream-of-consciousness string of commonplace reflections on life and religion; or to draw distinctions between Greek and barbarian when we think of the wandering priests of Atargatis taking their Syrian goddess and their oracle through the countryside of the Greek mainland (Apuleius, *Metamorphoses* 8.27).

It is now two decades since Liebeschuetz was able to write a substantial treatment of 'Continuity and Change in Roman Religion' (1979). We might be tempted to ask why there has been no comparable treatment for Greek religion. The very diffuseness of the whole concept is partly to blame, but it is not perhaps the whole story. We are left with a number of interrelated questions: What makes conservatism and radical renewal vital one moment and sterile the next? One might offer a variety of answers: one of these might be 'the arrow which killed the emperor Julian', and so secured the consolidation of Constantine's Christianizing state.

E.R. Dodds's memorable title *Pagan and Christian in an Age of Anxiety* (1968) has supplied both an ethos and a challenge for the latter

---

42. Philostratus, *Lives of the Sophists* 533; *Life of Apollonius* 4.16.

half of our period: the divisions he makes, 'man and the material world', 'man and the daemonic world', 'man and the divine world', are not open to challenge, but the illustration of the categories is through the eyes of a scholar with Neo-Platonic tastes and sympathies. There are a great many more ways in which such a series of perspectives might be applied. We should find a subtly different picture of the same period if we were to replace 'man and the material world' with 'the god and the individual's private affairs'. And it is not difficult to invent others, not least 'the god and his *polis*'—to say nothing of 'the holy man between human and divine'. But the ultimate challenge to the scholar is to reconstruct the mental horizons of late antique individuals from any level of society for whom religious experience may have had the thrill of the totally uncharacterized. There could always be some new revelation, some new divine combination about to make the world fall into place.

By contrast Robin Lane Fox (1986) offers a mosaic of pagan experience not only rich but unusually sympathetic: oracles are genuinely seen as the gods speaking, dreams as seeing the gods. Where Dodds stressed Christian charity and community, Lane Fox stresses the impact of martyrdom in the final victory of Christianity. There is moreover no lack of consensus that much remained unchanged between paganism and Christianity; that the study of religious forces is part of the study of power in the operations of society. Dodd's own thesis, so far as it can be disentangled from his illustrations, seems to see a pagan failure of spiritual nerve in the increasing pressures of the third century, and an elitist mysticism too esoteric to compete. I am inclined to revert to the agnosticism of Macmullen (1981) in the face of too many unknowns, though with a feeling that empire-wide persecution proves a costly mistake for the imperial system; and where Constantine's overt change in material encouragement for Christianity did irreversible damage. If we put it another way: after the Milvian Bridge, the crops still grew, the festivals still took place, the cities survived: the pagan gods did not depose Constantine, while the Christians themselves took up the struggle against the maleficent among the demons. Uncommitted pagans could draw their conclusions accordingly.

More recent discussions have often underlined several tendencies: one is recognition of the anti-pagan Christian-inspired stereotype encountered in traditional accounts, in which paganism is seen to be in a terminal decline, maintaining meaningless rituals; the antidotes are often the insistence on some redefinition of the relationship between spiritual and material in ancient societies, and the search for some kind of power that will explain the place of religion in the social fabric. The first approach is not difficult to affirm on the basis of the kinds of example I have offered; the second is more elusive, though perhaps no less real on that account. It is very difficult, to my mind, either to define or locate the sources of religious power precisely, Christian or pagan. We could follow Justin Martyr or Augustine through a series of encounters and perspectives and still not find the kind of answers in which they prided themselves. Religious power may subsist in varying degrees in traditional religious ties, or in the impact of the activist who dares to break them; in the capacity of the local deity to look after the needs of the worshipping community over a long period, or in the smart answer of an oracle in time of crisis; it may be seen in the action of an emperor determined to maintain or subvert the status quo, or in the defiance of an opponent. It may be pointed out in a sense of well-being with the *pax deorum*, or a sense that one has been cured of a headache by Asclepius or by the relic of a martyr.

Rightly or wrongly, such figures as Lucian and Plutarch, from their very different perspectives, could each paint a picture of traditional religion in the doldrums;[43] it was very good at riding out such doldrums, but not in the face of positive and dynamic competition. It is worth recollecting the celebrated anti-Christian caricature of an itinerant eschatological preacher supplied by Celsus towards the end of the second century: the Platonist intellectual has nothing but contempt for what he sees as the sheer effrontery of the intermediary who proclaims the imminent end of the world and then demands worship (Origen, *Contra Celsum* 7.9): this is perhaps the religious equivalent of the doorstep insurance salesman, but it shows the attempt to answer anxiety, or to foment it for one's own religious ends—and that many decades before the material and political anarchy in which physical and social insecurities might multiply.

The insoluble question of motivation still hangs over the whole subject. Questions put to oracles might be said to reflect genuine concerns of specific individuals, but almost any other religious act may be

---

43. Especially *de Defectu Oraculorum*; Lucian, *Icaromenippus* 24; further references in Levin (1989).

felt as ambiguously motivated. Do people commit suicide out of religious *kenodoxia*? Is conversion political and public rather than personal and sincere? Are sacrifices acts of traditional cultural affirmation rather than simply feeding the god and the excuse for a good meal? In almost no cases can such obvious questions be answered.

I end as I began, with a council of the gods: the emperor Julian, looking back to the Lucian passage with which we began, has Roman emperors invited to a banquet of the gods:[44] At the end individual emperors are invited to adopt their tutelary deities, after it has been already determined that Marcus Aurelius has satisfied the gods as being first among emperors on all counts:

> After this announcement, Alexander ran to Heracles, Octavian to Apollo, but Marcus stuck closely to Zeus and Kronos. Mighty Ares took pity on Caesar, who kept wandering about and running around, and he and Aphrodite called him to them. Trajan ran over to Alexander and sat down with him. But Constantine, not finding among the gods the model for his own life, caught sight of Pleasure close by and ran to her. She gave him a tender welcome and wrapping him in multicoloured robes and dressing him up she led him to Incontinence, where Constantine found him in residence and calling to all: whoever is a rapist, a murderer, a sacrilegious villain, let him come with impunity!... But the avenging deities all the same punished both him and his sons for their impiety, and punished them for the murder of their own family, until Zeus gave them respite on account of Claudius and Constantius (*Caesares* 335D–336B).

We are at once reminded both of the end of Plato's myth of afterlife in *Republic* X, and its imitation in Plutarch's *de Sera Numinis Vindicta*, where Nero is the natural villain, though he too is granted respite for services to Hellenism. As it happens, Nero's persecution of the Christians escapes Plutarch's notice: now it is Christian persecution that is to be punished. What both pictures have in common is that they were overtaken by events; Lucian's picture by much more varied and vibrant pagan activity, Julian's by its failure.

---

44. On the historical aspects of the *Caesares*, Bowersock (1982: 159-72).

GNOSTICISM

Robert McL. Wilson

1. The traditional view 'from Irenaeus to Harnack'[1] saw in Gnosticism a rather bizarre and outlandish Christian heresy, resulting from a fusion of the Christian faith with Greek philosophy and combated by such early Fathers as Irenaeus, Hippolytus, Tertullian and Epiphanius. Over a century ago, Charles Bigg could write:

> There is a certain wild poetical force in Valentinus, but otherwise their world-philosophy is purely grotesque. The ordinary Christian controversialist felt that he had nothing to do but set out at unsparing length their tedious pedigrees, in the well-grounded confidence that no one would care to peruse them a second time.[2]

We should, however, note what follows a few lines later:

---

1. R.P. Casey, 'The Study of Gnosticism', *JTS* 36 (1935), pp. 45-60, quoting Harnack, *History of Dogma*, I (ET; London: Williams & Norgate, 1897), p. 226 ('the acute Hellenization of Christianity'). For a survey of the heresiological literature and the earlier history of research see K. Rudolph, *Die Gnosis* (Göttingen: Vandenhoeck & Ruprecht, 1990 [1977]), pp. 13-39 (ET *Gnosis* [Edinburgh: T. & T. Clark, 1983], pp. 9-34; with abundant literature). For bibliography see R.McL. Wilson, 'Gnosis/Gnostizismus II: Neues Testament, Judentum, Alte Kirche', *TRE* 13 (1985), pp. 535-50; D.M. Scholer, *Nag Hammadi Bibliography*. I. *1948–1969* (Leiden: E.J. Brill, 1971); II. *1970–1995* (Leiden: E.J. Brill, 1997) (updated annually in *Novum Testamentum*). K. Rudolph presents a collection of studies, ranging from F.C. Baur in 1843 to H.J.W. Drijvers in 1967/68, in *Gnosis und Gnostizismus* (Darmstadt: Wissenschaftliche Buchgesellschaft, 1975) (English and French articles translated into German). See also his *Forschungsberichte* in *ThR* 34 (1969), pp. 121-75, 181-231, 358-361; 36 (1971), pp. 1-61, 89-124; 37 (1972), pp. 289-360; 38 (1973), pp. 1-25; and the bibliography of Rudolph's own works in H. Preissler and H. Seiwert (eds.), *Gnosisforschung und Religionsgeschichte* (Marburg: Diagonal-Verlag, 1994), pp. 17-33.

2. C. Bigg, *The Christian Platonists of Alexandria* (Oxford: Clarendon Press, 1886), p. 28.

It was an attempt, a serious attempt, to fathom the dread mystery of sorrow and pain, to answer that spectral doubt, which is mostly crushed down by force—can the world as we know it have been made by God?[3]

The emphasis here is on the second-century systems, for the resources then available scarcely extended beyond the patristic refutations, and the gnostics were regarded, as, for example, by F.C. Burkitt later,[4] as Christians who sought to present their faith 'in a form untrammeled by the Jewish envelope in which they had received it.' This view, which sees the gnostic movement as originating within Christianity, has had some more recent advocates in Alan Richardson, R.P. Casey, Simone Pétrement, H. Langerbeck, Barbara Aland and A.H.B. Logan,[5] but is today rather a minority opinion. It should be added that even those who claim that Gnosticism in this sense presupposes Christianity, and originated within it, generally recognize the presence in the background of the New Testament of trends and tendencies in a 'gnostic' direction. At the very least, as Robert Law put it,[6] Paul's Corinthian correspondence shows 'into how congenial a soil the seeds of Gnosticism were about to fall'.

3.   Cf. G.A.G. Stroumsa, *Another Seed: Studies in Gnostic Mythology* (Leiden: E.J. Brill, 1984), p. 17: 'At the root of the Gnostic rejection of the material world and its creator lies an obsessive preoccupation with the problem of evil.' On the following page Bigg writes: 'The effort is one that must command our respect, and the solution is one that a great writer of our own time [a footnote refers to J.S. Mill] thought not untenable.'

4.   *Church and Gnosis* (Cambridge: Cambridge University Press, 1932). Burkitt's argument for the essential Christianity of Valentinus is accepted by C.H. Dodd, *The Interpretation of the Fourth Gospel* (Cambridge: Cambridge University Press, 1953), p. 100 n. 4. Cf. Dodd's discussion, pp. 97-114, and for knowledge of God in the Fourth Gospel, pp. 151-69.

5.   A. Richardson, *Introduction to the Theology of the New Testament* (London: SCM Press, 1958) (see index s.v.); R.P. Casey, 'Gnosis, Gnosticism and the New Testament', in W.D. Davies and D. Daube (eds.), *The Background of the New Testament and its Eschatology* (Cambridge: Cambridge University Press, 1964), pp. 52-80; S. Pétrement, *Le Dieu Séparé* (Paris: Cerf, 1984) (ET *A Separate God* [London: Darton, Longman & Todd, 1991]); Hermann Langerbeck, *Aufsätze zur Gnosis* (Göttingen: Vandenhoeck & Ruprecht, 1967); B. Aland, 'Gnosis und Christentum', in B. Layton (ed.), *The Rediscovery of Gnosticism*, I (2 vols.; Leiden: E.J. Brill, 1980), pp. 319-42; A.H.B. Logan, *Gnostic Truth and Christian Heresy* (Edinburgh: T. & T. Clark, 1996).

6.   *The Tests of Life* (Edinburgh: T. & T. Clark, 1909), p. 28.

2. W.W. Harvey in the introduction to his edition of Irenaeus[7] already refers at various points to 'oriental theosophy', and there have long been advocates of the view that eastern religions contributed to the origins of Gnosticism, but it was the rise of the *religionsgeschichtliche Schule*[8] at the end of the nineteenth century that brought into prominence the contribution of other religions of the ancient Near East. The influence of this school can be traced in much of later scholarship, for example in the work of Rudolf Bultmann[9] and his pupils. Its representatives were undoubtedly right to widen the range, to take in a broader background, but pioneers are often in danger of giving too great an emphasis to their discoveries, and some aspects of their work are open to criticism.[10]

For one thing, there is the danger of 'motif methodology':[11] identifying terms and concepts as 'gnostic' on the strength of their

7. *Sancti Irenaei Libros quinque adversus Haereses* (Cambridge: Cambridge University Press, 1857).

8. E.g. R. Reitzenstein, *Poimandres* (Leipzig: Teubner, 1904); *idem, Die hellenistischen Mysterienreligionen* (Leipzig: Teubner, 3rd edn, 1927); W. Bousset, *Hauptprobleme der Gnosis* (Göttingen: Vandenhoeck & Ruprecht, 2nd edn, 1973 [1907]). For criticism, see C. Colpe, *Die religionsgeschichtliche Schule* (Göttingen: Vandenhoeck & Ruprecht, 1961).

9. E.g. *Das Urchristentum im Rahmen der antiken Religionen* (Zürich: Artemis Verlag, 1949) (ET *Primitive Christianity in its Contemporary Setting* [London: Thames & Hudson, 1956]); *idem, Theologie des Neuen Testaments* (Tübingen: J.C.B. Mohr, 6th edn, 1968 [1953]) (ET; 2 vols.; London: SCM Press, 1952, 1955). The works of his disciples (e.g. G. Bornkamm, E. Käsemann, H. Koester, J.M. Robinson) are too numerous to be listed in detail. The most extreme is W. Schmithals, *Die Gnosis in Korinth* (Göttingen: Vandenhoeck & Ruprecht, 3rd edn, 1969 [1956]) (ET; Nashville: Abingdon Press, 1971); *idem, Paulus und die Gnostiker* (Hamburg-Bergstedt: Herbert Reich-Evangelischer Verlag, 1965) (ET; Nashville: Abingdon Press, 1972]); cf. J.M. Robinson in A.H.B. Logan and A.J.M. Wedderburn (eds.), *The New Testament and Gnosis* (Edinburgh: T. & T. Clark, 1983), pp. 2-3, but see also W. Schmithals, *Neues Testament und Gnosis* (Darmstadt: Wissenschaftliche Buchgesellschaft, 1984). For criticism of Bultmann's Redeemed Redeemer myth cf. Colpe, *Die religionsgeschichtliche Schule*, p. 191.

10. Cf. H.A.A. Kennedy, *St Paul and the Mystery Religions* (London: Hodder & Stoughton, 1913), p. viii: 'The natural tendency of explorers in remote areas is to over-estimate the significance of their discoveries. This temptation, I believe, has not been escaped by the pioneer workers in the province of Hellenistic religion.'

11. Cf. R. Haardt, 'Bemerkungen zu den Methoden der Ursprungsbestimmung von Gnosis', in U. Bianchi (ed.), *Le origini dello Gnosticismo* (Leiden: E.J. Brill,

occurrence in the context of the classic gnostic systems, going on to assume that they are also gnostic when they occur earlier, and so finding the origins of Gnosticism far back in the mists of history. But are these terms and concepts 'gnostic' apart from the gnostic context in which we find them in the second century? The word πλήρωμα for example is a technical term in Valentinianism, for the totality of the aeons who emanate from Bythos, the primal ground of being, or more broadly for the heavenly realm in which they dwell; but in classical Greek it can mean the complement of a ship, its crew or its cargo, and it is frankly difficult to find any gnostic significance in some New Testament cases (in Mt. 9.16 [par. Mk 2.21] it is the new patch sewn on an old garment).[12] The word does occur at an earlier period, but it does not necessarily have its gnostic connotations. Here we need to have due regard for chronology, for otherwise we are in danger of reading first-century documents (e.g. the New Testament) with second-century spectacles.[13]

In this connection reference should be made to the vexed question of a pre-Christian Gnosticism.[14] M. Friedländer, for example, argued for a pre-Christian Jewish Gnosticism,[15] Reitzenstein for an origin in Egypt or Persia, while others have looked to Orphism or the Essenes.[16] There

1967), pp. 161-74; *idem*, 'Zur Methodologie der Gnosisforschung', in K.W. Tröger (ed.), *Gnosis und Neues Testament* (Berlin: Evangelische Verlagsanstalt, 1973), pp. 183-202; H.A. Green, 'Gnosis and Gnosticism: A Study in Methodology', *Numen* 24 (1977), pp. 95-134.

12. Cf. G. Delling in *TWNT*, VI, pp. 297-304 (for Gnosticism see pp. 299-300; for the New Testament see pp. 300-304).

13. Cf. Richardson's criticism of Bultmann (*Introduction*, pp. 41-43). Casey ('Gnosis, Gnosticism', p. 53) writes of Reitzenstein: 'In matters of chronology he was singularly cavalier and raised the subjective criticism of documents to a high imaginative art.'

14. Cf. E.M. Yamauchi, *Pre-Christian Gnosticism* (Grand Rapids: Baker Book House, 2nd edn, 1983).

15. *Der vorchristliche jüdische Gnosticismus* (Farnborough: Gregg, 1972 [1898]). Cf. B.A. Pearson, 'Friedländer Revisited: Alexandrian Judaism and Gnostic Origins', *Studia Philonica* 2 (1973), pp. 23-39 (reprinted with other relevant essays in *idem*, *Gnosticism, Judaism and Egyptian Christianity* [Minneapolis: Fortress Press, 1990], pp. 10-28).

16. For example, F. Legge, *Forerunners and Rivals of Christianity* (New York: University Books, 1964 [1915]) devotes chapters in his first volume to the Orphici, the Essenes and Simon Magus as 'pre-Christian Gnostics', and deals with 'post-Christian Gnostics' in his second volume. Gilles Quispel (*Gnosis als Weltreligion*

are certainly some affinities and similarities,[17] but while such movements may have contributed to the rise of Gnosticism they do not show
the full development that we find in the 'classic' systems of the second
century. As Hans Jonas put it, 'A Gnosticism without a fallen God,
without benighted creator and sinister creation, without alien soul, cosmic captivity and acosmic salvation, without the self-redeeming of the
Deity—in short: a Gnosis without divine tragedy will not meet speci-
fications.'[18]

One particular aspect of this debate is the relation between the New
Testament and Gnosticism. The second-century systems obviously cannot have influenced the New Testament authors in the first century, but
there are similarities that have suggested to some scholars that there
was some influence from an earlier pre-Christian Gnosticism, particularly in Paul and John. Paul's Corinthian correspondence, Colossians, 1
John and some of the later writings like the Pastorals, Jude and 2 Peter
have been thought to reflect reaction against gnostic teaching, and it
has even been suggested that in some cases the New Testament author
is to some extent influenced by the ideas he is opposing.

Here something depends on our definition of Gnosticism.[19] British

[Zürich: Origo, 1951], p. 9) remarks that practically the entire Near East belongs
among the ancestors of Gnosticism. In the early stages, the Dead Sea scrolls were
sometimes claimed as the long-sought evidence for a pre-Christian Jewish Gnosticism, but such claims soon subsided.

17. For Philo of Alexandria and Gnosticism cf. R.McL. Wilson, *The Gnostic
Problem* (London: Mowbray, 1958); M. Simon, 'Eléments gnostiques chez Philon',
in U. Bianchi (ed.), *Le origini dello Gnosticismo* (Leiden: E.J. Brill, 1967), pp. 359-
74; B.A. Pearson, 'Philo and Gnosticism', *ANRW*, II.21.1, pp. 295-342; R.McL.
Wilson, 'Philo and Gnosticism', *Studia Philonica Annual* 5 (1993), pp. 84-92.

18. In J.P. Hyatt (ed.), *The Bible in Modern Scholarship* (Nashville: Abingdon
Press, 1965), p. 293. This was originally directed against Gershom Scholem's use of
the terms Gnosis and Gnosticism to describe his Hekhaloth mysticism (*Jewish
Gnosticism, Merkabah Mysticism and Talmudic Tradition* [New York: Jewish Theological Seminary, 1950]), but is capable of wider application.

19. The Messina Colloquium in 1966 sought to distinguish Gnosticism, defined
in terms of the second-century systems, and Gnosis, defined as a knowledge reserved
for an élite (Bianchi, *Le origini*, pp. xx-xxxii), but this distinction has found little
favour. 'Gnosticism' should certainly be reserved for the classic second-century
systems, but there is no doubt that there was a kind of 'Gnosis' already current in
the first century. French-speaking scholars have long made this distinction, and A.D.
Nock wrote that 'in general apart from the Christian movement there was a Gnostic

scholars tend to think in terms of the traditional definition, and see it as a movement of the second century, but German scholars take a somewhat wider view. They prefer to speak of *Die Gnosis*, referring to the whole movement from its earliest beginnings even in the first century, which is not in all respects identical with what their British colleagues mean by Gnosticism. The trouble comes when a German book is translated, and *Die Gnosis* is uniformly rendered by 'Gnosticism'—Richardson probably would not have criticized Bultmann the way he does had he realized that! The problem is that it is difficult to give any firm shape or contours to the incipient Gnosis of the first century without drawing upon our knowledge of the developed Gnosticism of the second century; but an acorn is not yet an oak.

3. A new phase was introduced by Hans Jonas, in one of the most widely influential books in the field.[20] His existentialist approach did not find favour with some English-speaking reviewers, who frankly found it difficult.[21] In that respect his English version *The Gnostic Religion* (Boston 1956) is much more 'reader-friendly'. His approach is from the side of phenomenology, which leads to the association of similar concepts and ideas from various sources in order to understand the movement as a whole, but without always considering the relative chronology—that is, it is philosophical rather than historical. What is important here is the recognition that Gnosticism involved something of a new way of thinking, a new attitude and outlook. The gnostics certainly took over much from Judaism, from the contemporary world, and eventually also from Christianity—hence the similarities that led

---

way of thinking, but no Gnostic movement with its "place in the sun" ' (Z. Stewart [ed.], *Essays on Religion and the Ancient World*, II [Oxford: Clarendon Press, 1972], p. 958). Cf. R.McL. Wilson, 'Gnosis and Gnosticism: The Messina Definition', in G. Sfameni Gasparro (ed.), Ἀγαθὴ ἐλπίς (Festschrift U. Bianchi; Rome: Bretschneider, 1994), pp. 539-51. For somewhat divergent approaches to the question of the New Testament and Gnosticism, cf. R.McL. Wilson, *Gnosis and the New Testament* (Oxford: Basil Blackwell, 1968) and J.M. Robinson, 'Gnosticism and the New Testament', in B. Aland (ed.), *Gnosis* (Göttingen: Vandenhoeck & Ruprecht, 1978), pp. 123-43.

20. *Gnosis und Spätantiker Geist* (2 vols.; Göttingen: Vandenhoeck & Ruprecht, 1934, 1954); cf. K. Rudolph, *Gnosis* (ET; Edinburgh: T. & T. Clark, 1983), pp. 33-34.

21. Cf. A.D. Nock's review in *Gnomon*, reprinted in Stewart, *Essays*, I, pp. 441-51, and R.M. Grant, Review of Hans Jonas, *Gnosis und Spätantiker*, *JTS* 7 (1956), pp. 308-13.

scholars to think of 'gnostic' influences in the New Testament and elsewhere—but in the context of the developed gnostic systems these terms and concepts take on a new significance.[22] It is not enough to identify 'gnostic' terminology and concepts in an earlier period; we have to endeavour to see how the ideas were transmitted (e.g. from Persia through Judaism, or from Judaism through early Christianity; LXX was after all the Bible of the early church) and also what changes have been introduced in the process. To some extent the similarities are due to the fact that gnostics and 'orthodox' Christians (and others) are using the current language and concepts of their time.

A further complication arises with the recognition that Manicheism, Mandeism and the Hermetica have some connection with Gnosticism.[23] The question is precisely what that connection is. Manicheism later became a world religion in its own right, while Mandeism has survived into modern times, but the origins of the first and the documentation for the second belong well into the Christian era, and these for present purposes may be left aside. It has long been a debated question how far the Hermetica should be considered gnostic, but this has at least to some extent been resolved by the discovery of Hermetic documents among the Nag Hammadi texts (see below).[24] If that collection was the library of a gnostic group, they found Hermetica congenial; if it was

22. A. Böhlig in his Messina paper (Bianchi [ed.], *Le origini*, pp. 109-40, reprinted as two chapters in Böhlig, *Mysterion und Wahrheit* [Leiden: E.J. Brill, 1968], pp. 80-111) writes (p. 101): '...die Gnosis mit der Umwertung der religiösen Traditionen aus dem Judentum zwar Vorstellungen übernommen, aber aus ihnen Neues geschaffen hat.'

23. For Mandeism, see numerous works by K. Rudolph, listed in his *Festschrift*: *Gnosisforschung und Religionsgeschichte*; for Manicheism, see, for example, G. Widengren, *Mani and Manicheism* (ET; London: Weidenfeld & Nicolson, 1965; Stuttgart: W. Kohlhammer, 1961). A special interest attaches to the much-discussed Cologne Mani Codex (ed. and trans. R. Cameron and A.J. Dewey; Missoula, MT: Scholars Press, 1979). For the Hermetica, cf. the article H.J. Sheppard, R.McL. Wilson and A. Kehl, 'Hermetik', *RAC* 110 (1986), cols. 780-808 (esp. 795-808). The Hermetic Poimandres is frequently included in anthologies of gnostic texts. References could of course be multiplied. At a later period there are the Bogomils in the Balkans (cf. D. Obolensky, *The Bogomils* [Cambridge: Cambridge University Press, 1948]), and the Cathari and Albigensians (cf. S. Runciman, *The Mediaeval Manichee* [Cambridge: Cambridge University Press, 1947]).

24. Cf. J.-P. Mahé, *Hermès en Haute-Egypte* (2 vols.; Quebec: Les Presses de l'Université Laval, 1978, 1983).

made for heresiological purposes, the compilers thought Hermetica relevant. Yet another complication arises from the fact that Irenaeus in his refutation expressly refers to 'the gnosis falsely so called' (1 Tim. 6.20), which implies that there can be an orthodox gnosis as well as a heretical; Clement of Alexandria can speak quite happily of the 'true gnostic', meaning a perfectly orthodox Christian.[25] The gnostic problem is rather more complex than is sometimes realized.

4. Among modern studies, reference has already been made to the work of F.C. Burkitt, published before the discoveries of recent years, and to Jonas's book *The Gnostic Religion,* which could take account of only some of them (his original German book was criticized by Schmithals for the extensive use made of Mandean and Manichean materials). Some Nag Hammadi texts were taken into consideration by R.M. Grant and R.McL. Wilson,[26] but the first comprehensive study taking the Nag Hammadi texts fully into account is that of Kurt Rudolph; the most recent book on Gnosticism was published by G. Filoramo.[27] Useful anthologies of gnostic texts have been produced by R.M. Grant, Robert Haardt (the English translation is unfortunately unsatisfactory) and Werner Foerster (vol. I for patristic sources, vol. II for Nag Hammadi and Mandaic texts; vol. III [German only] deals with Manicheism).[28] The number of books and articles on various aspects is quite enormous: at the latest count, Scholer's bibliography lists 9846 items; this, however, includes reviews, some of which are not significant.

5. Nag Hammadi: down to 1955, the sources available to scholars were practically limited to the reports of the early Fathers, and such extracts from gnostic texts as they chose to incorporate, and hence were open to suspicion as the propaganda of the winning side in the conflict.

25. Cf. W. Völker, *Der wahre Gnostiker nach Klemens Alexandrinus* (TU, 57; Berlin: Akademie-Verlag, 1952).

26. R.M. Grant, *Gnosticism and Early Christianity* (New York: Columbia University Press, 2nd edn, 1966 [1958]); Wilson, *The Gnostic Problem*; see also Wilson, *Gnosis and the New Testament* (Oxford: Basil Blackwell, 1968).

27. Rudolph, *Gnosis*; G. Filoramo, *A History of Gnosticism* (ET; Oxford: Basil Blackwell, 1990).

28. R.M. Grant, *Gnosticism: An Anthology* (London: Collins, 1961); R. Haardt, *Die Gnosis* (Salzburg: O. Muller, 1967); W. Foerster, *Die Gnosis*, I (Zürich: Artemis Verlag, 1969; ET; Oxford: Clarendon Press, 1972); II (ed. M. Krause and K. Rudolph; Zürich: Artemis Verlag, 1971; ET; Oxford: Clarendon Press, 1974); III (ed. A. Böhlig and J.P. Asmussen; Zürich: Artemis Verlag).

The only authentic gnostic documents were those contained, in Coptic, in the Bruce and Askew codices—from a time when Gnosticism had long run to seed.[29] The Berlin gnostic codex 8502 was known in 1896, but not published until 1955.[30] The new discovery (1945)[31] yielded some 40 documents not previously known—some in duplicate or even triplicate. Not all of them are gnostic (one, NHC VI, 5, is a poor version of part of Plato's Republic!); some are perfectly orthodox, while others as already indicated are Hermetic. M. Krause[32] distinguished four groups: (1) non-Christian gnostic works, with no Christian elements, although they may contain Old Testament or Jewish material; (2) Christian gnostic texts, subdivided into (a) works originally non-Christian but subsequently Christianized, and (b) works of Christian gnostic origin; (3) Hermetic texts; and (4) wisdom literature and philosophical

29. Cf. W.C. Till, 'Die Gnosis in Ägypten', *La Parola del Passato* 12 (1949), pp. 231-50. English translations of the text from these codices were published by V. MacDermot: *Pistis Sophia* (Leiden: E.J. Brill, 1978); *The Books of Jeu and the Untitled Text in the Bruce Codex* (Leiden: E.J. Brill, 1978).

30. W.C. Till, *Die gnostischen Schriften des koptischen Papyrus Berolinensis 8502* (Berlin: Akademie Verlag, 2nd rev. edn, 1972 [1955]). Three further copies of one of the texts, the Apocryphon of John, are contained in the Nag Hammadi library, and were published by M. Krause and P. Labib (*Die drei Versionen des Apokryphon des Johannes im Koptischen Museum zu Alt-Kairo* [Wiesbaden: Otto Harassowitz, 1962]); a synopsis of all four versions was published by M. Waldstein and F. Wisse (*The Apocryphon of John* [Leiden: E.J. Brill, 1995]). A second text, the Sophia Jesu Christi, is contained in Nag Hammadi Codex III (NHC III, 4; published with the related Epistle of Eugnostus [NHC III, 3; V, 1] and a Greek fragment from POx 1081 in *Nag Hammadi Codices III, 3-4 and V, 1* [ed. D.M. Parrott; Leiden: E.J. Brill, 1991]).

31. For the significance of this discovery cf. Rudolph, 'Die Nag-Hammadi Texte und ihre Bedeutung für die Gnosisforschung', *ThR* 50 (1985), pp. 1-40; G.W. MacRae, 'Nag Hammadi and the New Testament', in Aland (ed.), *Gnosis*, pp. 144-57; R.McL. Wilson, 'Nag Hammadi and the New Testament', *NTS* 27 (1982), pp. 289-302. There is a complete facsimile edition, *The Facsimile Edition of the Nag Hammadi Codices* (Leiden: E.J. Brill, 1972–1984) (for the story of the discovery cf. the Introduction [1984], pp. 3-24, and *The Nag Hammadi Library in English* [Leiden: E.J. Brill, 3rd rev. edn, 1988 (1977)]). For detailed bibliography see Scholer, *Nag Hammadi Bibliography*. See also *The Nag Hammadi Library after Fifty Years. Proceedings of the 1995 Society of Biblical Literature Commemoration* (ed. J.D. Turner and Anne McGuire; Leiden: E.J. Brill, 1997).

32. Cf. e.g. 'Der Stand der Veröffentlichung der Nag-Hammadi Texte', in U. Bianchi (ed.), *Le origini dello Gnosticismo* (Leiden: E.J. Brill), pp. 67-68; also in Foerster, *Die Gnosis*, II, pp. 7-8.

texts; but other classifications have been suggested.[33] The one thing that is clear is that the texts do not fit the heresiological categories derived from the refutations of the Fathers;[34] we have to develop a new classification based on the texts themselves, and here the simplest classification would seem to be according to content.

The documents are in Coptic, and written by several different hands, in two Coptic dialects. Fragments used to stiffen the binding of Codex VII contain dates around 340 CE, which gives a *terminus post quem* for the manufacture of this codex. The texts themselves, however, are translations of older Greek originals, which may go back to the second century; we therefore have to allow for transmission both in Greek and in Coptic, and for the translation process, all of which leaves ample scope for error and corruption in the texts. Again, some of the manuscripts have been quite severely damaged, although others are more or less complete. It is not clear why they should have been hidden, although it has been suggested that there may be some connection with Athanasius's Festal Letter of 367, with its catalogue of the books that were to be considered canonical. That might suggest the purging of a monastic library, or concealment by the owners of books now suspect. It is not, however, clear who were the original owners, or what was the purpose of the collection: was it the library of a gnostic group, or of an individual? In view of some factors that suggest a monastic origin, it has been thought that it may have been a collection made for heresiological purposes, but on such questions it is difficult to reach any definite conclusion.[35]

Space does not permit of detailed discussion of all these texts, but a few may be mentioned because of their significance. Krause[36] noted

33. Cf. L. Painchaud and A. Pasquier (eds.), *Les textes de Nag Hammadi et le problème de leur classification* (Quebec: Presses de l'Université Laval/Louvain: Peeters, 1995).

34. Cf. F. Wisse, 'The Nag Hammadi Library and the Heresiologists', *VC* 25 (1971), pp. 205-33; also *idem*, 'Gnosticism and Early Monasticism in Egypt', in Aland (ed.), *Gnosis*, pp. 431-40.

35. Cf. T. Säve-Söderbergh, 'Gnostic and Canonical Gospel Traditions', in U. Bianchi (ed.), *Le origini dello Gnosticismo* (Leiden: E.J. Brill, 1967), pp. 552-62; *idem*, 'Holy Scriptures or Apologetic Documentations?', in J.E. Ménard (ed.), *Les textes de Nag Hammadi* (Leiden: E.J. Brill, 1975), pp. 3-14; but see also Wisse, 'Gnosticism'. A. Khosroyev, *Die Bibliothek von Nag Hammadi* (Altenberge: Oros Verlag, 1995), takes a critical view of the various theories.

36. See his Introduction in Foerster, *Die Gnosis*, II, p. 8.

that it would be possible to compile a gnostic 'New Testament' from the contents of the library: there are gospels, acts, epistles and apocalypses. A closer inspection, however, reveals that the texts are very different from their New Testament counterparts. None of the four 'gospels', for example, is a gospel in the canonical sense: they contain little or nothing of the life and teaching of Jesus, his death and resurrection. The Gospel of Truth is a meditation on the theme of the gospel message, the Gospel of Thomas a collection of sayings, the Gospel of Philip a rather meandering discourse that seems to owe such continuity as it possesses to catchwords and association of ideas.[37] The Gospel of the Egyptians, also entitled 'The Holy Book of the Great Invisible Spirit' and unrelated to the GosEgypt known from patristic sources, has been described as 'a gnostic salvation history'.[38] H.C. Puech[39] described a number of the texts as 'typical gnostic gospels', but these are rather revelation gospels, in which the risen Jesus appears to one or more disciples and engages them in dialogue; hence they are sometimes classed as 'dialogues of the redeemer'. There is an 'orthodox' example in the apocryphal Epistula Apostolorum.[40] These texts incidentally raise questions in regard to the definition of 'apocalypse': they are books of revelation (in Greek, ἀποκάλυψις), but they are not of the type usually described as 'apocalyptic'. One point that deserves to be noted therefore is that the titles are not always a reliable guide to the content of the texts. Some of the 'epistles', again, begin as letters but (like the Epistula Apostolorum) soon pass over into the form of the dialogue. The Apocryphon of John already mentioned was long ago identified as the source of a section in Irenaeus,[41] but subsequent

37. But see now M.L. Turner, *The Gospel according to Philip: The Sources and Coherence of an Early Christian Collection* (Leiden: E.J. Brill, 1996).

38. A. Böhlig and F. Wisse, *The Nag Hammadi Library in English*, p. 208.

39. See his 'Gnostic Gospels and Related Documents', in E. Hennecke and W. Schneemelcher (eds.), *New Testament Apocrypha*, I (London: Lutterworth, 1963), pp. 231-362. Cf. H. Koester, 'One Jesus and Four Primitive Gospels', in J.M. Robinson and H. Koester, *Trajectories through Early Christianity* (Philadelphia: Fortress Press, 1971), p. 194 n. 122.

40. Grouped with other 'dialogues of the Redeemer' in the revised edition of *New Testament Apocrypha*, I (ET; Cambridge: James Clarke & Co., 1991), pp. 228-353 (at pp. 249-84). On the treatment of Puech's contribution in this revision see the note by W. Schneemelcher, pp. 345-55.

41. Carl Schmidt, 'Ein vorirenäisches gnostisches Originalwerk in koptischen

studies have modified that conclusion: we now have four copies, representing two different versions, and, moreover, there are several other Nag Hammadi texts that seem to belong in the same context.[42] This raises interesting questions about their relationship, and the development of this particular gnostic system. Again, the Trimor-phic Protennoia shows what have been claimed as 'stupendous parallels' to the Prologue of the Fourth Gospel.[43] This does not mean that TriProt is to be taken as a source for John's Gospel; rather it points, at the very least, to a common background in the Jewish Wisdom literature.[44] At least two of the texts, Zostrianos (NHC VIII, 1) and Allogenes (NHC XI, 3), appear to have been known to the Neo-Platonist Porphyry, who says that Plotinus attacked certain gnostics who produced 'revelations by Zoroaster and Zostrianos and Nicotheos and Allogenes and Messos and other such people'.[45] In general, some texts have been identified as Valentinian (e.g. the Gospel of Truth, the Letter to Rheginus, the Gospel of Philip, the Tripartite Tractate), while others in view of the prominence given to Seth have been characterized as Sethian.[46] There

Sprache', in *Sitzungsbericht der Kgl. Preussischen Akademie der Wissenschaften zu Berlin* (Berlin, 1896), pp. 839-47; *idem*, 'Irenäus und seine Quelle in *adv. haer.* I 29', in A. Harnack *et al.* (eds.), *Philotesia: Paul Kleinert zum 70. Geburtstag dargebracht* (Berlin: Trowzisch, 1907), pp. 317-36.

42. For a study of this and related texts, in particular challenging the priority of the version in Irenaeus, cf. Logan, *Gnostic Truth and Christian Heresy.*

43. The phrase is Carsten Colpe's, in 'Heidnische, jüdische und christliche Überlieferung in den Schriften aus Nag Hammadi III', *JAC* 17 (1974), pp. 122-24. The first translation was published by Gesine Schenke in *TLZ* 99 (1974), pp. 731-46, and prompted a lively discussion, partly due to misunderstanding of what was intended (cf. J.M. Robinson, 'The Sethians and Johannine Thought', in *The Redis-covery of Gnosticism*, II (Leiden: E.J. Brill, 1980), pp. 643-70. Robinson, however, failed to realize that one of his targets actually intended to suspend judgment pending full presentation of the case). See now Dr Schenke's published edition, *Die dreigestaltige Protennoia* (TU, 132; Berlin: Akademie Verlag, 1984).

44. For similarities between John and the Wisdom literature, cf. already Dodd, *Interpretation*, pp. 274-75.

45. The point was already noted by Jean Doresse in one of the earliest studies, *Les livres secrets des gnostiques d' Egypte* (Paris: Librairie Plon, 1958) (ET *The Secret Books of the Egyptian Gnostics* [London: Hollis & Carter, 1960], see index). For Zostrianus see now J.D. Turner's introduction and commentary in C. Barry *et al.* (eds.), *Zostrien* (BCNH section 'textes', 24; Quebec: Presses de l'Université Laval; Louvain: Peeters, 2000).

46. Cf. B. Layton (ed.), *The Rediscovery of Gnosticism* (2 vols.; Leiden: E.J.

is debate as to whether there actually was a Sethian sect,[47] but there is no doubt about the place given to Seth in a large number of these texts.

A special interest attaches to the Gospel of Thomas in view of its parallels with the canonical Gospels, but here there are many problems. It can be read as a gnostic document, but was it composed by a gnostic? Do the parallels indicate dependence on our Gospels? Or has Thomas drawn upon independent tradition? In nearly every case of a parallel there are changes, which cannot always be explained as made for gnostic purposes. Those who maintain its dependence commonly point to cases where Thomas appears to follow Matthaean or Lukan redaction against Mark; those who argue for independence point to the differences, and to the widely variant order of the material. We are still not in a position to think that the last word has been written on the subject, but probably the development was rather more complex than is sometimes allowed for.[48]

For several years the texts were locked away in the Coptic Museum

Brill, 1980): the first volume of the proceedings of the Yale Colloquium in 1978 is devoted to Valentinianism, the second to Sethian Gnosticism. Other colloquia were held at Messina (1966), Stockholm (1973), Strasbourg (1974) and Quebec (1978, 1993). For texts grouped as 'Sethian' cf. H.M. Schenke, 'The Phenomenon and Significance of Gnostic Sethianism', in Layton (ed.), *Rediscovery*, II, pp. 588-616.

47. Cf. H.M. Schenke, 'Das sethianische System nach Nag-Hammadi-Handschriften', in P. Nagel (ed.), *Studia Coptica* (Berlin: Akademie Verlag, 1974), pp. 165-73, and Schenke, 'The Phenomenon', pp. 588-616; F. Wisse, 'The Sethians and the Nag Hammadi Library' (SBLSP, 1972), pp. 601-607, and 'Stalking Those Elusive Sethians', in B. Layton (ed.), *The Rediscovery of Gnosticism*, II (Leiden: E.J. Brill, 1980), pp. 563-76; M. Tardieu, 'Les livres mis sous le nom de Seth et les Séthiens de l'hérésiologie', in M. Krause (ed.), *Gnosis and Gnosticism* (Leiden: E.J. Brill, 1977), pp. 204-10 (note p. 210): 'Il n'y a donc pas sur cette base de système proprement 'séthien', mais seulement, des livres mis sous le nom de Seth [séthiens ou non] et des livres qui, sans lui être attribués, rendent compte de sa fonction [séthiens ou non]'.

48. The latest monograph, by S.J. Patterson (*The Gospel of Thomas and Jesus* [Sonoma: Polebridge Press, 1993]; reviewed in *JTS* 45 [1994], pp. 262-67), argues for an autonomous tradition rather than complete independence, and admits the possibility of influence from the canonical Gospels at a late stage. Cf. also R.McL. Wilson, 'The Gospel of Thomas Reconsidered', in C. Fluck *et al.* (eds.), *Divitiae Aegypti* (Wiesbaden: Reichert, 1995), pp. 331-36 for a broader survey and further literature. More recent studies include R. Uro (ed.), *Thomas at the Cross-roads* (Edinburgh: T. & T. Clark, 1998) and T. Zöckler, *Jesu Lehren im Thomasevangelium* (Leiden: E.J. Brill, 1999).

in Cairo, and more or less inaccessible. One codex, however, was smuggled out of Egypt and eventually purchased for the Jung Institute in Zürich (it has now been returned to Cairo). The first study in English was a slim volume, *The Jung Codex,* containing three articles by H.C. Puech, G. Quispel and W.C. van Unnik,[49] followed a few years later by Doresse's *Secret Books.* The Gospel of Truth from the Jung Codex was published in 1956, but the process of editing and translating the other treatises was not completed until 1975. A few texts from the Cairo codices were published by M. Krause and A. Böhlig, in collaboration with Pahor Labib, Director of the Coptic Museum, but it was only in 1970 that, thanks to the initiative and persistence of James M. Robinson, steps were taken that finally led to the production of a facsimile edition. The last volume of the edited texts appeared in 1995.[50]

6. The main characteristics of gnostic teaching, common to all the developed systems, may be briefly summarized as: (a) a radical cosmic dualism that rejects this world and all that belongs to it: the body is a prison from which the soul longs to escape. The root of evil is not in 'man's first disobedience' but in a pre-cosmic fall. (b) a distinction between the unknown and transcendent true God and the creator or Demiurge, who is commonly identified with the God of the Old Testament. The latter is not always actually hostile to humanity, but imagines himself to be supreme, and seeks to hold humanity in thrall. A corollary to this is that his commands are not binding upon the gnostic, who may even have a positive duty to disobey him. (c) the belief that the human race is essentially akin to, consubstantial with, the divine, being a spark of heavenly light imprisoned in a material body. Here Gnosticism takes over Hellenistic ideas of the descent of the soul from its heavenly origin, and develops them further. (d) a myth, often narrating the premundane fall of some heavenly being, to account for the human predicament. The onus for the origin of evil is thus removed

49. *The Jung Codex* (trans. and ed. F.L. Cross; London: Mowbray; New York: Morehouse–Goreham, 1955). Puech and Quispel also contributed several articles to *Vigiliae Christianae.* See further G. Quispel, *Gnostic Studies* (2 vols.; Istanbul: Nederlandes Historisch-Archaeologisch Instituut in het Nabije Oosten, 1974–75) (he wrote much on the Gospel of Thomas).

50. Reference should also be made to the German translations and editions published by the Berlin *Arbeitskreis* under the leadership of H.M. Schenke, to the French and Canadian collaboration in the Bibliothèque Copte de Nag Hammadi series, and to the studies of M. Tardieu.

from the shoulders of humanity, but God is still not responsible for it; he is beyond all possibility of reproach. (e) the saving *gnosis* by which deliverance is effected and the gnostic awakened to the knowledge of his or her true nature and heavenly origin. A place is often accorded to Jesus, but it is as the revealer of this gnosis, not as redeemer through his death and resurrection.[51]

> It is not only the washing (i.e. Baptism) that is liberating, but the knowledge of who we were, and what we have become, where we were or where we were placed, whither we hasten, from what we are redeemed, what birth is and what rebirth.[52]

This outline may be illustrated by a summary of the Valentinian system as described by Irenaeus (other 'schools' have their own myths, presenting a sometimes bewildering array of variations): Bythos, the primal ground of being, produces a series of emanations or aeons, 30 in all, who form the Pleroma or totality of divine being. Sophia, the last of these, and therefore the furthest removed from the primal Being, is guilty of a fault, variously described, and gives birth to the Demiurge (in the Tractatus Tripartitus, Sophia is replaced by a Logos). Then, repenting of her error, she is restored to the Pleroma. Unaware of any higher power, the Demiurge thinks himself supreme, and sets about the creation of a world. The first man, as part of this creation, remains inert and lifeless until the Demiurge breathes into him a part of the spirit that he has received from Sophia (clearly 'reinterpreting' Genesis). Human beings fall into three classes: those who are merely choic, earthly, who have no hope of salvation; those who possess the spirit, the pneumatic, who alone are assured of salvation and of return to the Pleroma; and

---

51. Cf. Rudolph's discussion of the gnostic doctrine of redemption and the Redeemer, *Gnosis*, pp. 113-71, and for the figure of Christ in *Gnosis*, pp. 148-71. The Apocalypse of Peter (NHC VII, 3: 74.13-15) speaks of those who 'will hold fast to the name of a dead man, thinking that they will become pure' (cf. TreatSeth, NHC VII, 2: 60.21-22), and later (81.15-20) presents the Saviour's interpretation of Peter's vision of the crucifixion: 'He whom you see above the cross, glad and laughing, is the living Jesus. But he into whose hands and feet they are driving the nails is his fleshly part.' This recalls the teaching of Basilides, who according to Irenaeus (1.24.4) said that Simon of Cyrene was crucified in error instead of Jesus, who took the form of Simon and stood by mocking; he who confessed the crucified was still under the power of those who created the body.

52. *Excerpta ex Theodoto* 78.2 (trans. R.P. Casey; London: Christophers, 1934), p. 89.

between them the psychic, commonly identified as non-gnostic Christians, who may attain to a partial salvation outside the Pleroma if they fulfil the proper conditions. The rest of the myth concerns Sophia's attempts to recover her true progeny, in the face of the Demiurge's efforts to maintain his dominance. Sometimes a part of the saving gnosis relates to the passwords that guarantee safe passage through the heavens on the ascent of the soul to the Pleroma.

According to the heresiologists, gnostics are 'saved by nature', because they possess the divine spark. Conduct is therefore irrelevant, and ethics a matter of no importance: they may do as they please, even to defiance of the law, which is the creation of the Demiurge. Rudolph however observes that 'thus far no libertine writings have appeared even among the plentiful Nag Hammadi texts'.[53] On the contrary, salvation is not independent of the conduct of the believer: 'The pneumatic element cannot perish and its entry into the Pleroma is preordained, but the why and the how are not independent of the right conduct of its bearer.'

The Gospel of Truth (NHC I, 3) derives its title from the opening words: 'The gospel of truth is joy for those who have received from the Father of truth the grace of knowing him, through the power of the Word that came forth from the Pleroma.' Later at several points (e.g. 21.30–22.20; 28.32–30.16; 42.12-38) it contrasts the lot of the 'ignorant' and those who have gnosis: for the latter it is the dawn of a new aeon, an awakening from nightmare dreams, from sleep and intoxication. There are similar passages in the Gospel of Philip (e.g. the closing pages, NHC II, 3: 84.34–86.18). These and other passages give us a glimpse of what Gnosticism meant to a gnostic: it was not a counsel of despair, but a religion of hope and deliverance, at least for those who were fortunate enough to possess the divine spark, to hear and respond to the call of the gnostic redeemer. It was an attempt, a

---

53. *Gnosis* 117-18, 252-72 (quotations from pp. 254 and 117; for libertinism see pp. 255-57. Such tendencies are ascribed by the Fathers to the Carpocratians and the Cainites, and to some groups described by Epiphanius, who is not the most reliable of witnesses). See also F. Wisse, 'Die Sextus-Sprüche und das Problem der gnostischen Ethik', in A. Böhlig and F. Wisse, *Zum Hellenismus in den Schriften von Nag Hammadi* (Göttinger Orientforschungen, 6th series, vol. 2; Wiesbaden: Otto Harrassowitz, 1975), pp. 55-86; R.McL. Wilson, 'Ethics and the Gnostics', in W. Schrage (ed.), *Studien zum Text und zur Ethik des Neuen Testaments* (Berlin: W. de Gruyter, 1986), pp. 440-49.

serious attempt, to deal with real and vital issues, even though the early Fathers found it at variance with their developing 'orthodox' teaching.

7. Background and sources: as already indicated, the question of the origins of Gnosticism has been much debated. It is easy enough to identify parallels, but the vital question is: What do these parallels signify? Are they merely parallels, which might arise between two quite independent movements by pure coincidence, or are they such as to suggest that one movement has influenced the other, or is even the source from which it has drawn? Is it possible to trace lines of connection between movements that appear to be in some way related? For example, some modern writers have consciously drawn upon gnostic motifs and ideas that they found in ancient sources, but is it possible to identify such older sources in the case of Gnosticism itself? In recent years there has been an increasing tendency to stress the Jewish element, although caveats have been entered by Hans Jonas and W.C. van Unnik.[54] The presence of Jewish features is beyond doubt, but the real question is how they got there. Do they point, as some have argued, to a pre-Christian Jewish Gnosticism, or is there some other explanation? If, as in the traditional theory, Gnosticism is the result of a fusion of Christianity and Greek philosophy, the obvious place to look for a pre-Christian Jewish Gnosticism would be in the Jewish Diaspora, and that means Philo of Alexandria; but it is now commonly agreed that Philo is not himself a gnostic.[55] In any case, whatever the elements that were taken over from Jewish sources, they were often subjected to a radical reinterpretation.

A second source often referred to, from the time of the heresiologists

---

54. The 'Jewish thesis' has been strongly argued by G. Quispel, B.A. Pearson and others (cf. most recently Pearson, *Gnosticism, Judaism and Egyptian Christianity*), but cf. also the reservations expressed by Jonas (e.g. in J.P. Hyatt [ed.], *The Bible in Modern Scholarship* [Nashville: Abingdon Press, 1965], pp. 286-93) and van Unnik (e.g. 'Gnosis und Judentum', in Aland [ed.], *Gnosis*, pp. 65-86). Cf. also R.McL. Wilson, ' "Jewish Gnosis" and Gnostic Origins: A Survey', *HUCA* 45 (1974), pp. 177-89; K.W. Tröger, 'The Attitude of the Gnostic Religion towards Judaism', in B. Barc (ed.), *Colloque international sur les textes de Nag Hammadi* (Quebec: Presses de l'Université Laval; Louvain: Peeters, 1981), pp. 86-98; *idem,* 'Gnosis und Judentum', in K.W. Tröger (ed.), *Altes Testament, Frühjudentum, Gnosis* (Gütersloh: Gütersloher Verlagshaus, 1980).

55. Cf. the references in n. 17 above.

on, is Greek philosophy,[56] but today we should no longer apply the methods of a Hippolytus, who sought to identify a specific philosophical school as the 'source' of each of the gnostic sects. Today the emphasis would be rather on the Platonic tradition, and particularly Middle Platonism, and here we may have a pointer to stages in the development of Gnosticism: at what stage does the 'Platonic' element become prominent? Here we also have to take into account the reaction of philosophers like Plotinus, who attacked the gnostics for their misuse of the philosophical tradition. Once again, if there is borrowing, there is also reinterpretation.

Whatever may be thought of the earliest stages, and even if there was an incipient form of Gnosis apart from Christianity, there is no question that a major factor in the development of the classic second-century systems was the Christian movement. Gnosticism may not have originated, in its first beginnings, within the church, but it certainly soon came into contact with the developing Christian movement, and the two interacted in various ways. We have still a long way to go before we can finally claim to have traced out all the lines of development on either side.

56. Cf., e.g., A.H. Armstrong, 'Gnosis and Greek Philosophy', in Aland (ed.), *Gnosis*, pp. 87-124; B.A. Pearson, 'The Tractate Marsanes (NHC X) and the Platonic Tradition', in Aland (ed.), *Gnosis*, pp. 373-84. See also J. Zandee, *The Terminology of Plotinus and of Some Gnostic Writings, Mainly the Fourth Treatise of the Jung Codex* (Istanbul: Nederlandes Historisch-Archaeologisch Instituut in het Nabije Oosten, 1961) (the 'fourth treatise' is actually the fifth, the Tractatus Tripartitus); C. Elsas, *Neuplatonische und gnostische Weltablehnung in der Schule Plotins* (Berlin: W. de Gruyter, 1975). The tractate Zostrianus is one of a group of Sethian texts which J.D. Turner, Introduction, p. 144, assigns to a late phase when Sethianism 'has become strongly attracted by the individualistic contemplative practices of second and third century Platonism'.

John M. Court

> Hail to Mithra, the Lord of Wide Pastures, who has a thousand ears and ten thousand eyes! Thou art worthy of sacrifice and prayer: mayest thou have sacrifice and prayer in the houses of men! Hail to that man who shall offer thee a sacrifice, with the holy wood in his hand, Barsman-twigs in his hand, the holy meat in his hand, the holy pestle and mortar in his hand, with his hands well washed, with the pestle and mortar well washed, with the Barsman-twigs spread out, the Haoma stalk uplifted, and the Ahuna Vairya sung through.[1]

I sense in myself a fascination with the cult of Mithras since the day when I stood on the bleak line of Hadrian's Wall in Northumbria and surveyed the traces on the ground of the small Mithraeum at Carrawburgh. It needed an exercise of the imagination to link this ground plan with the artefacts from the site and their colourful reconstructions to be found in the museum some miles to the east at the University of Newcastle upon Tyne. But from such traces, associated in the mind with other Mithraic discoveries in the province of Britannia and elsewhere in the Roman world, it is possible to build up at least an archaeologist's impression of what it felt like to be a worshipper of Mithras.

The direct relevance of Mithraism and other ancient Mystery Religions for the student of the New Testament remains a highly debated area among scholars. The over-enthusiastic comparison of Christianity with the Mysteries by the Religionsgeschichtliche Schüle in Germany between 1880 and 1920 provoked an opposite reaction. A prominent Pauline scholar once declared that 'this subject need be considered only at the level of popular misconception'. One issue concerns the adequacy of the data for study; the other issue is whether this is a real and meaningful question to ask of the New Testament world. Can the

---

1. *Mihir Yast* 10. In the form edited by Geshevitch, the *Avestan Hymn to Mithra* dates from the fifth century BCE.

amount of authenticated information about the ancient cults at least lift
the subject out of the realm of popular Romanticism, where eighteenth-
century enthusiasts succeeded in producing largely imaginative
reconstructions of comparable religious movements, such as the Druids
and the Knights Templar? Clearly one needs to take a critical view of
such popular hypotheses and employ research techniques that can
distinguish later mythologies from any original basis in fact.

Other scholars are much more positive on the usefulness of investigating the Mysteries. Some are studying particular contexts, such as the
early Christian churches in Corinth or in Thessalonica, where the evidence suggests that a comparison with the practices of the ancient cults
could prove helpful. And some find room for the Mysteries because
such alternative religions are a necessary feature of their hypothesis.
An example of the latter would be the work of the Jewish scholar
Hyam Maccoby,[2] or before him Leo Baeck.[3] In his attitude to Paul,
Baeck changed his mind from an attitude of polemic to the recognition
of a great Jewish brother (even though Paul was responsible for taking
the community of Jesus' followers out of the context of Jewish life).
Paul was Jewish (indissolubly rooted in Israel's life as Rom. 11 shows),
because 'only a Jew would always be aware that the revelation entailed
the mission'. But in developing that mission Paul transformed the Jewish faith into something akin to the mystery religions of the Hellenistic
world. 'The old theocentric faith of Judaism is superseded by a new
Christ-centred faith' that entailed preaching a Messiah to a pagan
world in romantic terms, akin to (or borrowed from) pagan salvation
mysteries.

Karl Donfried[4] argued that the history of Thessalonica in the first
century BCE and the first century CE, and especially knowledge of the
cults, both political and religious, practised in that place and period,
would be vital for a fuller understanding of the correspondence of Paul
with the Thessalonian church. The politically motivated civic cults,
designed to include a proper acknowledgment of the goddess Roma
alongside the local deities, are not so relevant for our present purpose
as are the references to the cults of Sarapis, Isis, Dionysus and Cabirus,

2.   Hyam Maccoby, *Paul and Hellenism* (London: SCM Press, 1991).
3.   See, e.g., A. Friedlander, *Leo Baeck* (London: Routledge & Kegan Paul,
1973).
4.   K.F. Donfried, 'The Cults of Thessalonica and the Thessalonian Correspondence', *NTS* 31.3 (1985), pp. 336-56.

and the mysteries of Samothrace.[5] Meanwhile, as regards Corinth, interest focuses on a text such as 1 Cor. 10.27: 'If an unbeliever invites you to a meal and you are disposed to go, eat whatever is set before you without raising any question on the ground of conscience.'[6] The comparison suggested here is with invitations to a banquet found in standardized form in the Oxyrhynchos papyri from Egypt, for example, 'Herais asks you to dine in the (dining-) room of the Sarapeion at a banquet of the lord Sarapis tomorrow, namely the 11th, from the 9th hour.'[7] These are invitations to banquets involving the god Sarapis; such meals would have a fundamentally religious character, since the deity was regarded as being present for the dinner.

> Trivial and ephemeral as the invitations may appear to be, they reflect some of the most pervasive and persistent religious ideals of their time, as well as the mutual penetration and interaction of Greek and native elements in the daily life and civilisation [of the Graeco-Roman world].[8]

Modern investigation of the Mysteries should acknowledge not only their cultural importance, but also their variety. The concluding section of Apuleius's, *The Golden Ass*[9] is a useful text, because it offers an accessible description of the supposed experience of an initiate in the worship of Isis, but its authenticity is open to dispute, and anyway it should not be regarded as typical of all such experiences. Nevertheless the underlying question as to how early practitioners of any cult would have viewed their religious experience must be fundamental to the enquiry. It is also worth asking whether we can speak of a common culture of the language of the Mysteries, a kind of common denominator for these cults, as mediated to us perhaps through Hellenistic Christianity. This would be to generalize, not on the basis of individual cults, but about their influence in culture. Such an academic abstraction or synthesis could be particularly valuable if our knowledge of individual cults is limited and closed (there is an imbalance between recently rediscovered cult-objects and fragmentary or allusive texts that are

5.   See, e.g., 1 Thess. 1.9; 2.7-8; 4.1-9; 5.5-7; 19-22.
6.   Other relevant texts for comparison are 1 Cor. 8.10; 11.17-22.
7.   See G.H.R. Horsley (ed.), *New Documents Illustrating Early Christianity* (NSW, Australia: Macquarie University, 1976).
8.   J.F. Gilliam, *P.Coll.Youtie*, p. 314 n. 1.
9.   Translated by Robert Graves (Harmondsworth: Penguin Books, 1950 and subsequent editions), ch. xviii.

bound to a discipline of secrecy). It may also correspond to an effective synthesis between cults, as they interacted with one another, borrowing features and fusing together as they spread in the Mediterranean world.

Another question concerns the points at which the Mysteries might be claimed to intersect with Christianity. For example, with the apostle Paul, the Mysteries may be influential at an earlier stage in transmission upon material that he uses later. So he may echo an indirect awareness of the Mysteries in the imagery of Romans 6, for instance. Alternatively the Mysteries may be reflected at a later stage of the Pauline tradition, in such Deutero-Pauline texts as the Pastoral Epistles or Ephesians. It is possible that 'mystery' groups might have arisen in areas of Christianity, just like the 'gnostic' groups that can be seen in 1 Jn 2.19. These are further dimensions of connection with the Mysteries worth considering, beyond the most direct possibility of an influence upon Paul himself. Even if his ideas as a whole are less likely to be influenced by the Mysteries, certain motifs in his thought may derive from such a source. It is also true that direct influence may be detected in a negative mode: to react strongly against something is also in a sense to be influenced by it. But the critical question is how much could Paul have known of what actually took place in a Mystery cult?

Popular philosophies, such as the contemporary versions of Platonism, certainly had an appeal in the Graeco-Roman world, as going beyond the limits of traditional religion, but this would engage only a comparatively small segment of the more intellectual members of society. More people, including many women, looked to the Mystery cults as offering comfort and a way of salvation.

> Superstition and notions of fate, the yearning for miracles and fascination with astrology and magic, all of which found numerous adherents in the Hellenistic period, make it evident that people were in the throes of deep anxiety and uncertainty about life. Threatened by powers and demons, by illnesses and unforeseen strokes of fate, one lived in suspense and fear, and felt subject to overpowering forces against which one could not assert oneself. People strove, through all sorts of practices and precautionary measures, to arm and protect themselves against fate.[10]

This widespread attitude, which Gilbert Murray characterized as a

---

10. Eduard Lohse, *The New Testament Environment* (London: SCM Press, 1976), pp. 232-33.

'failure of nerve',[11] found numerous resolutions, as Oriental cults spread through the Mediterranean in the Hellenistic era. Transmission of these cults could be by soldiers or travellers, but especially accompanied the great waves of immigrants from the East who invaded the city of Rome from the middle of the second century BCE onwards. From Egypt came the cult of Isis and her husband Osiris (or Serapis, to use the Hellenistic name). Another cult of a mother-goddess was that of Cybele and her consort Attis, which originated in Phrygia and was introduced to Rome during the final crisis of the Punic War (205–204 BCE). The traditional religion of Orpheus from Greece was revived as a cult (and seems to have spread as far as Britain, to judge by the frequency of Orpheus figures in British mosaics). Mithraism originated from Persia, and the cult of Adonis from Syria/Palestine. The Bacchic cult of Dionysus had reached Italy as early as the second century BCE and it was regarded as beneficial to the Roman community, except when it degenerated into orgies that could cloak conspiracy and needed to be suppressed. Pythagoreanism (associated with the Greek colony of Croton in Italy) was a religious society founded by Pythagoras, the philosopher/mathematician who himself worshipped Apollo, and it was revived as a 'native' mystery in the first century BCE. Naturally, the later 'westernized' version of these cults might bear scant resemblance to their origins; for example, Roman Mithraism might differ profoundly from the Persian religion, although superficially Mithras wears Persian dress and a Phrygian cap.[12]

The hold that Mystery Religions could exercise upon their worshippers, even among civilized Romans, can be illustrated by Juvenal's description (c. 120 CE) of a pious adherent of Isis:

> Three times in the depths of winter the devotee of Isis will dive into the chilly waters of the Tiber, and, shivering with cold, will drag herself around the temple with bleeding knees; if the goddess commands, she will go to the bounds of Egypt and take water from the Nile and empty it within the sanctuary.[13]

11. Gilbert Murray, *Five Stages of Greek Religion* (Oxford: Clarendon Press, 1925, Ch. 4.

12. In some modern theories astronomical interpretation of the iconography has been used to sever the connection of Mithras with Iran; see, e.g., David Ulansey, *The Origins of the Mithraic Mysteries: Cosmology and Salvation in the Ancient World* (Oxford: Oxford University Press, 1990).

13. *Satires* 6.523ff.

The dominance of a particular cult over its adherents seems to have transcended normal social barriers, embracing free men and slaves, men and women, Greeks and barbarians as equally acceptable. But a few Mysteries (such as that of Eleusis) did operate specific conditions of exclusion, such as no barbarians or murderers.

Apuleius's work *The Golden Ass* (already referred to) tells the entertaining and racy story of Lucius, a devotee of Isis who offers sacrifice and obedience to the goddess known as the Queen of Heaven:

> At last the day came for taking my vows. As evening approached a crowd of priests came flocking to me from all directions, each one giving me congratulatory gifts, as the ancient custom is. Then the high priest ordered all uninitiated persons to depart, invested me in a new linen garment and led me by the hand into the inner recesses of the sanctuary itself. I have no doubt, curious reader, that you are eager to know what happened when I entered. If I were allowed to tell you, and you were allowed to be told, you would soon hear everything; but, as it is, my tongue would suffer for its indiscretion and your ears for their inquisitiveness.
>
> However, not wishing to leave you, if you are religiously inclined, in a state of tortured suspense, I will record as much as I may lawfully record for the uninitiated, but only on condition that you believe it. *I approached the very gates of death and set one foot on Proserpine's threshold, yet was permitted to return, rapt through all the elements. At midnight I saw the sun shining as it were noon; I entered the presence of the gods of the underworld and the gods of the upper-world, stood near and worshipped them.*
>
> Well, now you have heard what happened, but I fear you are still none the wiser.[14]

Such religions are of course referred to as 'mysteries' because their adherents maintained silence to the uninitiated about the content and significance of their activities, a discipline that seems to have been largely effective. Lucius provides the reader with an enigmatically (or satirically) allusive description of religious experience as a descent to the underworld ('the threshold of Proserpine') and an ascent to the higher levels of heaven.

The way of salvation from evil is provided in the Mystery Religions by what could be loosely termed 'sacramental' means. The focus of the

14. Lucius Apuleius, *The Transformations of Lucius, Otherwise Known as The Golden Ass* (trans. Robert Graves; Harmondsworth: Penguin Books, 1950), pp. 285-86.

cult is often on a dramatic enactment of the fate of the deity. This happens in two distinguishable aspects of cult ritual: first is the initiation of the believer in a ceremony that incorporates her or him into the divine activity (e.g. the Mithraic taurobolium or bull-slaying that is central to that Mystery's mythology); second is the ritual meal, or a mystical communion, which gives the believer a strong sense of unity with the deity. Thus the adherent is given an assurance of immortality. In the words of Plutarch, 'I conquer fate and fate obeys me.'[15] Firmicus Maternus, a Christian convert from the Mysteries, described the whole process: 'Salvation comes to God. You, his initiates, are comforted; salvation from your woes is granted also to you.'[16] The mythology of a saviour deity probably originated in the annual cycle of nature and fertility, while the traditional legends were refined in terms of growth and rebirth, probably with influences from Babylonian religion and Hinduism. Particular legends have a quasi-historical appearance (e.g. the account of Mithras's exploits, like the stories told of Krishna), but scholars usually declare that 'the cultic myth…is not related to a particular historical event, but illustrates an always valid truth'.[17] Such a view is convenient for Christian apologists, but can also be supported by quoting words of Sallust, *Of Gods and of the World*: 'these things never happened, but are always'.[18]

The Roman Empire experienced major problems in working out a tolerable relationship between official religion, including the imperial cult, and the Mysteries. Roman religion was nationalistic, but not inhospitable to other religions; the authorities recognized the right of subject peoples and allies to their own worship, which might mean leaving the door ajar to such ideas among the Roman populace. Pragmatic considerations applied in distinguishing between foreign religions and undesirable religions. If the result of tolerance was a scandal or a conspiracy, then a particular cult might be suppressed, as well as the adherents being punished. Although individuals were punished and religious practices supervised, it was comparatively unusual for a whole religion to be proscribed. In any event a suppressed religion tended to re-establish itself. The centuries either side of the birth of

---

15. *Praises of Isis and Osiris* 46-47.
16. *De Errore* 22.1-3.
17. Lohse, *The New Testament Environment*, p. 235.
18. Book IV.

Christianity saw a bewildering succession of persecution, tolerance and official favour of particular religions.

The ideas of various Mystery Religions may well have exerted influence on many an infant Christian community, either unconsciously as Christian worship activities were interpreted in accordance with the example of the Mysteries, or by conscious reference to the views of these cults. Christian baptism could be interpreted as an incorporation into the destiny of the deity, in parallel to the cultic drama of the mystic. The language of Paul's letter to the Roman church (6.1-5) speaks of baptism into Christ as incorporation into his death and resurrection. But it is significant that Paul is obliged to combat the view that the Christian is already thereby raised to a life that cannot be lost. In discussing with the church at Corinth the ritual meal of the Lord's Supper (1 Cor. 10.1-13), Paul opposes the belief that in this meal the Christian has received a salvation, both tangible and material, which sets her or him free to do, or not to do, anything they please. Just as it was thought that a permanent bond was established between the mystagogue, who imparted the cultic initiation, and the mystic, who received it, so many Christians seem to have thought that the person baptized was forever linked with the baptizer as a result of the act by which salvation was imparted. Paul strongly contests this view in the opening chapter of 1 Corinthians (especially 1.12).

Such misleading ideas could have crept in surreptitiously, although it is also likely that some Christians arrogantly claimed the saving power, imparted to the believer, as a possession to be employed at will. Paul was fierce in his opposition to such assumptions, emphasizing that baptism and the communion meal do not bestow a material gift of salvation, but rather subject the Christian to the lordship of Christ, in order that one day they might be raised from the dead and united with Christ. For the mystic a divine vital power was imparted in relation to the order of nature; in contrast through baptism the Christian is related to the historically unique events of the death and resurrection of Christ. The Christian emphasis on the proclaimed word of the Gospel could be contrasted with the dramatic rituals of the Mystery cult. But there is clear evidence that individual Christians also encountered mystical and esoteric experiences; Paul's allusive description in the third person, of a mystical ascent to the third heaven (see 2 Cor. 12.1-4), bears comparison with the quotation above of Lucius's experiences in Apuleius' *The Golden Ass*.

In the final section of this chapter the focus of attention returns to Mithraism, from which the survey began. The particular justification for this is the fact that Mithraism was one of Christianity's closest rivals in the first four centuries CE. In the words of John D. North,

> Its [Mithraism's] theology, with its planetary pantheon, was very easily absorbed by Roman society, and what it might have lacked in the way of Christianity's equity and uncomplicated morality it compensated for by its cult of mystery. The secret teachings of the cult were apparently never committed to writing, but it left behind an abundance of richly symbolic archaeological remains and inscriptions.[19]

Mithraism and Christianity both operated with a 'sacramental' system of initiatory ritual and community meal. Perhaps as early as the second century CE both religions may have held celebrations to coincide with the winter solstice (on 25 December). There may also have been a strongly eschatological emphasis in Mithraism, comparable with Christianity. And both religions saw their deity as a saviour figure, although the means of salvation were different.

Whatever weight is placed on the Iranian origins or Indian references concerning Mithras, the significant fact for the future of the Mystery cult is the worship of Mithras in Asia Minor well before the arrival of Christianity. In the East Mithra was the warrior deity of truth, the god of light associated with the sun; while in the West he became the focal point of a secret cult. The transition seems to have taken place during the last two centuries BCE, and Franz Cumont argued that it was the Hellenized 'Magi' or priest-figures of Asia Minor who developed the Mystery cult. Such Mysteries were certainly known to the Cilician pirates who had threatened Rome's security in the first century BCE (Plutarch's *Life of Pompey* 24.5 refers to strange mysteries practised by the pirates 'among which those of Mithras continue to the present time, having been first instituted by them'). According to Appian, the pirates had been introduced to the mysteries by the Parthian troops left behind from the defeated army of Mithridates Eupator. As the Parthians probably fought under the banner of Mithras, it must have seemed that Mithras was the deity who led the opposition to the Romans.

The earliest evidence for the worship of Mithras in Rome itself comes at the end of the first century CE. The Roman poet Statius has seen representations of Mithras as the bull-slayer; he describes the god

19. *TLS*, 27 July–2 August 1990.

as one who 'twists the unruly horns beneath the rocks of a Persian cave'.[20] Franz Cumont believed that Tiridates of Armenia wished to initiate the emperor Nero into the Mithras cult on his visit to Rome in 66 CE. According to Pliny's version of events, this involved magical banquets ('magicisque cenis initiaverat'), which Cumont then interprets as the Mithraic ritual. Tiridates was believed to be a Magus, and brought other Magi with him; he travelled to Rome, for his coronation by the emperor Nero, by an overland route so as not to pollute the sacred element of water. During the ceremony he is supposed to have declared to Nero: 'I am the ruler, descendant of Arsakos, of the kings Vologeses and Pakorus (his brother), but I am your slave and I come to you, my Lord, to worship you, as if you were Mithras himself.' Nero was certainly captivated by the occult and may well have hoped that the Magi would enlighten him in their eastern practices. Nero insisted on being worshipped as the sun-god; in his Domus Aurea he had a statue of himself in this role. During the festivities with Tiridates, a purple cloth was stretched over the theatre of Pompey on the Campus Martius, and on this had been painted a representation of Nero in the solar chariot, surrounded by golden stars.

Mithras had been characterized as a warrior even in the Iranian form of his worship. In the Roman world the military connotations were obvious; not only did the cult of Mithras follow the march of Roman armies to the furthest outposts of the empire, but the Roman form of the cult also used the metaphor of military service. One of the grades of initiation was that of 'miles' (or foot-soldier), but cavalry and bowmen also followed Mithras. The god is frequently depicted as the divine archer (armed with a bow from the moment of birth!) and as a mounted deity. At Dura Europos in Syria he was shown as a huntsman with bow and arrows; on a relief from Neuenheim in Germany he appears as a powerful horse-rider, holding a globe in his right hand and attended by a lion and a snake.

The Mithraic temple was designed as a cavern structure; where possible a natural cave was preferred. The cavern roof symbolized the vault of the heavens, and so it would often be decorated with stars and planets (represented by deities). At Capua the figure of Luna (the moon) was also depicted in a chariot drawn by oxen. To judge from the

---

20. 'Persei sub rupibus antri Indignata sequi torquantem cornua Mithram' (*Thebaid* 1.717).

later examples of the Mithraeum that have been excavated, every sanctuary would have its own representation of Mithras slaying the bull (the outstanding exploit of the deity in the mythology and an important part of the cultic ritual). While hundreds of examples of this image are found in the Roman Empire, there is no reference in the Iranian traditions to an act of bull-slaying. This fact poses in the sharpest way the historical questions of continuity and of the origin of this image.

The most likely answer is in the interaction of Iranian beliefs with Mesopotamian astrology during the Hellenistic period. According to Franz Cumont's classical theory:

> The mysteries of Mithra imported into Europe this composite theology, offspring of the intercourse between Magi and Chaldeans; and the signs of the zodiac, the symbols of the planets, the emblems of the elements, appear time after time on the bas-reliefs, mosaics and paintings of their subterranean temples.[21]

Another typical relief shows the birth of Mithras from a rock. He is seen as symbolizing the elements of light and fire; he holds a globe to signify a cosmic event; with his other hand he touches the circle of the zodiac. The 4 elements, the 7 planets (including sun and moon, as protectors of the seven grades of initiation), and the 12 signs of the zodiac, are all important in this Mithraic iconography. The Mithraeum at Ostia has a sophisticated design of the 7 spheres; at Modena (and similarly at the Walbrook Mithraeum in London) Mithras is portrayed as god of time encircled by the signs of the zodiac.

Within this astrological background it is plausible to look for the origin of the central image of the tauroctony. But unless the cultural context of the bull-slaying can first be identified it is risky to attempt to decode the various details of the picture in astronomical terms and then 'prove' the constellation under which this image arose; such astronomical details can be made to fit into too many different constellations. What one can say (with appropriate caution, since the final meaning of this central image of the cult is so elusive) would be to suggest that the shedding of the bull's blood is first linked with ideas of fertility. This suggestion is supported by the luxuriant vegetation displayed on the reliefs around the wound from which the victim's blood pours. Subsequently the new vegetative life can be interpreted spiritually, as a way

---

21. *Astrology and Religion among the Greeks and Romans* (New York: Dover, 1960 [1912]), p. 91.

of ensuring immortality. According to the Church father Tertullian (*De Praescr. Haeret.* 40), the tauroctony was regarded as an image of resurrection. In Mithraic ritual the bull's blood could be mixed with the white juice of the Haoma (Vedic 'soma'—a sacred herb, variously identified according to locality) in a liquor fermented to make a beverage for immortality. The bull personifies brute force and vitality; its death releases concentrated power for the benefit of mankind: 'You have saved men by the spilling of the eternal blood.'[22]

The underlying context of the natural order of human life is reaffirmed by the fact (already mentioned) that the cavern of the Mithraeum represents the vault of the heavens over the earth. The solar chariot (or the Asia Minor variant of the sun as a horseman) crosses the heavens in the daily course. Mithras is described as 'deus sol invictus' (the invincible solar deity). Together with his two attendants, the torch-bearers ('dadophori') Cautes, with his torch raised as a symbol of hope (the rising sun), and Cautopates, the sorrowful figure with the torch down (the setting sun), Mithras (as the full force of the midday sun) could represent the entire course of the sun from morning to evening. But the solar deity could also be depicted as additional to Mithras and quite distinct, sometimes as a superior and sometimes a subordinate figure.

The original sacred meal in Mithraism seems to have been envisaged on a divine level, as a meal shared by Mithras and the sun-god, ritually dining off the slain bull. However in the Mystery cult the worshippers imitated the deity, and community representatives would take the places of the deities, sharing in a symbolic meal to commemorate the god's exploits. Originally the meal was one of meat and blood, but later evidence (including some Christian writings) suggests that subsequently bread and wine could have been used. There do seem to have been considerable variations in the pattern and practice of the ritual, especially when a variety of other deities, Hellenistic and eastern, have become incorporated in the cult.

There were seven grades of initiate, each one under the protection of a planet. The sequence remained constant throughout the Roman empire, to judge from inscriptions from East and West. According to Porphyry in the third century CE, the three lowest grades, Raven

---

22. 'Viros servasti eternali sanguine fuso.'

(Mercury), Mystic Bride (Venus),[23] and Soldier (Mars), could only act as attendants at the ritual, while the higher grades were the true participants. However the evidence from archaeology has shown that the lowest grades were also able to participate in the meal. The four higher grades were Lion (Jupiter), Perses or the Persian (Moon), Heliodromus or Courier of the Sun (Sun) and Pater or Father (Saturn). One of the most interesting representations of the sequence of initiation is found in a third century CE floor mosaic from the Mithraeum of Felicissimus at Ostia. This shows a Mithraic ladder leading from the elements of fire, water and air, through the grades up to paradise. Each of the grades is illustrated with symbols: (1) the caduceus or herald's staff and a cup; (2) diadem and lamp; (3) spear, helmet and wallet; (4) fire-shovel, sistrum or rattle, and thunderbolt; (5) sword, scythe and crescent; (6) radiate crown, torch and whip; and (7) spear, helmet, sickle and dish. The process of initiation from grade to grade is believed to have been accompanied by rites that might test the courage and endurance, and could sometimes be barbarous. Perhaps the less seemly survivals from the past, such as being thrown over a pit of water with the hands bound in chicken entrails, would have been dropped by the decorous patrician communities of Rome.

The eschatological thought associated with Mithraism is to be found in Pahlavi (Middle Persian) texts. According to *Bundahishn* 30.10, good and evil powers would be separated after a final battle. Mithras was one of three who pass judgment on individual souls when the dead arrive at the bridge Cinrât; but at the end of time it is Mithras who will guide the good souls through the blazing stream that has intelligence to harm only the evil ones. The present world is to last for six thousand years, then to be followed by an age of gold, a millennium of happiness under the Sun's influence. After this will come the burning and destruction of all elements, under the rule of the 'eternal heaven'; then the whole creative process begins anew, with a new world coming from the ashes. This scheme is reminiscent of the Babylonian seven-part cycle. Information about Mithraic eschatological beliefs is supposed to be derived from the Apocalypse of Hytaspes, a first-century BCE source used by Lactantius in the 4th century CE. If this source is reproduced accurately, then there are obvious parallels with Jewish apocalyptic thought of the period, and such similarities may well be due to similar

23. Cf. Gryphon in Rudyard Kipling, *Puck of Pook's Hill.*

indebtedness to Iranian or Babylonian influences. But considerable doubt must remain as to how far the sources for Mithraic thought can be trusted. The Pahlavi texts that are the most substantial witness to this material come from the third–seventh centuries CE and may therefore reflect borrowings from Christian traditions.

Mithraism was a masculine preserve.The faithful worshipper of Mithras accepted an austere moral code, in an ardent zeal for moral purity, secured by an attitude of belligerence. The most admired virtues were the strength and courage displayed by Mithras himself. Such a cult would have a special appeal to the military mind, given its cultivation of belligerence and the practical advantages in the exclusion of women. There would be mystical appeal in the rites of initiation and sacred meals, as well as with the esoteric mythology imparted with each advance in membership. Morality, courage, equality of brotherhood, assurance of a celestial after-life, with the additional encouragement of some imperial support (although probably not extensive participation), all made Mithraism an attractive faith. This is not to follow Ernst Renan all the way in his romantic assertion that Mithraism was the prime competitor of Christianity. But three hundred years after the death of Christ, it certainly looked as if 'Sol invictus' would indeed prove invincible. Then, almost abruptly, the tables were turned and it was Christ 'the pale Galilean' who had effectively conquered the Roman Empire and secured the future faith of the western world, against the competition of Roman paganism and the major Mystery Cults.

BIBLIOGRAPHY

Aland, B.
1980 'Gnosis und Christentum', in B. Layton (ed.), *The Rediscovery of Gnosticism* (2 vols.; Leiden: E.J. Brill, 1980): 319-42.

Aland, B. (ed.)
1978 *Gnosis* (Göttingen: Vandenhoeck & Ruprecht).

Albani, M.
1999 'Horoscopes in the Qumran Scrolls', in Flint and VanderKam 1999: II, 279-330.

Albright, W.F.
1957 *From the Stone Age to Christianity* (New York: Doubleday, 2nd edn [1947]).

Alcock, S.
1993 *Graecia Capta: The Landscapes of Roman Greece* (Cambridge: Cambridge University Press).

Alcock, S., and R. Osborne (eds.)
1994 *Placing the Gods: Sanctuaries and Sacred Space in Ancient Greece* (Oxford: Clarendon Press).

Anderson, G.
1994 *Sage Saint and Sophist: Holy Men and their Associates in the Early Roman Empire* (London: Routledge).

Applebaum, S.
1979 *Jews and Greeks in Ancient Cyrene* (Leiden: E.J. Brill).

Apuleius, L.
1950 *The Transformations of Lucius, Otherwise Known as The Golden Ass* (trans. Robert Graves; Harmondsworth: Penguin Books).

Arafat, K.
1996 *Pausanias' Greece: Ancient Artists and Roman Rulers* (Cambridge: Cambridge University Press).

Armstrong, A.H.
1978 'Gnosis and Greek Philosophy', in Aland 1978: 87-124.

Athanassiadi-Fowden, P.
1981 *Julian and Hellenism: An Intellectual Biography* (Oxford: Clarendon Press).

Audet, J.P.
1958 *La Didachè: Instruction des apôtres* (Paris: Lecoffre).

Aune, D.
1980 'Magic in Early Christianity', *ANRW*, II.23.2: 1507-57.

Avigad, N.

1983   *Discovering Jerusalem* (Nashville: Abingdon Press).

Bagnall, R.S.

1993   *Egypt in Late Antiquity* (Princeton: Princeton University Press).

Bar-Adon, P.

1977   'Another Settlement of the Judaean Desert Sect at 'En el-Ghuweir on the Shores of the Dead Sea', *BASOR* 227: 1-25.

Barclay, J.M.G.

1995   'Deviance and Apostasy: Some Applications of Deviance Theory to First Century Judaism and Christianity', in P.F. Esler (ed.), *Modelling Early Christianity* (London: Routledge): 114-27.

1996   *Jews in the Mediterranean Diaspora from Alexander to Trajan (323 BCE–117 CE)* (Edinburgh: T. & T. Clark).

Bardtke, H.

1961   'Die Rechtsstellung der Qumrangemeinde', *TLZ* 86: 93-104.

Barnett, P.W.

1980–81   'The Jewish Sign Prophets—A.D. 40–70: Their Intentions and Origin', *NTS* 27: 679-97.

Barry, C. *et al.*

2000   *Zostrien* (BCNH section 'textes', 24; Quebec: Presses de l'Université Laval; Louvain: Peeters).

Barth, Fredrik (ed.)

1969   *Ethnic Groups and Boundaries: The Social Organization of Culture Difference* (Boston: Little, Brown and Co.).

Bauckham, Richard

1988   'Jesus' Demonstration in the Temple', in Barnabas Lindars (ed.), *Law and Religion: Essays on the Place of the Law in Israel and Early Christianity* (Cambridge: James Clarke): 72-89.

Bauer, W.

1924   'Essener', in W. Kroll (ed.), *Pauly-Wissowa, Real-Encyclopädie der classischen Altertumswissenschaft* (Stuttgart: Metzler), supplement vol. IV, cols. 386-430.

Baumgarten, J.M.

1980   'The Pharisaic–Sadducean Controversies about Purity and the Qumran Texts', *JJS* 31: 157-70.

1992   'The Disqualifications of Priests in 4Q Fragments of the "Damascus Document", a Specimen of the Recovery of pre-Rabbinic Halakha', in Trebolle Barrera and Vegas Montaner 1992: II, 503-13.

1994   'Sadducean Elements in Qumran Law', in E. Ulrich and J.C. VanderKam (eds.), *The Community of the Renewed Covenant: The Notre Dame Symposium on the Dead Sea Scrolls* (Notre Dame: Notre Dame University Press): 27-36.

Baur, F.C.

1878   *The Church History of the First Three Centuries* (London: Williams & Norgate [1st German edn, 1860]).

Beall, T.S.

1988   *Josephus' Description of the Essenes Illustrated by the Dead Sea Scrolls* (SNTSMS, 58; Cambridge: Cambridge University Press).

Beard, M., and J. North (eds.)
1990   *Pagan Priests* (London: Gerald Duckworth; Ithaca, NY: Cornell University Press).
Beck, Roger
1984   'Mithraism since Franz Cumont', *ANRW*, II.17.4.
1988   *Planetary Gods and Planetary Orders in the Mysteries of Mithras* (Études Préliminaires aux Religions Orientales dans l'Empire Romain, 109; Leiden: E.J. Brill).
Becker, J.
1993   *Paul: Apostle to the Gentiles* (Louisville, KY: Westminster/John Knox Press).
Beker, J.C.
1980   *Paul the Apostle: The Triumph of God in Life and Thought* (Philadelphia: Fortress Press, 1980).
Belo, F.
1974   *Lecture matérialiste de l'évangile de Marc: Récit pratique-idéologie* (Paris: Cerf) (ET *A Materialistic Reading of the Gospel of Mark* [New York: Orbis Books, 1981]).
Berardino, A. Di, and W.H.C. Frend (eds.)
1991   *Encyclopedia of the Early Church* (Cambridge: James Clarke & Co.).
Bergmeier, R.
1993   *Die Essener-Berichte des Flavius Josephus: Quellenstudien zu den Essenertexten im Werk des jüdischen Historiographen* (Kampen: Kok Pharos).
Behr, C.
1968   *Aelius Aristides and the Sacred Tales* (Amsterdam: Hakkert).
Betz, O., and R. Riesner
1994   *Jesus, Qumran, and the Vatican: Clarifications* (London: SCM Press).
Bianchi, Ugo (ed.)
1967   *Le origini dello Gnosticismo* (Leiden: E.J. Brill).
1976   *The Greek Mysteries* (Iconography of Religions, 17.3; Leiden: E.J. Brill).
1979   *Mysteria Mithrae (Proceedings of the International Seminar on the 'Religio-Historical Character of Roman Mithraism, with particular reference to Roman and Ostian Sources', Rome and Ostia 28–31 March 1978)* (Études Préliminaires aux Religions Orientales dans l'Empire Romain, 80; Leiden: E.J. Brill).
Bickerman, E.J.
1939   *Der Gott der Makkabäer* (translated as *The God of the Maccabees* [Leiden: E.J. Brill, 1979]).
Bigg, C.
1886   *The Christian Platonists of Alexandria* (Oxford: Clarendon Press).
Bilde, P.
1998   'The Essenes in Philo and Josephus', in F.H. Cryer and T.L. Thompson (eds.), *Qumran between the Old and New Testaments* (JSOTSup, 290; Copenhagen International Seminar, 6; Sheffield: Sheffield Academic Press): 32-68.

Bingham, J.
1870   *Origines Ecclesiasticae: The Antiquities of the Christian Church* (2 vols.;
            London: Henry G. Bohn).
Birge, D.
1994   'Trees in the Landscape of Pausanias' *Periegesis*', in Alcock and
            Osborne 1994: 231-45.
Blomberg, C., and S. Goetz
1981   'The Burden of Proof', *JSNT* 11: 39-63.
Bockmuehl, M.
1994   *This Jesus: Martyr, Lord, Messiah* (Edinburgh: T. & T. Clark).
Böhlig, A.
1968   'Der Jüdische Juden-Christliche Hintergrund in Gnostischen Texten von
            Nag Hammadi', in Bianchi 1967: 109-40 (reprinted in A. Böhlig,
            Mysterion und Wahrheit [Leiden: E.J. Brill]: 80-111).
Böhlig, A., and F. Wisse
1988   *The Nag Hammadi Library in English* (Leiden: E.J. Brill, 3rd rev edn).
Bohn, Henry
1870   *Origines Ecclesiasticae: The Antiquities of the Christian Church* (2 vols.;
            London).
Bonani, G., *et al.*
1992   'Radiocarbon Dating of Fourteen Dead Sea Scrolls', *Radiocarbon* 34:
            843-49.
Bond, H.K.
1998   *Pontius Pilate in History and Interpretation* (Cambridge: Cambridge
            University Press).
Borg, M.J.
1987   *Jesus: A New Vision* (San Francisco: Harper).
1994   *Jesus in Contemporary Scholarship* (Valley Forge, PA: Trinity Press
            International).
1994   *Meeting Jesus Again for the First Time* (San Francisco: Harper).
1998   'Jesus and the Revisioning of Theology', *Dialog* 37: 9-14.
Borgen, P.
1992   ' "There Shall Come Forth a Man": Reflections on Messianic Ideas in
            Philo', in Charlesworth 1992: 341-61.
Boring, E
1996   'The "Third Quest" and the Apostolic Faith', *Int* 50: 341-54.
Bornkamm, E.
1960   *Jesus of Nazareth* (New York: Harper & Row).
Bousset, W.
1973   *Hauptprobleme der Gnosis* (Göttingen: Vandenhoeck & Ruprecht
            [1907]).
Bousset, W., and H. Gressmann
1926   *Die Religion des Judentums im späthellenistischen Zeitalter* (Tübingen:
            J.C.B. Mohr [Paul Siebeck]).
Bowersock, G.W.
1968   *Greek Sophists in the Roman Empire* (Oxford: Clarendon Press)
1978   *Julian the Apostate* (London: Gerald Duckworth).
1982   'The Emperor Julian on his Predecessors', *YCS* 27: 159-72.

Bowker, John
    1973   *Jesus and the Pharisees* (Cambridge: Cambridge University Press).
Box, G.H.
    1918   *The Apocalypse of Abraham* (London: SPCK).
Boyarin, D.
    1994   *A Radical Jew: Paul and the Politics of Identity* (Berkeley: University of
                California Press).
Braaten, C.
    1994   'Jesus and the Church', *Ex Auditu* 10: 59-71.
Brandon, S.
    1967   *Jesus and the Zealots* (Manchester: University of Manchester Press).
Brenk, F.
    1977   *In Mist Apparelled: Religious Themes in Plutarch's Moralia and Lives*
                (Leiden: E.J. Brill).
Broshi, M.
    1992   'Anti-Qumranic Polemics in the Talmud', in Trebolle Barrera and Vegas
                Montaner 1992: II, 589-600.
Broshi, Magen
    1987   'The Role of the Temple in the Herodian Economy', *JJS* 38: 31-37.
Brown, C.
    1988   *Jesus in European Protestant Thought* (Grand Rapids: Baker Book House,
                2nd edn).
    1992   'Historical Jesus, Quest of', in J.B. Green, S. McKnight and I.H.
                Marshall (eds.), *Dictionary of Jesus and the Gospels* (Leicester: Inter-
                Varsity Press): 326-41.
Brown, P.R.L.
    1969   'The Diffusion of Manichaeism in the Roman Empire', *JRS* 59: 92-103.
    1992   *Power and Persuasion in Late Antiquity: Towards a Christian Empire*
                (Madison: University of Wisconsin Press).
Buber, M.
    1951   *Two Types of Faith* (London: Routledge & Kegan Paul).
Bultmann, R.
    1926   *Jesus and the Word* (ET; New York: Charles Scribner's Sons, 1958 [Ger-
                man, 1926]).
    1949   *Das Urchristentum im Rahmen der antiken Religionen* (Zürich: Artemis
                Verlag) (ET *Primitive Christianity in its Contemporary Setting* [London:
                Thames & Hudson, 1956]).
    1953   *Theologie des Neuen Testaments* (Tübingen: J.C.B. Mohr) (ET; 2 vols.;
                London: SCM Press, 1952, 1955).
    1956   *Primitive Christianity in its Contemporary Setting* (London: Thames &
                Hudson).
    1963   *The History of the Synoptic Tradition* (ET; New York: Harper & Row
                [German, 1921]).
    1964   'The Primitive Christian Kerygma and the Historical Jesus', in C.E.
                Braaten and R.A. Harrisville (eds. and trans.), *The Historical Jesus and
                the Kerygmatic Christ* (New York: Abingdon Press): 15-42.
Burkert, W.
    1985   *Greek Religion* (ET; Oxford: Basil Blackwell [German, 1977]).

Burkitt, F.C.
    1932   *Church and Gnosis* (Cambridge: Cambridge University Press).
Byrskog, S.
    1994   *Jesus the Only Teacher: Didactic Authority and Transmission in Ancient Israel, Ancient Judaism and the Matthean Community* (ConBNT, 24; Stockholm: Almqvist & Wiksell).
Cameron, Averil
    1991   *Christianity and the Rhetoric of Empire* (Berkeley: University of California Press).
Cameron, R., and A. Dewey (eds.)
    1979   *Cologne Mani Codex* (Missoula, MT: Scholars Press).
Campbell, A. LeRoy
    1968   *Mithraic Iconography and Ideology* (Études Préliminaires aux Religions Orientales dans l'Empire Romain, 11; Leiden: E.J. Brill).
Carleton-Paget, J.
    1996   'Jewish Proselytism at the Time of Christian Origins: Chimera or Reality?', *JSNT* 62: 65-103.
Carr, E.H.
    1964   *What is History?* (repr.; Harmondsworth: Penguin Books).
Casey, R.P.
    1935   'The Study of Gnosticism', *JTS* 36: 45-60.
    1964   'Gnosis, Gnosticism and the New Testament', in W.D. Davies and D. Daube (eds.), *The Background of the New Testament and its Eschatology* (Cambridge: Cambridge University Press): 52-80.
Caster, M.
    1938   *Études sur Alexandre ou le faux prophète de Lucien* (Paris: Les Belles Lettres).
Chalk, H.H.O.
    1960   'Eros and the Lesbian Pastorals of Longus', *JHS* 80: 32-51.
Chaney, Marvin L.
    1989   'Bitter Bounty: The Dynamics of Political Economy Critiqued by the Eighth-Century Prophets', in R. Stivers (ed.), *Reformed Faith and Economics* (Lanham, MD: University Press of America): 15-30.
Charles, R.H.
    1973   *The Apocrypha and Pseudepigrapha of the Old Testament in English with Introductions and Critical and Explanatory Notes to the Several Books* (2 vols.; Oxford: Oxford University Press [1913]).
Charlesworth, J.H.
    1980   'The Origin and Subsequent History of the Authors of the Dead Sea Scrolls: Four Transitional Phases Among the Qumran Essenes', *RevQ* 10: 213-33.
Charlesworth, James H. (ed.)
    1983   *The Old Testament Pseudepigrapha*. I. *Apocalyptic Literature and Testaments* (London: Darton, Longman & Todd).
    1985   *The Old Testament Pseudepigrapha*. II. *Expansion of the 'Old Testament' and Legends, Wisdom and Philosophical Literature, Prayers, Psalms and Odes, Fragments of Lost Judeo-Hellenistic Works* (London: Darton, Longman & Todd).

1992   *The Messiah: Developments in Earliest Judaism and Christianity* (The
            First Princeton Symposium on Judaism and Christian Origins; Philadel-
            phia: Fortress Press).

Chuvin, P.
1990   *A Chronicle of the Last Pagans* (trans. B.A. Archer; Cambridge, MA:
            Harvard University Press).

Cohen, S.J.D.
1989   'Crossing the Boundary and Becoming a Jew', *HTR* 92: 13-33.
1990   'The Modern Study of Ancient Judaism', in S.J.D. Cohen and E.L.
            Greenstein (eds.), *The State of Jewish Studies* (Detroit: Wayne State
            University Press): 55-73.

Cohen, S.J.D., and E.S. Frerichs (eds.)
1993   *Diasporas in Antiquity* (Atlanta: Scholars Press).

Cohen, S.J.D.
1984   'The Significance of Yavneh: Pharisees, Rabbis and the End of Jewish
            Sectarianism', *HUCA* 55: 27-53.
1999   *The Beginnings of Jewishness: Boundaries, Varieties, Uncertainties*
            (Berkeley: University of California Press).

Collins, John J., and George W.E. Nickelsburg (eds.)
1980   *Ideal Figures in Ancient Judaism: Profiles and Paradigms* (Chico, CA:
            Scholars Press).

Collins, J.J.
1984   *The Apocalyptic Imagination* (New York: Crossroad).
1986   *Between Athens and Jerusalem: Jewish Identity in the Hellenistic Dias-
            pora* (New York: Crossroad).
1989   'The Origin of the Qumran Community: A Review of the Evidence', in
            M.P. Horgan and P.J. Kobelski (eds.), *To Touch the Text: Biblical and
            Related Studies in Honor of Joseph A. Fitzmyer* (New York: Crossroad):
            159-78.

Colpe, C.
1961   *Die religionsgeschichtliche Schule* (Göttingen: Vandenhoeck &
            Ruprecht).
1974   'Heidnische, jüdische und christliche Überlieferung in den Schriften aus
            Nag Hammadi III', *JAC* 17: 122-24.

Colson, F.H., and G.H. Whitaker
1929–43   *Philo* (10 vols.; LCL; London: William Heinemann; Cambridge, MA:
            Harvard University Press).

Conzelmann, H.
1973   *Jesus* (ed. J. Reumann; Philadelphia: Fortress Press) (reprint of article in
            RGG 3 (1959): 97-116.

Cross, F.L. (trans. and ed.)
1955   *The Jung Codex* (London: Mowbray; New York: Morehouse–Gorham).

Cross, F.M.
1961   'The Development of Jewish Scripts', in G.E. Wright (ed.), *The Bible and
            the Ancient Near East* (Garden City, NY: Doubleday, 1961): 133-202.
1995   *The Ancient Library of Qumran* (Sheffield: Sheffield Academic Press,
            rev. 3rd edn).

1999   'Palaeography and the Dead Sea Scrolls', in Flint and VanderKam 1999:
            I, 379-402.

Crossan, J.
1993   *The Historical Jesus: The Life of a Mediterranean Jewish Peasant* (San
            Francisco: Harper).
1994   *Jesus: A Revolutionary Biography* (San Francisco: Harper).
1998   *The Birth of Christianity* (San Francisco: HarperSanFrancisco)

Cumont, Franz
1956a   *The Mysteries of Mithras* (New York: Dover [1903]).
1956b   *Oriental Religions in Roman Paganism* (New York: Dover [1911]).
1960   *Astrology and Religion among the Greeks and Romans* (New York:
            Dover [1912]).

Daniels, Charles
1962   *Mithras and his Temples on the Wall* (Museum of Antiquities of the
            University of Durham and Society of Antiquaries of Newcastle upon
            Tyne).

Davenport, Gene L.
1980   ' "The Anointed of the Lord" in Psalms of Solomon 17', in Collins and
            Nickelsburg 1980: 67-92.

Davies, P.R.
1977   'Hasidim in the Maccabean Period', *JJS* 28: 127-40.
1982   *Qumran* (Cities of the Biblical World; Guildford: Lutterworth).
1988   'How Not to Do Archaeology: The Story of Qumran', *BA* 51: 203-207.
1996   'Sadducees in the Dead Sea Scrolls', in *idem, Sects and Scrolls: Essays
            on Qumran and Related Topics* (South Florida Studies in the History of
            Judaism, 134; Atlanta: Scholars Press): 127-38.

de Jonge, M.
1991   *Jesus, the Servant Messiah* (New Haven: Yale University Press).

Dillon, M.
1997   *Pilgrims and Pilgrimage in Ancient Greece* (London: Routledge).

Dodd, C.H.
1953   *The Interpretation of the Fourth Gospel* (Cambridge: Cambridge Univer-
            sity Press).

Dodds, E.R.
1968   *Pagan and Christian in an Age of Anxiety* (Cambridge: Cambridge Uni-
            versity Press).

Donaldson, T.L.
1997   *Paul and the Gentiles: Remapping the Apostle's Convictional World*
            (Philadelphia: Fortress Press).

Donfried, K.F.
1985   'The Cults of Thessalonica and the Thessalonian Correspondence', *New
            Testament Studies* 31.3: 336-56.

Doresse, J.
1958   *Les livres secrets des gnostiques d'Egypte* (Paris: Librairie Plon, 1958)
            (ET *The Secret Books of the Egyptian Gnostics* [London: Hollis & Carter,
            1960]).

Doudna, G.
1999   'Dating the Scrolls on the Basis of Radiocarbon Analysis', in Flint and VanderKam 1999: II, 430-71.

Dowd, S.
1996   'Which Jesus? A Survey of the Controversy over "The Historical Jesus" ', *Lexington Theological Quarterly* 31: 87-186.

Downing, F.G.
1988   *Christ and the Cynics: Jesus and Other Radical Preachers in First Century Tradition* (Sheffield: Sheffield Academic Press, 1988).

Duling, Dennis C., and Norman Perrin
1994   *The New Testament: Proclamation and Parenesis, Myth and History* (Fort Worth: Harcourt Brace College Publishers).

Dunn, J.D.G.
1990   *Unity and Diversity in the New Testament: An Inquiry into the Character of Earliest Christianity* (London: SCM Press; Valley Forge, PA: Trinity Press International, 2nd rev. edn).
1991   *The Partings of the Ways between Christianity and Judaism and their Significance for the Character of Christianity* (London: SCM Press; Philadelphia: Trinity Press International).
1998a   'Paul: Apostate or Apostle of Israel', *ZNW* 89: 256-71.
1998b   *The Theology of Paul the Apostle* (Grand Rapids: Eerdmans).

Dunn, J.
1985   *The Evidence for Jesus* (Philadelphia: Westminster Press).

Dupont-Sommer, A.
1961   *The Essene Writings from Qumran* (ET G. Vermes; Oxford: Basil Blackwell).

Duthoy, Robert
1969   *The Taurobolium: Its Evolution and Terminology* (Études Préliminaires aux Religions Orientales dans l'Empire Romain, 10; Leiden: E.J. Brill).

Easterling, P., and J.V. Muir (eds.)
1985   *Greek Religion and Society* (Cambridge: Cambridge University Press).

Ebeling, G.
1963   *Word and Faith* (Philadelphia: Fortress Press).

Elliott, John
1995   *Social-Scientific Criticism of the New Testament: An Introduction* (London: SPCK).

Elsas, C.
1975   *Neuplatonische und gnostische Weltablehnung in der Schule Plotinus* (Berlin: W. de Gruyter).

Epp, E.J.
1995   'The Papyrus Manuscripts of the New Testament', in B.D. Ehrman and M.W. Holmes (eds.), *The Text of the New Testament in Contemporary Research: Essays on the Status Quaestionis* (Grand Rapids: Eerdmans): 3-21.

Esler, Philip F.
1987   *Community and Gospel in Luke–Acts: The Social and Political Motivations of Lucan Theology* (Cambridge: Cambridge University Press).

1994	*The First Christians in their Social Worlds: Social-Scientific Approaches to New Testament Interpretation* (London: Routledge).
1995b	'God's Honour and Rome's Triumph: Responses to the Fall of Jerusalem in 70 CE in Three Jewish Apocalypses', in Esler 1995a: 239-58.
1998a	*Galatians* (London: Routledge).
1998b	'Poverty and Riches in the Bible and the Third World', in Philip F. Esler (ed.), *Christianity for the Twenty-First Century* (Edinburgh: T. & T. Clark): 145-79.

Esler, Philip F. (ed.)

1995a	*Modelling Early Christianity: Social-Scientific Studies of the New Testament in its Context* (London and New York: Routledge).

Evans, C.A.

1989a	'Authenticity Criteria in Life of Jesus Research', *CSR* 19: 6-31.
1989b	'Jesus' Action in the Temple and Evidence of Corruption in the First-Century Temple', in David J. Lull (ed.), *Society of Biblical Literature 1989 Seminar Papers* (Atlanta, GA: Scholars Press): 522-39.
1993	'Life-of-Jesus Research and the Eclipse of Mythology', *TS* 54: 3-26.
1996	*The Historical Christ and the Jesus of Faith: The Incarnational Narrative as History* (Oxford: Clarendon Press).

Evans-Pritchard, E.E.

1976	*Witchcraft and Oracles among the Azande* (Oxford: Clarendon Press, abridged edn).

Falk, H.

1985	*Jesus the Pharisee: A New Look at the Jewishness of Jesus* (New York: Paulist Press, 1985).

Faraone, C.A., and D. Obbink (eds.)

1991	*Magika Hiera* (Oxford: Oxford University Press).

Feldman, Louis H.

1990	'Some Observations on the Name of Palestine', *HUCA* 61: 1-23.
1993	*Jew and Gentile in the Ancient World* (Princeton: Princeton University Press).

Ferguson, J.

1970	*The Religions of the Roman Empire* (Aspects of Greek and Roman Life; Ithaca, NY: Cornell University Press).

Festugière, A.

1954	*Personal Religion among the Greeks* (Berkeley: University of California Press).

Fiensy, David A.

1991	*The Social History of Palestine in the Herodian Period: The Land Is Mine* (Studies in the Bible and Early Christianity, 20; Lewiston, NY: Edwin Mellen Press).

Filoramo, G.

1990	*A History of Gnosticism* (ET; Oxford: Basil Blackwell).
1992	'Nag Hammadi Writings', in A. Di Berardino and W.H.C. Frend (eds.), *The Encyclopedia of the Early Church II* (Cambridge: James Clarke & Co.): 579.

Fiorenza, E.S.
    1994   *Jesus: Miriam's Child, Sophia's Prophet: Critical Issues in Feminist Christology* (New York: Continuum).
Fitzmyer, J.A.
    1995   'The Qumran Community: Essene or Sadducean?', *HeyJ* 36: 467-76.
Flesher, Paul M.
    1995   'Palestinian Synagogues before 70 C.E.: A Review of the Evidence', in Urman and Flesher 1995: I, 27-39.
Flint, P. and J.C. VanderKam (eds.)
    1999   *The Dead Sea Scrolls after Fifty Years: A Comprehensive Assessment* (2 vols.; Leiden: E.J. Brill).
Foerster, W.
    1969   *Die Gnosis*, I (Zürich: Artemis Verlag, 1969; ET Oxford: Clarendon Press, 1972).
    1972   *Die Gnosis*, II (ed. M. Krause and K. Rudolph; Zürich: Artemis Verlag, 1971; ET Oxford: Clarendon Press, 1974).
Fowl, S.
    1989   'Reconstructing and Deconstructing the Quest of the Historical Jesus', *SJT* 42: 319-33.
Francis, J.A.
    1995   *Subversive Virtue: Ascetics and Authority in the Second-Century Pagan World* (University Park: Pennsylvania State University Press).
Frend, W.H.C.
    1996   *The Archaeology of Early Christianity* (London: Geoffrey Chapman).
Frey, J.
    1997   'Different Patterns of Dualistic Thought in the Qumran Library. Reflections on their Background and History', in M. Bernstein, F. García Martínez and J. Kampen (eds.), *Legal Texts and Legal Issues: Proceedings of the Second Meeting of the International Organization for Qumran Studies Published in Honour of Joseph M. Baumgarten* (STDJ, 23; Leiden: E.J. Brill): 275-335.
Freyne, Sean
    1980   *Galilee from Alexander the Great to Hadrian 323 B.C.E. to 135 C.E.: A Study of Second Temple Judaism* (Wilmington, DE: Michael Glazier; Notre Dame, IN: University of Notre Dame Press).
    1995   'Herodian Economics in Galilee: Searching for a Suitable Model', in Esler 1995a: 23-46.
    2000   *Galilee and Gospel: Collected Essays* (WUNT, 125; Tübingen: Mohr–Siebeck).
Friedländer, M.
    1905   *Die religiösen Bewegungen innerhalb des Judentums im Zeitalter Jesu* (Berlin: Georg Reimer).
Friedlander, A.
    1972   *Der vorchristliche judische Gnosticismus* (Farnborough: Gregg [1898]).
    1973   *Leo Baeck* (London: Routledge & Kegan Paul).
Fuchs, E.
    1964   *Studies in the Historical Jesus* (SBT, 42; London: SCM Press).

Funk, R.
1996   *Honest to Jesus: Jesus for a New Millennium* (San Francisco: Harper).
Funk, R. (ed.)
1998   *Acts of Jesus* (San Francisco: HarperSanFrancisco).
Funk R., and R. Hoover (eds.)
1993   *The Five Gospels: The Search for the Authentic Words of Jesus* (New York: Macmillan).
Gager, J.G.
1983   *The Origins of Anti-Semitism: Attitudes towards Judaism in Pagan and Christian Antiquity* (Oxford: Oxford University Press).
1992   *Curse Tablets and Binding Spells from the Ancient World* (Oxford: Oxford University Press).
García Martínez, F.
1988   'Qumran Origins and Early History: A Groningen Hypothesis', *Folia Orientalia* 25: 113-36.
García Martínez F., and A.S. van der Woude
1990   'A "Groningen" Hypothesis of Qumran Origins and Early History', *RevQ* 14: 521-41.
Georgi, D.
1964   *Die Gegner des Paulus im 2. Korintherbrief* (trans. and updated as *The Opponents of Paul in Second Corinthians* [Edinburgh: T. & T. Clark, 1987]).
Gerhardsson, B.
1961   *Memory and Manuscript: Oral Tradition and Written Transmission in Rabbinic Judaism and Early Christianity* (Uppsala and Lund: C.W.K. Gleerup), now reissued with his *Tradition and Transmission in Early Christianity* (Grand Rapids: Eerdmans, 1998).
Golb, N.
1980   'The Problem of Origin and Identification of the Dead Sea Scrolls', *Proceedings of the American Philosophical Society* 124: 1-24.
1995   *Who Wrote the Dead Sea Scrolls?* (London: O'Mara).
Goodblatt, D.
1989   'The Place of the Pharisees in First Century Judaism: The State of the Debate', *JSJ* 20: 12-30.
Goodenough, E.R.
1953–68 *Jewish Symbols in the Greco-Roman Period* (13 vols.; New York: Pantheon; ed. J. Neusner; Princeton: Princeton University Press, 1988).
Goodman, M.
1994   *Mission and Conversion: Proselytizing in the Religious History of the Roman Empire* (Oxford: Clarendon Press).
Goodman, M.D.
1987   *The Ruling Class of Judaea: The Origins of the Jewish Revolt against Rome A.D. 66–70* (Cambridge: Cambridge University Press).
1994   'Sadducees and Essenes after 70 CE', in S.E. Porter, P. Joyce and D.E. Orton (eds.), *Crossing the Boundaries: Essays in Biblical Interpretation in Honour of Michael D. Goulder* (Leiden: E.J. Brill): 347-65.
1995   'A Note on the Qumran Sectarians, the Essenes and Josephus', *JJS* 46: 161-66.

Grabbe, Lester L.
   1994   *Judaism from Cyrus to Hadrian* (London: SCM Press, one-vol. edn [1992]).
   1995   'Synagogues in Pre-70 Palestine: A Re-Assessment', in Urman and Flesher 1995: 16-26 (reprinted from *JTS* 39 [1989]: 401-10).
   1996   *An Introduction to First Century Judaism: Jewish Religion and History in the Second Temple Period* (Edinburgh: T. & T. Clark).
Grant, F.C. (ed.)
   1957   *Ancient Roman Religion* (Library of Liberal Arts; New York: Bobbs-Merrill).
Grant, R.M.
   1956   Review of Hans Jonas, *Gnosis und Spätantiker Geist*, *JTS* 7: 308-13.
   1961   *Gnosticism: An Anthology* (London: Collins).
   1966   *Gnosticism and Early Christianity* (New York: Columbia University Press, 1966, 2nd edn [1958]).
Graves, Robert (trans.)
   1950   *Apuleius: The Golden Ass* (Harmondsworth: Penguin Books).
Gray, Rebecca
   1993   *Prophetic Figures in Late Second Temple Jewish Palestine: The Evidence from Josephus* (Oxford: Oxford University Press).
Green, H.
   1977   'Gnosis and Gnosticism: A Study in Methodology', *Numen* 24: 95-134.
Griffiths, J. Gwyn
   1995   'Egypt and the Rise of the Synagogue', in Urman and Flesher 1995: 3-16 (reprinted from *JTS* 38 [1987]: 1-15).
Groh, Dennis E.
   1995   'The Stratigraphic Chronology of the Galilean Synagogue from the Early Roman Period through the Early Byzantine Period (ca. 420 C.E.)', in Urman and Flesher 1995: 51-69.
Haardt, R.
   1967a   'Bemerkungen zu den Methoden der Ursprungsbestimmung von Gnosis', in Bianchi 1967: 161-74.
   1967b   *Die Gnosis* (Salzburg: O. Muller).
   1973   'Zur Methodologie der Gnosisforschung', in K.W. Tröger, *Gnosis und Neues Testament* (Gütersloh: Gütersloher Verlagshaus): 183-202.
Habicht, C.
   1985   *Pausanias' Guide to Ancient Greece* (Berkeley: California University Press).
Hagner, D.
   1984   *The Jewish Reclamation of Jesus* (Grand Rapids: Zondervan).
Hall, Jonathan M.
   1997   *Ethnic Identity in Greek Antiquity* (Cambridge: Cambridge University Press).
Hansen, W.
   1998   *Anthology of Ancient Greek Popular Literature* (Bloomington: Indiana University Press).

Hanson, K.C., and Douglas E. Oakman
  1998   *Palestine in the Time of Jesus: Social Structures and Social Conflicts* (Philadelphia: Fortress Press).
Harnack, A. von
  1897   *History of Dogma* (ET; London: Williams & Norgate, 1897).
Harnack, A. von *et al.* (eds.)
  1907   *Philotesia: Paul Kleinert zum 70. Geburtstag dargebracht* (Berlin: Trowzisch, 1907).
Harrisville, R., and W. Sundberg
  1995   *The Bible in Modern Culture: Theology and Historical-Critical Method from Spinoza to Käsemann* (Grand Rapids: Eerdmans).
Harvey, A.
  1982   *Jesus and the Constraints of History* (London: Gerald Duckworth).
Harvey, Graham
  1996   *The True Israel: Uses of the Names Jew, Hebrew and Israel in Ancient Jewish and Early Christian Literature* (Leiden: E.J. Brill).
Harvey, W.
  1857   *Sancti Irenaei Libros quinque adversus Haereses* (Cambridge: Cambridge University Press).
Hempel, C.
  1997   'Qumran Communities: Beyond the Fringes of Second Temple Society', in S.E. Porter and C.A. Evans (eds.), *The Scrolls and the Scriptures: Qumran Fifty Years After* (Roehampton Institute London Papers, 3; JSPSup, 26; Sheffield: Sheffield Academic Press): 43-53.
  1999   'Community Origins in the *Damascus Document* in the Light of Recent Scholarship', in D.W. Parry and E. Ulrich (eds.), *The Provo International Conference on the Dead Sea Scrolls: Technological Innovations, New Texts and Reformulated Issues* (STDJ, 30; Leiden: E.J. Brill): 316-29.
  2000   *The Damascus Texts* (Guides to the Qumran Scrolls, 1; Sheffield: Sheffield Academic Press).
Hengel, M.
  1961   *Die Zeloten* (Leiden: E.J. Brill).
  1969   *Judentum und Hellenismus* (trans. from 2nd edn as *Judaism and Hellenism* [London: SCM Press, 1974]).
  1974   *Judaism and Hellenism: Studies in their Encounter in Palestine during the Early Hellenistic Period* (London: SCM Press, one-vol. edn).
  1978   'Qumran und der Hellenismus', in M. Delcor (ed.), *Qumrân: Sa piété, sa théologie et son milieu* (Paris: Duculot; Leuven: Leuven University Press): 333-72.
Hengel, Martin
  1961   *Die Zeloten* (Leiden: E.J. Brill).
  1966   'Die Synagogeninschrift von Stobi', *ZNW* 57: 145-83.
  1971   'Proseuche und Synagoge: Jüdische Gemeinde, Gotteshaus und Gottesdienst in der Diaspora und in Palästina', in Gert Jeremias, Heinz-Wolfang Kuhn and Hartmut Stegemann (eds.), *Tradition und Glaube: Das frühe Christentum in seiner Umwelt. Festgabe für Karl Georg Kuhn zum 65. Geburtstag* (Göttingen: Vandenhoeck & Ruprecht): 157-84.

Hennecke, E., and W. Schneemelcher (eds.)
    1963   *New Testament Apocrypha* (2 vols.; London: Lutterworth).
Hinnells, John R. (ed.)
    1975   *Mithraic Studies* (Proceedings of the First International Congress of
                Mithraic Studies; 2 vols.; Manchester: Manchester University Press).
Hobsbawm, Eric J.
    1981   *Bandits* (New York: Pantheon, rev. edn).
Holladay, Carl R.
    1983   *Fragments from Hellenistic Jewish Authors*. I. *Historians* (Texts and
                Translations, 20; Pseudepigrapha Series, 10; Atlanta: Scholars Press).
Horbury, W., and D. Noy
    1992   *Jewish Inscriptions of Graeco-Roman Egypt* (Cambridge: Cambridge
                University Press).
Horsley, R.A.
    1985   *Bandits, Prophets and Messiahs: Popular Movements of the Time of Jesus*
                (with J.S. Hanson; Minneapolis: Winston).
    1989   *Sociology and the Jesus Movement* (New York: Crossroad).
    1993   *Jesus and the Spiral of Violence* (San Francisco: Harper).
Horsley, G.H.R. (ed.)
    1976   *New Documents Illustrating Early Christianity* (NSW, Australia: Mac-
                quarie University).
Hyatt, J.P. (ed.)
    1965   *The Bible in Modern Scholarship* (Nashville: Abingdon Press).
Jefford, C.N.
    1995   *The Didache in Context: Essays on its Text, History and Transmission*
                (Leiden: E.J. Brill).
Johnson, L.T.
    1995   *The Real Jesus: The Misguided Quest for the Historical Jesus and the
                Truth of the Traditional Gospels* (San Francisco: Harper).
Johnson, P.
    1992   Review of B. Thiering, *Jesus the Man: A New Interpretation from the
                Dead Sea Scrolls* (New York: Doubleday), in the *Sunday Telegraph*, 13
                Sept. 1992.
Jonas, H.
    1934, 1954 *Gnosis und Spätantiker Geist* (2 vols.; Göttingen: Vandenhoeck &
                Ruprecht).
    1965   'Response to G. Quispel's *Gnosticism and the New Testament*', in J.P.
                Hyatt (ed.), *The Bible in Modern Scholarship* (Nashville: Abingdon
                Press): 286-93.
Jones, C.P.
    1978   *The Roman World of Dio Chrysostom* (Cambridge, MA: Harvard Univer-
                sity Press).
    1986   *Culture and Society in Lucian* (Cambridge, MA: Harvard University
                Press).
Jull, A.J.T. *et al.*
    1996   'Radiocarbon Dating of Scrolls and Linen Fragments from the Judaean
                Desert', *'Atiqot* 28: 1-7.

Juster, J.
  1914   *Les Juifs dans l'Empire Romain* (2 vols.; Paris: P. Geuthner).
Käsemann, E.
  1954   'The Problem of the Historical Jesus', *ZTK* 51: 125-53 (ET in *Essays on New Testament Themes* [SBT, 41; London: SCM Press, 1964]: 15-47).
Kasher, A.
  1985   *The Jews in Hellenistic and Roman Egypt: The Struggle for Equal Rights* (Tübingen: J.C.B. Mohr [Paul Siebeck]).
Kasher, Aryeh
  1995   'Synagogues as "Houses of Prayer" and "Holy Places" in the Jewish Communities of Hellenistic and Roman Egypt', in Urman and Flesher 1995: 205-20.
Kautsky, John H.
  1982   *The Politics of Aristocratic Empires* (Chapel Hill: University of North Carolina Press).
Kearns, E.
  1995   'Order, Interaction, Authority: Ways of Looking at Greek Religion', in A. Powell (ed.), *The Greek World* (London: Routledge).
Keck, L.
  1994   'The Second Coming of the Liberal Jesus?', *Christian Century* 111: 784-87.
Keck, L.E.
  1982   *Paul and his Letters* (Philadelphia: Fortress Press).
Kennedy, H.
  1913   *St Paul and the Mystery Religions* (London: Hodder & Stoughton).
Khosroyev, A.
  1995   *Die Bibliothek von Nag Hammadi* (Altenberge: Oros Verlag).
Knibb, M.A.
  1983   'Exile in the Damascus Document', *JSOT* 25: 99-117.
Koester, E.
  1992   'Jesus the Victim', *JBL* 111: 3-15.
Koester, H.
  1972   'One Jesus and Four Primitive Gospels', in J. Robinson and H. Koester, *Trajectories through Early Christianity* (Philadelphia: Fortress Press): 158-204.
Kraabel, A.T.
  1981   'The Disappearance of the "God-Fearers" ', *Numen* 28: 113-26.
  1982   'The Roman Diaspora: Six Questionable Assumptions', *JJS* 33: 445-64.
  1983   'Impact of the Discovery of the Sardis Synagogue', in G.M.A. Hanfmann (ed.), *Sardis from Prehistoric to Roman Times: Results of the Archaeological Exploration of Sardis, 1958–1975* (Cambridge, MA: Harvard University Press): 178-90.
Kraeling, C.H.
  1956   *The Synagogue* (Excavations at Dura Europos, 8.1; New Haven: Yale University Press).
Kraft, Robert A., and G.W.E. Nickelsburg (eds.)
  1986   *Early Judaism and its Modern Interpreters* (Atlanta: Scholars Press).

Krause, M.
    1967   'Der Stand der Veröffentlichung der Nag-Hammadi Texte', in Bianchi
                1967: 67-68.
Krause, M., and P. Labib
    1962   *Die drei Versionen des Apokryphon des Johannes im Koptischen Museum
                zu Alt-Kairo* (Wiesbaden: Otto Harrassowitz).
Kuhn, T.S.
    1970   *The Structure of Scientific Revolutions* (Chicago: University of Chicago
                Press, 2nd edn).
Lagrange, M.-J.
    1931   *Le Judaïsme avant Jésus-Christ* (Paris: J. Gabalda).
Lane Fox, R.
    1986   *Pagans and Christians* (Harmondsworth: Viking Press).
Langerbeck, H.
    1967   *Aufsätze zur Gnosis* (Göttingen: Vandenhoeck & Ruprecht).
Lapide, P.
    1976   'Two Famous Rabbis', *ASTI* 10: 97-109.
Law, R.
    1909   *The Tests of Life* (Edinburgh: T. & T. Clark, 1909).
Layton, B. (ed.)
    1980   *The Rediscovery of Gnosticism* (2 vols.; Leiden: E.J. Brill).
Legge, F.
    1915   *Forerunners and Rivals of Christianity* (New York: University Books,
                1964).
LeMoyne, J.
    1972   *Les Sadducéens* (Paris: Etudes Bibliques).
Lenski, Gerhard, and Jean Lenski
    1982   *Human Societies: An Introduction to Macrosociology* (New York:
                McGraw–Hill).
Leon, H.J.
    1960   *The Jews of Ancient Rome* (Philadelphia: Jewish Publication Society of
                America) (repr.; Peabody, MA: Hendrickson, 1995).
Levin, S.
    1989   'The Old Greek Oracles in Decline', *ANRW*, II.18.2: 1599-649.
Levinskaya, I.
    1996   *The Book of Acts in its Diaspora Setting* (Grand Rapids: Eerdmans;
                Carlisle: Paternoster Press).
Lewis, Jack P.
    1992   'Jamnia (Jabneh), Council of', *ABD*, III: 634-37.
Lewis, N.
    1983   *Life in Egypt under Roman Rule* (Oxford: Clarendon Press).
Lieberman, S.
    1962   *Hellenism in Jewish Palestine* (New York: Jewish Theological Seminary
                of America).
Liebeschuetz, W.
    1979   *Continuity and Change in Roman Religion* (Oxford: Clarendon Press).

Lieu, S.
1985   *Manichaeism in the Later Roman Empire and Medieval China: A His-
            torical Survey* (Manchester: Manchester University Press).
Lightley, J.W.
1925   *Jewish Sects and Parties in the Time of Jesus* (London: Epworth Press).
Logan, A.H.B.
1996   *Gnostic Truth and Christian Heresy* (Edinburgh: T. & T. Clark).
Logan, A.H.B., and A.J.M. Wedderburn
1983   *The New Testament and Gnosis* (Edinburgh: T. & T. Clark).
Lohse, E.
1976   *The New Testament Environment* (London: SCM Press).
Lüderitz, G.
1983   *Corpus jüdischer Zeugnisse aus der Cyrenaika* (appendix by J. Reynolds;
            Wiesbaden: L. Reichert).
1994   'What Is the Politeuma?', in J.W. van Henten and P.W. van der Horst
            (eds.), *Studies in Early Jewish Epigraphy* (Leiden: E.J. Brill): 183-225.
Lowenthal, D.
1985   *The Past Is a Foreign Country* (Cambridge: Cambridge University Press).
Maccoby, H.
1973   *Revelation in Judea: Jesus and the Jewish Resistance* (London: Orbach
            & Chambers).
1991   *Paul and Hellenism* (London: SCM Press).
MacDermot, V.
1978   *The Books of Jeu and the Untitled Text in the Bruce Codex* (Leiden: E.J.
            Brill).
1978   *Pistis Sophia* (Leiden: E.J. Brill).
Mack, B.L.
1988   *A Myth of Innocence: Mark and Christian Origins* (Philadelphia: Fortress
            Press).
1993   *The Lost Gospel: The Book of Q and Christian Origins* (San Francisco:
            Harper).
Macmullen, R.
1981   *Paganism in the Roman Empire* (New Haven: Yale University Press).
1984   *Christianising the Roman Empire* (New Haven: Yale University Press).
MacRae, G.
1978   'Nag Hammadi and the New Testament', in Aland 1978: 144-57.
Magness, J.
1994   'The Community at Qumran in Light of its Pottery', in M.O. Wise *et al.*
            (eds.), *Methods of Investigation of the Dead Sea Scrolls and the Khirbet
            Qumran Site: Present Realities and Future Prospects* (ANYAS, 722;
            New York: New York Academy of Sciences): 39-50.
Mahé, P.J.
1983   *Hermés en Haute-Egypte* (2 vols.; Quebec: Les Presses de l'Université
            Laval, 1978–83).
Malina, Bruce J.
1986   'Religion in the World of Paul: A Preliminary Sketch', *BTB* 16: 92-101.
1993   *The New Testament World: Insights from Cultural Anthropology*
            (Louisville, KY: Westminster/John Knox Press [1981]).

1994   'Religion in the Imagined New Testament World: More Social Science
             Lenses', *Scriptura* 51: 1-26.
1996   'Mediterranean Sacrifice: Dimensions of Domestic and Political
             Religion', *BTB* 26: 26-44.
Martinez, Florentino García
1994   *The Dead Sea Scrolls Translated: The Qumran Texts in English* (Leiden:
             E.J. Brill).
Mason, Steve
1991   *Flavius Josephus on the Pharisees: A Composition-Critical Study* (SPB,
             39; Leiden: E.J. Brill).
Maurer, C.
1963   'Gospel of Peter', in Hennecke and Schneemelcher 1963: I, 179-83.
McDonald, Lee M.
1995   *The Formation of the Christian Biblical Canon* (Peabody, MA: Hendrick-
             son, rev. and expanded edn).
McKnight, S.
1991   *A Light among the Gentiles: Jewish Missionary Activity in the Second
             Temple Period* (Philadelphia: Fortress Press).
Meeks, W.A.
1983   *The First Urban Christians: The Social World of the Apostle Paul* (New
             Haven: Yale University Press).
Meeks, W.A., and R.L. Wilken
1978   *Jews and Christians in Antioch in the First Four Centuries of the Com-
             mon Era* (Missoula, MT: Scholars Press).
Meier, J.P.
1991   *A Marginal Jew.* I. *Rethinking the Historical Jesus* (New York:
             Doubleday).
1994   *A Marginal Jew.* II. *Mentor, Message, Miracle* (New York: Doubleday).
1996   'Dividing Lines in Jesus Research Today: Through Dialectical Negation
             to a Positive Sketch', *Int* 50: 355-72.
Ménard, J.E. (ed.)
1975   *Les textes de Nag Hammadi* (Leiden: E.J. Brill).
Merkelbach, R.
1988   *Die Hirten des Dionysos: Die Dionysos-Mysterien der roemischen
             Kaiserzeit und der bukolische Romans des Longus* (Stuttgart: Teubner).
Meyer, B.F.
1979   *The Aims of Jesus* (London: SCM Press).
Meyers, Eric M., and A. Thomas Kraabel
1986   'Archaeology, Iconography, and Nonliterary Written Remains', in Kraft
             and Nickelsburg 1986: 175-210.
Meyers, Eric M., and James F. Strange
1981   *Archaeology, the Rabbis and Early Christianity* (London: SCM Press).
Mikalson, J.D.
1983   *Athenian Popular Religion* (Chapel Hill: University of North Carolina
             Press).
Milik, J.T.
1959   *Ten Years of Discovery in the Wilderness of Judaea* (ET J. Strugnell;
             London: SCM Press).

Millar, F.G.B.
  1993   *The Roman Near East 31 BC–AD 337* (Cambridge, MA: Harvard University Press).
Miller, P.C.
  1994   *Dreams in Late Antiquity* (Princeton: Princeton University Press).
Mitchell, S.
  1993   *Anatolia: Land, Men and Gods in Asia Minor* (2 vols.; Oxford: Clarendon Press).
Modrzejewksi, J.M.
  1995   *The Jews of Egypt from Rameses II to Emperor Hadrian* (Edinburgh: T. & T. Clark).
Moeller, Walter O.
  1973   *The Mithraic Origin and Meanings of the Rotas-Sator Square* (Études Préliminaires aux Religions Orientales dans l'Empire Romain, 38; Leiden: E.J. Brill).
Montefiore, C.G.
  1914   'The Genesis of the Religion of St. Paul', in *idem, Judaism and St. Paul: Two Essays* (London: Max Goschen): 1-129.
Moore, G.F.
  1927–30   *Judaism in the First Centuries of the Christian Era in the Age of the Tannaim* (3 vols.; Cambridge, MA: Harvard University Press).
Murphy-O'Connor, J.
  1974   'The Essenes and their History', *RB* 81: 215-44.
  1996   *Paul: A Critical Life* (Oxford: Clarendon Press).
Murray, G.
  1925   *Five Stages of Greek Religion* (Oxford: Clarendon Press).
Nagel, P. (ed.)
  1974   *Studia Coptica* (Berlin: Akademie Verlag).
Neill, S., and T. Wright
  1988   *The Interpretation of the New Testament, 1861–1986* (Oxford: Oxford University Press).
Neusner, Jacob
  1971   *The Rabbinic Traditions about the Pharisees before 70* (3 vols.; Leiden: E.J. Brill).
  1973   *From Politics to Piety: The Emergence of Pharisaic Judaism* (Englewood Cliffs, NJ: Prentice–Hall).
Neusner, J., W.S. Green and E.S. Frerichs (eds.)
  1987   *Judaisms and their Messiahs at the Turn of the Christian Era* (Cambridge: Cambridge University Press).
Nickelsburg, George W.E.
  1981   *Jewish Literature between the Bible and the Mishnah* (Philadelphia: Fortress Press; London: SCM Press).
Nickelsburg, George W.E., with Robert A. Kraft
  1986   'Introduction: The Modern Study of Early Judaism', in Kraft and Nickelsburg 1986: 1-30.
Niederwimmer, K.
  1998   *The Didache: A Commentary* (Minneapolis: Fortress Press).

Nock, A.D.
    1933   *Conversion* (Oxford: Clarendon Press)
Nodet, E., and J. Taylor
    1998   *The Origins of Christianity: An Exploration* (Collegeville: Liturgical Press).
North, R.
    1955   'The Qumran Sadducees', *CBQ* 17: 164-88.
Noy, D.
    1993   *Jewish Inscriptions of Western Europe.* I. *Italy (Excluding the City of Rome), Spain and Gaul* (Cambridge: Cambridge University Press).
    1995   *Jewish Inscriptions of Western Europe.* II. *The City of Rome* (Cambridge: Cambridge University Press).
Oakman, Douglas E.
    1986   *Jesus and the Economic Questions of his Day* (Studies in the Bible and Early Christianity; Lewiston: Edwin Mellen Press).
Obolensky, D.
    1948   *The Bogomils* (Cambridge: Cambridge University Press).
Oesterley, W.O.E., and G.H. Box
    1907   *The Religion and Worship of the Synagogue: An Introduction to the Study of Judaism from the New Testament Period* (London: Pitman).
Oliver, J.H.
    1970   *Marcus Aurelius: Aspects of Civic and Cultural Policy in the East* (Princeton: American School of Classical Studies in Athens).
O'Loughlin, T.
    1988   'Medieval Church History: Beyond Apologetics, after Development, the Awkward Memories', *The Way* 38: 65-76.
Oster, R.E.
    1990   'Ephesus as a Religious Center under the Principate I: Paganism before Constantine', *ANRW*, II.18.3: 1661-728.
Overman, J. Andrew
    1993   'Recent Advances in the Archaeology of the Galilee in the Roman Period', *Currents in Research* 1: 35-57.
Padgett, A.G.
    1997   'Advice for Religious Historians: On the Myth of a Purely Historical Jesus', in S.T. Davis, D. Kendall and G. O'Collins (eds.), *The Resurrection: An Interdisciplinary Symposium on the Resurrection of Jesus* (Oxford: Oxford University Press): 287-307.
Painchaud, L., and A. Pasquier (eds.)
    1995   *Les textes de Nag Hammadi et le problème de leur classification* (Quebec: Presses de l'Université Laval; Louvain: Peeters).
Parke, H.W.
    1985   *The Oracles of Apollo in Asia Minor* (London: Croom Helm).
Parker, R.
    1995   *Athenian Religion: A History* (Oxford: Clarendon Press).
Parrott, D.M. (ed.)
    1991   *Nag Hammadi Codices Ill, 3–4 and V 1* (Leiden: E.J. Brill).

Patterson, S.J.
1993   *The Gospel of Thomas and Jesus* (Sonoma: Polebridge Press) (reviewed in *JTS* 45 [1994]: 262-67).

Pearson, B.A.
1973   'Friedländer Revisited: Alexandrian Judaism and Gnostic Origins', *Studia Philonica* 2: 23-39.
1978   'The Tractate Marsanes (NHC X) and the Platonic Tradition', in Aland 1978: 373-84.
1984   'Philo and Gnosticism', *ANRW*, II.21.1: 295-342.
1990   *Gnosticism, Judaism and Egyptian Christianity* (Minneapolis: Fortress Press).
1995   'The Gospel according to the Jesus Seminar', *Religion* 25: 317-38.
1997   *The Emergence of the Christian Religion: Essays on Early Christianity* (Harrisburg, PA: Trinity Press International).
1998   'An Exposé of the Jesus Seminar', *Dialog* 37: 28-35.

Perrin, N.
1967   *Rediscovering the Teaching of Jesus* (New York: Harper).

Pétrement, S.
1984   *Le Dieu Séparé* (Paris: Cerf) (ET *A Separate God* [London: Darton, Longman & Todd, 1991]).

Peuch, H.C.
1963   'Gnostic Gospels and Related Documents', in E. Hennecke and W. Schneemelcher (eds.), *New Testament Apocrypha*, I (2 vols.; London: Lutterworth): 231-362.

Phipps, W.E.
1977   'Jesus the Prophetic Pharisee', *JES* 14: 17-31.

Potter, C.
1963   *The Lost Years of Jesus* (New Hyde Park, NY: University Books).

Potter, D.
1994   *Prophets and Emperors: Human and Divine Authority from Augustus to Theodosius* (Cambridge, MA: Harvard University Press).

Preissler, H., and H. Seiwert (eds.)
1994   *Gnosisforschung und Religionsgeschichte* (Marburg: Diagonal-Verlag).

Price, S.R.
1984   *Rituals and Power: The Roman Imperial Cult in Asia Minor* (Cambridge: Cambridge University Press).

Puech, H.
1963   'Gnostic Gospels and Related Documents', in Hennecke and Schneemelcher 1963: I, 231-362.

Qimron E., and J. Strugnell
1994   *Qumran Cave 4*. V. Miqsat Ma'ase Ha-Torah (DJD, 10; Oxford: Clarendon Press).

Quispel, G.
1951   *Gnosis als Weltreligion* (Zürich: Origo).
1974–75   *Gnostic Studies* (2 vols.; Istanbul: Nederlands Historisch-Archaeologisch Institut in het Nabije Oosten).

Räisänen, H.
1983   *Paul and the Law* (Tübingen: J.C.B. Mohr).

Rajak, T.
1983   *Josephus: The Historian and his Society* (London: Gerald Duckworth).
1984   'Was There a Roman Charter for the Jews?', *JRS* 74: 107-23.
Redfield, R.
1956   *Peasant Society and Culture* (Chicago: University of Chicago Press).
Reif, S.
2000   'Cairo Genizah', in L.H. Schiffman and J.C. VanderKam (eds.), *Ency-clopedia of the Dead Sea Scrolls* (New York: Oxford University Press): 105-108.
Reimarus, H.S.
1970   *Fragments* (ed. C.H. Talbert; Philadelphia: Fortress Press).
Reitzenstein, R.
1904   *Poimandres* (Leipzig: Teubner).
1927   *Die hellenistischen Mysterienreligionen* (Leipzig: Teubner, 3rd edn).
Renan, Ernst
1882   *Marc-Aurèle et la fin du monde antique* (Paris).
Rengstorf, K.H.
1963   *Ḥirbet Qumrân and the Problem of the Library of the Dead Sea Scrolls* (Leiden: E.J. Brill).
Reynolds, J., and R. Tannenbaum
1987   *Jews and Godfearers at Aphrodisias* (Cambridge: Cambridge Philological Society).
Richardson, A.
1958   *Introduction to the Theology of the New Testament* (London: SCM Press).
Riesenfeld, H.
1993   'Kristologi och kontingens', *SEÅ* 58: 33-50.
Riesner, R.
1992·   'Essene Gate', in *ABD*, II: 618-19.
1988   *Jesus als Lehrer: Eine Untersuchungen zum Ursprung der Evangelien-Überlieferung* (WUNT, 2.7; Tübingen: J.C.B. Mohr, 3rd edn).
Riesner, Rainer
1995   'Synagogues in Jerusalem', in Richard Bauckham (ed.), *The Book of Acts in its First-Century Setting*. IV. *Palestinian Setting* (Grand Rapids: Eerdmans): 179-211.
Riessler P.
1966   *Altjüdisches Schrifttum ausserhalb der Bibel* (Heidelberg: Kerle Verlag, 1966 [1928]).
Robert, L.
1980   *A travers l'Asie Mineure: Poètes et prosateurs, monnaies grecques, voyageurs et géographie* (Athenes: Ecole Française d'Athenes).
Robinson, J.A.T.
1963   *Honest to God* (Philadelphia: Westminster Press).
Robinson, J.M.
1959   *A New Quest of the Historical Jesus* (SBT, 25; London: SCM Press).
1978   'Gnosticism and the New Testament', in Aland 1978: 123-43.
1980   'The Sethians and Johannine Thought', in Layton 1980: 643-70.

Robinson, J.M. *et al.*
1990   *The Nag Hammadi Library in English* (New York: HarperCollins).
Robinson, J.M., and H. Koester
1971   *Trajectories through Early Christianity* (Philadelphia: Fortress Press).
Roetzel, C.J.
1975   *The Letters of Paul: Conversations in Context* (Atlanta: John Knox Press).
Rogers, G.M.
1991   *The Sacred Identity of Ephesos: Foundation Myths of a Roman City* (London: Routledge).
Rowland, Christopher
1988   *Radical Christianity: A Reading of Recovery* (Cambridge: Polity Press).
Rudolph, K.
1969   *Festschrift: Gnosisforschung und Religionsgeschichte* in *TRE* 34: 121-75, 181-231, 358-61; 36 (1971): 1-61, 89-124; 37 (1972): 289-360; 38 (1973): 1-25.
1975   *Gnosis und Gnostizismus* (Darmstadt: Wissenschaftliche Buchgesellschaft (English and French articles translated into German).
1977   *Die Gnosis* (Göttingen: Vandenhoeck & Ruprecht, 1990 [1977]) (ET *Gnosis* [Edinburgh: T. & T. Clark, 1983]).
1983   *Gnosis* (Edinburgh: T. & T. Clark).
1985   'Die Nag-Hammadi Texte und ihre Bedeutung für die Gnosisforschung', *ThR* 50: 1-40.
Runciman, S.
1947   *The Mediaeval Manichee* (Cambridge: Cambridge University Press).
Russell, D.A.
1972   *Plutarch* (London: Gerald Duckworth).
1990   *Antonine Literature* (Oxford: Clarendon Press).
Rutgers, L.
1995   *The Jews in Late Ancient Rome* (Leiden: E.J. Brill).
Rutherford, R.B.
1989   *The Meditations of Marcus Aurelius: A Study* (Oxford: Oxford University Press).
Ryle, H.E.
1892   *The Canon of the Old Testament* (New York: Macmillan).
Saldarini, Anthony J.
1975   'Johanan ben Zakkai's Escape from Jerusalem: Origin and Development of a Rabbinic Story', *JSJ* 6: 189-204.
1988   *Pharisees, Scribes and Sadducees in Palestinian Society: A Sociological Approach* (Wilmington, DE: Michael Glazier).
Sanders, E.P., with A.I. Baumgarten and Alan Mendelson (eds.)
1981   *Jewish and Christian Self-Definition. II. Aspects of Judaism in the Graeco-Roman Period* (London: SCM Press).
Sanders, E.P.
1977   *Paul and Palestinian Judaism* (London: SCM Press).
1983   *Paul, the Law and the Jewish People* (Philadelphia: Fortress Press).
1985   *Jesus and Judaism* (Philadelphia: Fortress Press).

1990a   *Jewish Law from Jesus to the Mishnah: Five Studies* (London: SCM Press; Philadelphia: Trinity Press International).
1990b   'Did the Pharisees Have Oral Law?', in Sanders 1990a: 97-130.
1990c   'Did the Pharisees Eat Ordinary Food in Purity?', in Sanders 1990a: 131-254.
1991   *Paul* (Oxford: Oxford University Press).
1992   *Judaism: Practice and Belief* (London: SCM Press; Philadelphia: Trinity Press International).
1993   *The Historical Figure of Jesus* (London: Allen Lane; Penguin Press).
Save-Söderbergh, T.
1967   'Gnostic and Canonical Gospel Traditions', in Bianchi 1967: 552-62.
1975   'Holy Scriptures or Apologetic Documentations?', in J. Ménard (ed.), *Les textes de Nag Hammadi* (Leiden: E.J. Brill): 3-14.
Schäfer, P.
1995   *The History of the Jews in Antiquity* (Luxembourg: Harwood Academic Publishers).
Schalit, Abraham
1968   *Namenwörterbuch zu Flavius Josephus.* Supplement I to Karl Heinrich Rengstorf (ed.), *A Complete Concordance to Flavius Josephus* (Leiden: E.J. Brill).
Schechter, S.
1910   *Documents of Jewish Sectaries. I. Fragments of a Zadokite Work* (Cambridge: Cambridge University Press).
Schenke, G.
1984   *Die dreigestaltige Protennoia* (TU, 132; Berlin: Akademie Verlag).
Schenke, H.M.
1980   'The Phenomenon and Significance of Gnostic Sethianism', in Layton 1980: II, 588-616.
1974   'Das sethianische System nach Nag-Hammadi-Handschriften', in P. Nagel (ed.), *Studia Coptica* (Berlin: Akademie Verlag): 165-73.
Schiffman, L.H.
1985   *Who Was a Jew? Rabbinic and Halakhic Perspectives on the Jewish–Christian Schism* (New York: Ktav).
1990   'The New Halakhic Letter (4QMMT) and the Origins of the Dead Sea Sect', *BA* 53: 64-73.
1992   'Messianic Figures and Ideas in the Qumran Scrolls', in Charlesworth 1992: 116-29.
1993   'The Sadducean Origins of the Dead Sea Scroll Sect', in Shanks 1993: 35-49.
Schmidt, C.
1896   'Ein vorirenäisches gnostisches Originalwerk in koptischen Sprache', in *Sitzungsbericht der Kgl. Preussischen Akademie der Wissenschaften zu Berlin* (Berlin): 839-47.
1907   'Irenäus und seine Quelle in adv. haer. 1 29', in A. Harnack et al. (eds.), *Philotesia: Paul Kleinert zum 70. Geburtstag dargebracht* (Berlin: Trowzisch): 317-36.

Schmithals, W.

1965   *Paulus und die Gnostiker* (Hamburg-Bergstedt: Herbert Reich-Evangelischer Verlag) (ET; Nashville: Abingdon Press, 1972).

1969   *Die Gnosis in Korinth*, III (Göttingen: Vandenhoeck & Ruprecht) (ET; Nashville: Abingdon Press, 1971).

1984   *Neues Testament und Gnosis* (Darmstadt: Wissenschaftlicher Buchgesellschaft).

Scholem, G.

1950   *Jewish Gnosticism, Merkabah Mysticism and Talmudic Tradition* (New York: Jewish Theological Seminary).

Scholer, D.M.

1971   *Nag Hammadi Bibliography*. I. *1948–1969* (Leiden: E.J. Brill).

1997   *Nag Hammadi Bibliography*. II. *1970–1995* (Leiden: E.J. Brill).

Schürer, Emil

1898   *Geschichte des jüdischen Volkes im Zeitalter Jesu Christi*, II (Leipzig: J.C. Hinrichs, 3rd edn).

1973   *The History of the Jewish People in the Age of Jesus Christ (175 B.C.–A.D. 135)*, I (ed. Geza Vermes and Fergus Millar; Edinburgh: T. & T. Clark, rev. edn).

1979   *The History of the Jewish People in the Age of Jesus Christ (175 B.C.–A.D. 135)*, II (3 vols.; ed. Geza Vermes, Fergus Millar and Matthew Black; Edinburgh: T. & T. Clark, rev. edn).

Schweitzer, A.

1968   *The Quest of the Historical Jesus* (New York: Macmillan).

Scott, James C.

1985   *Weapons of the Weak: Everyday Forms of Peasant Resistance* (New Haven: Yale University Press).

Segal, A.F.

1990   *Paul the Convert: The Apostolate and Apostasy of Saul the Pharisee* (New Haven: Yale University Press).

Shaked, S.

1972   'Qumran and Iran: Further Considerations', *Israel Oriental Studies* 2: 433-46.

Shanks, H. (ed.)

1993   *Understanding the Dead Sea Scrolls* (London: SPCK).

Sheppard, H.J., R.McL. Wilson and A. Kehl

1986   'Hermetik', *RAC* 110, cols. 780-808.

Simon, M.

1948   *Verus Israel*, translated as *Verus Israel: A Study of the Relations between Christians and Jews in the Roman Empire (AD 135–425)* (Oxford: Oxford University Press).

1967   'Eléments gnostiques chez Philon', in Bianchi 1967: 359-74.

Smallwood, E.M.

1976   *The Jews under Roman Rule* (SJLA, 20; corrected reprint 1981; Leiden: E.J. Brill).

Smith, J.Z.

1990   *Drudgery Divine: On the Comparison of Early Christianities and the*

Religions of Antiquity (Jordan Lectures in Comparative Religion, 14; London: School of Oriental and African Studies).

Smith, M.
1978   *Jesus the Magician* (San Francisco: Harper).

Smith, R.
1995   *Julian's Gods: Religion and Philosophy in the Thought and Action of Julian the Apostate* (London: Routledge).

Sourvinou-Inwood, C.
1990   'What Is *Polis* Religion?', in O. Murray and S. Price (eds.), *The Greek City from Homer to Alexander* (Oxford: Clarendon Press): 295-322.

Spong, J.
1992   *Born of a Woman: A Bishop Rethinks the Birth of Jesus* (San Francisco: Harper).

Stegemann, H.
1992   'The Qumran Essenes—Local Members of the Main Jewish Union in Late Second Temple Times', in Trebolle Barrera and Vegas Montaner 1992: I, 83-166.

1998   *The Library of Qumran: On the Essenes, Qumran, John the Baptist, and Jesus* (Grand Rapids, MI: Eerdmans; Leiden: E.J. Brill).

Stein, R.
1980   'The "Criteria" for Authenticity', in R.T. France and D. Wenham (eds.), *Gospel Perspectives*, I (Sheffield: JSOT Press, 1980): 255-63.

Stemberger, Günther
1995   *Jewish Contemporaries of Jesus: Pharisees, Sadducees, Essenes* (ET Allan W. Mahnke; Philadelphia: Fortress Press).

Stendahl, K.
1976   *Paul among Jews and Gentiles* (Philadelphia: Fortress Press).

Stern, Menahem (ed.)
1974   *Greek and Latin Authors on Jews and Judaism. I. From Herodotus to Plutarch* (Jerusalem: Israel Academy of Sciences and Humanities).

1980   *Greek and Latin Authors on Jews and Judaism. II. From Tacitus to Simplicius* (Jerusalem: Israel Academy of Sciences and Humanities).

1984   *Greek and Latin Authors on Jews and Judaism. III. Appendices and Indexes* (Jerusalem: Israel Academy of Sciences and Humanities).

Stern, Sacha
1994   *Jewish Identity in Early Rabbinic Writings* (Leiden: E.J. Brill).

Stewart, Z. (ed.)
1972   *Essays on Religion and the Ancient World* (Oxford: Clarendon Press).

Stone, Michael E.
1981   'Reactions to Destructions [*sic*] of the Second Temple', *JSJ* 12: 195-204.

Stone, Michael E. (ed.)
1984   *Jewish Writings of the Second Temple Period* (CRINT, 2.2; Philadelphia: Fortress Press).

Stroumsa, G.
1984   *Another Seed: Studies in Gnostic Mythology* (Leiden: E.J. Brill).

Stuhlmacher, P.
1993   *Jesus of Nazareth—Christ of Faith* (ET; Peabody, MA: Hendrickson).

Sukenik, E.L.
1948   *Megillot genuzot* (Hidden scrolls), I (Jerusalem: Bialik Institute).

Sussman Y.
1994   'The History of the Halakhah and the Dead Sea Scrolls. Preliminary Talmudic Observations on *Miqṣat Ma'ase ha-Torah* (4QMMT)', in E. Qimron and J. Strugnell (eds.), *Qumran Cave 4. V. Miqṣat Ma'ase ha-Torah* (DJD, 10; Oxford: Clarendon Press, 1994): 179-200.

Sutcliffe, E.S.J.
1960   *The Monks of Qumran: The People of the Dead Sea Scrolls* (London: Burns & Oats).

Swerdlow, Noel
1991   'Review Article: On the Cosmical Mysteries of Mithras', *Classical Philology* 86: 48-63.

Talbert, C.H. (ed)
1970   *Reimarus: Fragments* (Philadelphia: Fortress Press).

Talmon, S.
1987   'Waiting for the Messiah: The Spiritual Universe of the Qumran Covenanters', in Neusner *et al.* 1987: 111-37.

Tardieu, M.
1977   'Les livres mis sous le nom de Seth et les Séthiens de l'hérésiologie', in M. Krause (ed.), *Gnosis and Gnosticism* (Leiden: E.J. Brill): 204-10.

Tcherikover, V.
1961   *Hellenistic Civilization and the Jews* (Philadelphia: Jewish Publication Society of America).

Tcherikover, V., and A. Fuks
1957–64   *Corpus Papyrorum Judaicarum* (3 vols.; Jerusalem: Magnes Press; Cambridge, MA: Harvard University Press).

Teixidor, J.
1977   *The Pagan God: Popular Religion in the Greco-Roman Near East* (Princeton: Princeton University Press).

Telford, W.R.
1994   'Major Trends and Interpretive Issues in the Study of Jesus', in C.A. Evans and B. Chilton (eds.), *Studying the Historical Jesus: Evaluation of the State of Current Research* (Leiden: E.J. Brill): 33-74.

Thackeray, H. St. John *et al.* (trans. and eds.)
1926–65   *Josephus* (LCL; 10 vols.; London: Heinemann; Cambridge, MA: Harvard University Press).
1972–84   *The Facsimile Edition of the Nag Hammadi Codices* (Leiden: E.J. Brill).
1988   *The Nag Hammadi Library in English* (Leiden: E.J. Brill; 3rd rev. edn [1977]).

Theissen, G.
1978   *Sociology of Early Palestinian Christianity* (Philadelphia: Fortress Press).
1982   *Essays on Corinth: The Social Setting of Pauline Christianity* (Edinburgh: T. & T. Clark).
1987   *The Shadow of the Galilean: The Quest of the Historical Jesus in Narrative Form* (Philadelphia: Fortress Press).
1999   *A Theory of Primitive Christian Religion* (London: SCM Press).

224   *Religious Diversity in the Graeco-Roman World*

Thiering, B
1992   *Jesus and the Riddle of the Dead Sea Scrolls: Unlocking the Secret of his Life Story* (San Francisco: Harper).
1992   *Jesus the Man: A New Interpretation from the Dead Sea Scrolls* (New York: Doubleday).
Till, W.C.
1949   'Die Gnosis in Ägypten', *La Parola del Passato* 12: 231-50.
1972   *Die gnostischen Schriften des koptischen Papyrus Berolinensis 8502* (Berlin: Akademie-Verlag, 2nd rev. edn [1955]).
Toynbee, J.M.C.
1986   *The Roman Art Treasures from the Temple of Mithras* (London and Middlesex Archaeological Society Papers, 7).
Trapp, M.B. (trans.)
1990   'Plato's *Phaedrus* in Second-Century Greek Literature', in D.A. Russell (ed.), *Antonine Literature* (Oxford: Clarendon Press): 141-73.
1997   *Maximus of Tyre: The Philosophical Orations* (Oxford: Clarendon Press).
Trebilco, P.
1991   *Jewish Communities in Asia Minor* (Cambridge: Cambridge University Press).
Trebolle Barrera, J., and L. Vegas Montaner (eds.)
1992   *The Madrid Qumran Congress: Proceedings of the International Congress on the Dead Sea Scrolls, Madrid 18–21 March 1991* (STDJ, 11; 2 vols.; Leiden: E.J. Brill).
Troeltsch, E.
1962   'Über historische und dogmatische Methode in der Theologie' (On historical and dogmatic method in theology), in *Gesammelte Schriften* (Aalen: Scientia Verlag [1922]): 729-53.
1977   *Writings on Theology and Religion* (trans. and ed. R. Morgan and M. Pye; Atlanta, GA: John Knox Press).
Tröger, K.W.
1973   *Gnosis und Neues Testament* (Berlin: Evangelische Verlagsanstalt).
1980   'Gnosis und Judentum', in *idem, Altes Testament, Frühjudentum, Gnosis* (Gütersloh: Gütersloher Verlagshaus).
1981   'The Attitude of the Gnostic Religion towards Judaism', in B. Barc (ed.), *Colloque international sur les textes de Nag Hammadi* (Quebec: Presses de l'Université Laval; Louvain: Peeters): 86-98.
Tuckett, C.M.
1986   *Nag Hammadi and the Gospel Tradition: Synoptic Tradition in the Nag Hammadi Library* (Edinburgh: T. & T. Clark).
Turcan, R.
1996   *The Cults of the Roman Empire* (trans. A. Nevill; Oxford: Basil Blackwell).
Turner, J.D.
2000   Introduction and commentary, in C. Barry *et al.* (eds.), *Zostrian* (BCNH section 'textes', 24; Quebec: Presses de l'Université Laval; Leuven: Peeters).

Turner, J.D., and Anne McGuire (eds.)
    1997   *The Nag Hammadi Library after Fifty Years: Proceedings of the 1995 Society of Biblical Literature Commemoration* (Leiden: E.J. Brill).

Turner, M.L.
    1996   *The Gospel according to Philip: The Sources and Coherence of an Early Christian Collection* (Leiden: E.J. Brill).

Tyrrell, G.
    1909   *Christianity at the Cross-Roads* (London: Longmans).

Udoh, Fabian Eugene
    1996   'Tribute and Taxes in Early Roman Palestine (63 B.C.E.–70 C.E.)' (PhD dissertation at Duke University under E.P. Sanders).

Ulansey, David
    1994   'Solving the Mithraic Mysteries', *BARev* 20.5 (Sept/Oct): 40-53. See also 'The Cosmic Mysteries of Mithras' on Internet page www.well.com/user/davidu/mithras.html.
    1989   *The Origins of the Mithraic Mysteries: Cosmology and Salvation in the Ancient World* (Oxford: Oxford University Press).

Urman, Dan, and Paul M. Flesher (eds.)
    1995   *Ancient Synagogues: Historical Analysis and Archaeological Discovery*, I (Leiden: E.J. Brill).

Uro, R. (ed.)
    1998   *Thomas at the Cross-Roads* (Edinburgh: T. & T. Clark).

Valantasis, R.
    1997   *The Gospel of Thomas* (London: Routledge).

van Unnik, W.C.
    1993   *Das Selbstverständnis der jüdischen Diaspora in der hellenistisch-römischen Zeit* (ed. P.W. van der Horst; Leiden: E.J. Brill).

VanderKam, J.C.
    1992   'Righteous One, Messiah, Chosen One and Son of Man in 1 Enoch 37–71', in Charlesworth 1992: 169-91.
    1993   'The People of the Dead Sea Scrolls: Essenes or Sadducees?', in Shanks 1993: 50-62.
    1994   *The Dead Sea Scrolls Today* (Grand Rapids: Eerdmans; London: SPCK).
    1999   'Identity and History of the Community', in Flint and VanderKam 1999: II, 487-533.

Vermaseren, Maarten J.
    1956, 1960 *Corpus Inscriptionum et Monumentorum Religionis Mithriacae* (2 vols.; Leiden: E.J. Brill).
    1977   *Cybele and Attis: The Myth and the Cult* (London: Thames & Hudson).

Vermes, G.
    1953   *Les manuscrits du désert de Juda* (Paris: Desclée de Brouwer).
    1960   'The Etymology of "Essenes"', *RevQ* 2: 427-43.
    1981   'The Essenes and History', *JJS* 32: 18-31.
    1983   *Jesus the Jew: A Historian's Reading of the Gospel* (New York: Macmillan, 2nd edn).
    1984   *Jesus and the World of Judaism* (Philadelphia: Fortress Press).
    1984   *The Religion of Jesus the Jew* (Minneapolis: Augsburg–Fortress).

1994   *The Dead Sea Scrolls: Qumran in Perspective* (London: SCM Press, rev. 3rd edn).

1995   *The Dead Sea Scrolls in English* (London: Penguin Books, 4th edn).

Vermes, G., and M.D. Goodman

1989   *The Essenes: According to the Classical Sources* (Oxford Centre Textbooks, 1; Sheffield: JSOT Press).

Vidman, L. (ed.)

1969   *Sylloge inscriptionum religionis Isiacae et Serapiacae* (Berlin: W. de Gruyter).

Vokes, F.E.

1938   *The Riddle of the Didache: Fact or Fiction, Heresy or Catholicism?* (London: SPCK).

Wagner, S.

1960   *Die Essener in der wissenschaftlichen Diskussion: Vom Ausgang des 18. bis zum Beginn des 20. Jahrhunderts* (Berlin: Alfred Töpelmann).

Waldstein, M., and F. Wisse

1995   *The Apocryphon of John* (Leiden: E.J. Brill).

Website of Cambridge University Library, Taylor–Schechter Unit: http://www.lib.cam. ac.uk/Taylor-Schechter

Wedderburn, A.J.M.

1989   *Paul and Jesus: Collected Essays* (Sheffield: Sheffield Academic Press).

Weinfeld, M.

1986   *The Organizational Pattern and the Penal Code of the Qumran Sect: A Comparison with Guilds and Religious Associations of the Hellenistic-Roman Period* (NTOA, 2; Göttingen: Vandenhoeck & Ruprecht; Fribourg: Editions Universitaires).

Weiss, J.

1971   *Jesus' Proclamation of the Kingdom of God* (ET; Minneapolis: Fortress Press [German, 1892]).

Wenham, D.

1995   *Paul: Follower of Jesus or Founder of Christianity?* (Grand Rapids: Eerdmans, 1995).

Whiston, William (trans.)

1987   *The Works of Josephus* (Peabody, MA: Hendrickson [1737]).

Whittaker, M.

1984   *Jews and Christians: Graeco-Roman Views* (Cambridge: Cambridge University Press).

Widengren, G.

1961   *Mani and Manicheism* (Stuttgart: W. Kohlhammer; ET London: Widenfeld and Nicholson, 1965).

Willoughby, Harold R.

1960   *Pagan Regeneration: A Study of Mystery Initiations in the Graeco-Roman World* (Chicago: Chicago University Press [1929]).

Wilson, A.N.

1992   *Jesus* (London: Sinclair–Atkinson).

Wilson, R.McL.

1958   *The Gnostic Problem* (London: Mowbray).

1968   *Gnosis and the New Testament* (Oxford: Basil Blackwell).

1974	' "Jewish Gnosis" and Gnostic Origins: A Survey', *HUCA* 45: 177-89.
1982	'Nag Hammadi and the New Testament', *NTS* 27: 289-302.
1985	'Gnosis/Gnostizismus II: Neues Testament, Judentum, Alte Kirche', *TRE* 13: 535-50.
1986	'Ethics and the Gnostics', in W. Schrage (ed.), *Studien zum Text und zur Ethik des Neuen Testaments* (Berlin: W. de Gruyter): 440-49.
1993	'Philo and Gnosticism', *Studia Philonica Annual* 5: 84-92.
1994	'Gnosis and Gnosticism: The Messina Definition', in G. Sfameni Gasparro (ed.), Ἀγατὴ ἐλπίς (Festscrift U. Bianchi; Rome: Bretschneider): 539-51.
1995	'The Gospel of Thomas Reconsidered', in C. Fluck *et al.* (eds.), *Divitiae Aegypti* (Wiesbaden: Reichert): 331-36.

Wilson, R.McL. (trans. and ed.)
| 1991 | *New Testament Apocrypha* (Cambridge: James Clarke). |

Wise, M.O.
| 1990 | 'The Teacher of Righteousness and the High Priest of the Intersacerdotium: Two Approaches', *RevQ* 14: 587-613. |

Wisse, F.
1971	'The Nag Hammadi Library and the Heresiologists', *VC* 25: 205-33.
1972	'The Sethians and the Nag Hammadi Library' (SBLSP).
1975	'Die Sextus-Sprüche und das Problem der gnostischen Ethik', in A. Böhlig and F. Wisse, *Zum Hellenismus in den Schriften von Nag Hammadi* (Göttinger Orientforschungen, 6th series, vol. 2; Wiesbaden: Otto Harassowitz): 55-86.
1978	'Gnosticism and Early Monasticism in Egypt', in Aland 1978: 431-40.
1980	'Stalking those Elusive Sethians', in Layton 1980: 563-76.

Witherington III, B.
1990	*The Christology of Jesus* (Philadelphia: Fortress Press).
1994	*Jesus the Sage: The Pilgrimage of Wisdom* (Minneapolis: Augsburg–Fortress).
1995	*The Jesus Quest: The Third Search for the Jew of Nazareth* (Downers Grove, IL: InterVarsity Press).
1996	'The Promise of History: Jesus and his Cultural Admirers', *Lexington Theological Quarterly* 31: 155-66.

Wolfson, H.A.
| 1948 | *Philo* (2 vols., Cambridge, MA: Harvard University Press). |

Wrede, W.
| 1971 | *The Messianic Secret* (ET; Cambridge: James Clark [German, 1901]). |

Wright, N.T.
1992a	*Who Was Jesus?* (London: SPCK).
1992b	'Jesus, Quest for the Historical', in *ABD*: III, 796-802.
1995	'Five Gospels but No Gospel: Jesus and the Seminar', in W.R. Farmer (ed.), *Crisis in Christology: Essays in Quest of Resolution* (Livonia: MI: Dove): 115-57.
1996a	*Jesus and the Victory of God* (Philadelphia: Fortress Press).
1996b	*The Original Jesus: The Life and Vision of a Revolutionary* (Grand Rapids: Eerdmans).

Yadin, Y.

1966   *Masada: Herod's Fortress and the Zealots' Last Stand* (London: Weidenfeld & Nicolson).

Yamauchi, E.M.

1983   *Pre-Christian Gnosticism* (Grand Rapids: Baker Book House).

Yonge, C.D.

1993   *The Works of Philo* (foreword by D.M. Scholer; Peabody, MA: Hendrickson).

Zandee, J.

1961   *The Terminology of Plotinus and of Some Gnostic Writings, Mainly the Fourth Treatise of the Jung Codex* (Istanbul: Nederlands Historisch-Archaeologisch Instituut in het Nabije Oosten).

Zissu B.

1998   ' "Qumran Type" Graves in Jerusalem: Archaeological Evidence of an Essene Community?', *DSD* 5: 158-71.

Zöckler, T.

1999   *Jesu Lehren in Thomasevangelium* (Leiden: E.J. Brill).

INDEX OF REFERENCES

BIBLE

INDEX OF AUTHORS

THE BIBLICAL SEMINAR